THIS IS
God's Path
FOR YOU

THIS IS
God's Path
FOR YOU

A collection of God's spiritual truth's
ascertained from the King James Version of the Bible.
Truths which can change your life. . .
if you chose to believe in them.

Ephesians 3:20 "Now to him who is able by power to do for us more than anyone else, and to do for us more than we ask or think, according to his mighty power that works in us." This scripture was taken from the Lamsa Bible which is translated from the Aramaic language. God is saying He will supply all our needs above and beyond what we can ask or think to help anyone who needs His love.

Koste J. Vlahos

Table of Contents

Dedication

To my loving and supportive wife Ginny who walks alongside of me in our journey to follow and be inspired by God's Word. I could not have achieved my present walk with God without her trust and commitment.

Preface

The primary reason for writing this book was to take the religion out of the Word of God so you can have a clearer understanding of what God really wants for you and how you can go about achieving it through His glorious Word. He wants you to know His will for you. He has a path for you to follow. He wants you to know who His Son is. He wants you to feel His Holy Spirit within your heart. And lastly He wants you to know who Satan is and how you can begin to defeat his works. This book is not a deep theological study of God's Word and it is not meant to be one.

This book is based on the scriptures seen in the King James Version of the Bible. I chose the King James Version for several reasons. It has stood the test of time, over 400 years. And this is the first Bible I learned to read and understand. Please listen to me. I am not a theologian. I have spent the last 38 years studying His Word and listening to many different teachers. When I was younger I attended a mid-western college for Fine Arts but after several tries I never finished. I joined the Navy and this changed my life from being undisciplined to disciplined. I married my college sweetheart but that did not last. 12 years later I was divorced. To make a long story short I went to my 20th year reunion. Met a lady whom I had one date with in high school. 12 months later we were married and that was 40 years ago. Six months into our marriage we came to God together and have been on the same page spiritually since then. I am just an ordinary retired fellow who is married with grown children, grown grandchildren and great grandchildren. We do the best we can to follow the truth of God's Word and live our lives for

Him. Finally after all these years of studying His Word I was inspired to put the truth of His Word as it was taught to me in a book.

The King James Version of the Bible is all prophecy and is totally spiritual. KJV published in 1614 was the first English translation to contain all of the Old and New Testament books. There were other versions before the KJV but they were not complete with all 66 books. The KJV is still being published today without any changes having been made to its original text.

This Bible is God's loving commands to help you with your walk in this world. Whether you have just begun your walk or are continuing your walk it is God's desire for you to follow His Word the best you can. He is a loving and forgiving God of many second chances. He will never leave nor forsake you. He will love you with a love which transcends all time.

All scriptures in this book are from the King James Version of the Bible with the exceptions of two scriptures: Genesis 9:11 and Matthew 27:46. These are from George Lamsa"s Holy Bible published by A.J.Holman Co., Nashville, TN, 1933.

Chapter One

How I became saved. . .

Quite simply back in 1979 I joined a ministry which was founded entirely on the principals of the King James Version of the Bible. They believed this version of the Bible was indeed the actual Word of God as He inspired holy men in old times to write His Word in their own style of speech.

This ministry sounded like the answer to my prayers. I was hungry to learn how to read the Bible. I had looked though not too hard to find an organized religion where I could learn the depth of the Word but there none teaching it. My family had several copies of the Bible in our home. Each was a dusty as the other. One was in Greek and belonged to my father when he lived in Sparta, Greece. Though I had a Greek background through my father who has since passed I never learned how to read Greek. So I could not read his Greek Bible but I did know the names of the usual food items like baklava and gyro's. I do remember the first time I opened an English translation of the King James Bible and it proved to be still *"Greek to me"* as the original Greek translation I tried to read earlier.

So when this ministry provided the opportunity to learn how to read the KJV of the Bible I was all onboard. Please understand this. I did not know one version from another. I was happy to be learning whatever version they offered, I just wanted to know God's Word. I have since found there are actually 65 different versions available on *"YouVerse"*. I have referenced an additional bible in this book which is no longer in print but is equally as powerful if not more so.

I found there were several important takeaway's from this ministry. One was the knowledge I was now an adopted son of God. Which meant that Jesus was my step brother, spiritually speaking. God had chosen me before the foundation of the universe and He knew in His foreknowledge I would make the commitment to follow His Son. I also learned I was saved when I made the commitment to follow Jesus Christ and accept him as my Lord and Saviour and even more. Being saved is another name for salvation. I also believed God raised Jesus from the dead while he was still in the tomb. One of the additional blessings of this commitment is I get to spend eternity with God and Jesus Christ as well as all the other *"born again"* saints.

Before I go too far it is very important you understand where and how God's word is made up. In **II Peter 1:20"Knowing this first, that no prophecy of the scripture is of any private interpretation."** When you begin any study concerning God's Word you should understand this one thing *"first."* The Bible is made up entirely of *"prophecies."* Webster defines this word as *"a prediction of things to come."* A great deal of the New Testament was written circa 50 A.D. The second most important fact is, none of the scriptures in the KJV of the Bible are of private interpretation. Meaning young, middle-aged or old people did not just sit around and make up these verses. The next verse is from **II Peter 1:2 "For the prophecy came not in old time by the will of man; but holy men of God spake as they were moved by the Holy Ghost."** As I said earlier, these holy men did not sit around the camp fires writing scriptures. These holy men of God were *"moved"* or inspired by revelation from God to speak exactly the words He wanted them to speak. Then those words were in turn written down just as God spoke them. Keep this in mind pencils and paper as you know them today did not exist so it took some time to acquire parchment and writing instruments. So how was God's Word spread to those who were eager to know about this Messiah. The Book of Acts is a history of the 1st century church spreading the Word of God. The 1st century church was basically made up of small groups of families coming together in one families home to hear the word spoken by someone who had personally witnessed Jesus or one of his disciples speaking.

Now, would you like to be saved?

Silly question, of course you want to be saved. God in all His spiritual glory will accept you just the way you are right now. Even though you may be imperfect, a sinner, rejected, confused, lonely, divorced, married, in jail, childless, on whatever drug of choice is happening in your body at this moment. It does not make any difference to God. He does not care what color or race nor ethnicity you are. God does not care about your sexual preferences or your present or past circumstances at this point in your life. He will accept you right now just the way you are and once He accepts you He will love you forever and He will never forsake or leave you. God says all this in His Word, the only hitch is you have to believe what He says.

This is **THE** game changing scripture; **Romans 10:9** in the New Testament of your KJV of the Bible. **"That if thou shalt confess with thy mouth the Lord Jesus, and shalt believe in thine heart that God hath raised him from the dead thou shalt be saved."** The word *"thou"* is old English for you. The word *"shalt"* is also old English and means an absolute promise from God to you. The word *"confess"* means you speak to God out loud or quietly whichever suits, stating you will accept Jesus Christ as your Lord and Master as well as your Saviour. Then you will try to do the best you can to follow him the rest of your life. Next you will need to believe God raised His Son Jesus from the dead. Jesus did not get up from the grave of his own accord. And this last verse you should look at to complete your transformation from a citizen of the world to a citizen of heaven. **Romans 10:10 "For with the heart man believeth unto righteousness; and with the mouth confession is made unto salvation."** This verse is telling you that with your commitment to follow Jesus Christ you are now as righteous as he is. Righteous means "as if you have never sinned." And with your mouth begin to confess silently or out loud *"all"* the sins you have ever committed up to your point of commitment. God will forgive and forgot every single one of them. **Psalms 103:12 "As far as the east is from the west, so far hath he removed our transgressions from us."** God also knows your confession will be a near impossible feat for you to perform considering you started out as an unbeliever. To try and remember all the sins you ever committed when you did not even know what a sin was, is a near impossibility. Even if you knew what sin was just trying to remember the few sins you performed this morning could have been difficult. So God has made it easy on you. Just speak these words," *please Father forgive all my past sins"* and He will make it so. Jesus gave up his life on the cross as the price for all of your past sins. The blood he shed before and during the crucifixion was for the remission of your sins. The word *"remission"* means the cancellation of a debt. Each sin you have ever committed was in fact a debt you would have to pay back to God. With Jesus shedding of his blood your debt was paid for in full. And there is more. Jesus was beaten by the Roman guards brutally and the stripes he bore on his back are symbols of the healing that is available for you and me to claim as we start our journey with God.

Now as you start out on your new walk you have a clean slate of no sins having been committed. God has forgiven you of all your past sins and He has forgotten all about them but there is an action you still need to take and that is repenting of all those sins you were just forgiven of. Repenting means you change the direction you were walking in your past life and turn around 180 degrees and begin your walk with God in the opposite direction. God forgave all those sins but you still need to be humble enough to thank Him for forgiving you of those sins, and thus you begin the process of repenting or changing the path your life was headed.

You are not perfect. . .

You are not perfect and never will be but that is ok! Jesus Christ was the only human being ever to walk on this earth who was perfect in all respects and was resurrected by His Father and now sits at the right hand of his Father in heaven. In the following scripture Jesus shares His Father's Word with us and recounts how Satan wants to steal, kill and destroy each of us. In **John 10:10a "The thief cometh not, but to steal and to kill and to destroy."** This verse describes what Satan wants to do to your life now that you are on the way to living your life as a believer. Please read this next verse **John 10:10b "I am come that they might have life, and that they might have it more abundantly."** Should you chose to believe this second verse though your walk here on earth is a physical one God through His Son Jesus will provide you with a life which is more spiritually abundant than you could ever imagine. You have nothing to fear concerning what Satan wants to do to you, your God, your new Father will never forsake you nor leave you. His Holy Spirit will be within your forever. The battles you will fight here on earth are all spiritually influenced by Satan. The fight will be between your ears, in your mind, in your thought processes. **Ephesians 6:12 "For we wrestle not against flesh and blood, but against principalities, against powers, against the rulers of the darkness of this world, against spiritual wickedness in high places."** Satan is going to do whatever he can to throw you off this wonderful path God has given you.

And because you are human, will you continue to sin. . .

God knows you very well and He also knows as the years go by in your walk with Him you will continue to sin again and again, sometimes intentionally and sometimes unintentionally. All those past sins have been forgiven and forgotten. And when you come to Him humbly He will forgive those sins which you will confess to Him.

In the very beginning of time when you were with God spiritually speaking He could have easily possessed your mind so you would love Him unconditionally. Instead He decided to give you a choice in the matter. He gave you *"free will."* There are some people who say you did not receive the gift of "free will" from God until you made the commitment to become "born again." Actually when you were with God before the foundation of the universe, He gave you your "free will" to make the choice of following Him or Satan. **Ephesians 1:4a "According as he***(God)* **hath chosen us in him before the foundation of the world,"**

You now have the opportunity to determine what path you are going to walk here on earth. Let's go to **Proverbs 3:5** and see what God would like you to do, **"Trust in the Lord***(God)* **with all thine heart; and lean not unto thine own understanding." 6 "In all thy ways acknowledge him and he shall direct thy paths."** To acknowledge Him means you will pray more and sing praises to Him and speak His Word to others. The more you study His Word which is His Will for you and make it your own the opportunity is greater He will speak to you spiritually. His Holy Spirit is within your spiritual heart. You received His Holy Spirit when you were born physically but you did not energize it until you made the commitment spiritually to follow Jesus Christ.

God is Spirit, **John 4:24a"God is Spirit;"** and God can only speak to what He is, Spirit, so He will be speaking into your spiritual heart His thoughts for you to consider. We will talk more about God's Holy Spirit later on.

God wants nothing more from you but to worship Him and help reconcile all those people who have fallen away back to Him. To accomplish this purpose He has given you His playbook for your lives, the Bible.

Here's something extra. . .concerning eternity

Matthew 5:3 "Blessed are the poor*(humble)* in spirit*(in their conscious minds)* for their is the kingdom of heaven."
Matthew 5:4 "Blessed are the meek for they shall inherit the earth*(new earth)*.

Chapter Two

Improving your prayers to God. . .

The goal of this chapter is to help you improve your prayer life with God. Whether you have just started to **talk** with God or have been a *"prayer warrior"* for many years, here are several helpful hints to bring about a more positive conclusion to your daily conversation with God.

Your beginning, believe then learn to talk. . .

Learning how to pray is not some mystical rite of passage you need to go through as a new Christian.

To those of you who have just begun this special journey, you have already given Jesus Christ and God your heart so you are now a *"born again"* believer. What is next?

Communicating with God is simply having a conversation with Him. Just as you sit and **talk** with your close friends, you can now begin to have a conversation with God the creator of the universe.

Here is a thought you could keep in mind when you are talking with God. He is omnipresent in the universe. Which means He is everywhere present in the universe at the same time including being within you.

Now what is wonderful about having a conversation with God is no one can hear you speaking because you are doing it with your spiritual heart. He will listen to every word you say. **I John 5:14 "And this is the confidence that we have in him, that if we ask anything according**

to his will, he heareth us." And He will answer all your prayers when He knows you are ready to receive the answer. Sometimes you may think you are ready for the answer but you are not and God knows the reasons. Not to worry. His timing is always perfect. God is never late. This scripture from the Old Testament in **Habakkuk 2:3** speaks to our waiting for God's answer with believing. **"For the vision is yet for an appointed time, but at the end it shall speak, and not lie; though it tarry, wait for it; because it will surely come, it will not tarry."** Let's break it down here; *"vision"* means your petition or prayer. And you have set an *"appointed time"* frame for the answer. God will answer in His time frame. God says He will absolutely speak to and not lie about the answer. **Numbers 23:19a "God is not a man, that he should lie."** He will give you an answer. He says it will *"tarry"* or wait, and He says again *"wait for the answer."* When God speaks anything twice in scriptures what He has spoken about becomes established. The answer will surely come and this time it will not *"tarry."* So God will answer your petition or prayer in His time and not yours

Next is listening. . .

Listening is a very important aspect of your journey towards a successful prayer life. After you lift or speak your petitions or prayers to God you should try to remain quiet for a short time afterwards because He may speak to you with His answer. Should you move on with your life right away you could miss His answer. His answers will not come when there is confusion about you, simply speaking because you could not hear Him.

Meaning if you are in a place where there are a lot of people around you making noise you will never be able to hear Him. There will be times when His answer will come in over *"quiet waters."* It's akin to being on a lake in the early morning hours when there's no sound or movement, not even the chirping of birds. This could be the case where stillness will be necessary to hear God's response and then there will be times when your very "first" thought after you have finished praying will be His answer. God is very specific when He answers prayers. I had a situation where I needed a new lawnmower. Yes, God is interested in lawn mowers. God is interested in anything you are concerned about. I had an name brand for years and it was falling apart. I was using duct tape to hold it together. I was actually considering buying a newer version of the same mower but this time I asked God to help me with the selection. The first word literally into my mind when I finished the request was "Toro." So I went to the local home improvement store and there in the lawn mower department sat the only non-riding Toro model they carried and it met all the specifications I needed.

God has lovingly told us in His Word we should end our prayers accordingly.

When you speak *"in the name of Jesus"* at the end of your prayers you are speaking to God directly through His Son Christ Jesus. He is your intercessor to the Father and he is seated at his Father's right hand. Christ Jesus will present your petitions to his Father for Him to consider.

When I came to the Lord in '79 I chose to end my prayers as He had asked. And to date virtually all my prayers both long and short term have been answered. Now I have found over the years of praying for my family, anytime my prayer deals with a specific relative who has not chosen to follow God or just is not at that place in their life, without God or Jesus in their life then His answer will take some time before coming. Why? Because God has to wait for the person involved to make up their mind which path they are going to chose to walk. Should this person chose not to follow Jesus or God then I have to keep on praying. Should they change their minds and chose God then I will get my answer. The choice is up to them and there is nothing I can do about it. But miracles are still available. What is wonderful when you chose to give your situation to God is the peace which will come over you after having released the burden of the situation to God. Basically you are giving God control over your life, your spiritual life which will eventually trickle down to your physical life.

Let's summarize now.

First; you have to believe.
Second; you have to talk.
Third; you have to end your prayer request accordingly.
Fourth; and you have to listen

I would like to explore a little more about your commitment to being *"born again."*

You have given your life to Jesus and God. The following scriptures in Romans hold the promises of remission, salvation and righteousness for you.

The first five books of the New Testament are Matthew, Mark, Luke and John followed by the book of Acts. The **next** nine books were written by the apostle Paul. *An apostle is one who brings new light to an already dark world.* God inspired Paul to write these books beginning around 59 A.D. So in this book of **Romans 10:9,10** is the key scripture for being "born again." Paul states this,

"That if*(a condition set by God in many of His scriptures which allows for your free will to be utilized.)* **thou***(you)* **shalt***(absolute promise from God)* **confess***(or speak)* **with thy***(your)* **mouth, the Lord***(master)* **Jesus."** We must acknowledge Jesus Christ, the Son of God as our Lord and Master.

"And shalt believe in thine*(your)* **heart***(spiritual)* **that God hath***(past tense)* **raised him***(Jesus)* **from the dead thou shalt be saved. "10"For with the heart** *(spiritual)* **man believeth unto righteousness** *(free from guilt or sin)* **and with the mouth confession is made unto salvation."***(all our past sins will be forgiven and forgotten, never to be remembered again by God)*

This is a critical point to remember. Making a covenant with God is **the** ultimate promise and should never be broken.

If you have chosen to believe Romans 10:9,10 then congratulations on being "born again." To accomplish this new spiritual condition you had to exercise your *"free will"* to become born again. So now what do you do.

Salvation, what is it. . .

You have just accepted Jesus as your Saviour. You have humbly confessed all your sins with your spiritual heart and God has forgiven your past history of sins up to the point of your commitment to Him and His Son. The spiritual heart you now have resides between your ears. This is your mind. It is the seat of all your thought processes and where you will store the Word of God you learn. **Ephesians 2:9 "Not of works, lest any man should boast."** You are saved by a gift from God, not by your works.

There three parts to salvation. . .

Let's take a look at the three parts of Salvation. *First,* there are the past sins which you and I have been forgiven of. *Secondly,* there are going to be some of those same old sin's you have carried your entire life which will still hang around. God forgave those sins. Now you have to forget about them also. You are still going to make every effort to get over them but some will continue to plague you. Satan does not want you to be completely free. You have an awesome Father who will continue to give you second and third and fourth and so on chances of forgiveness as long as you continue to remain faithful to Him. Christ is no longer available to sacrifice his life again. So you still must come humbly come to the Father and continue to confess your new sins and He being the wonderful Father He is will continue to forgive you. And *thirdly,* when you enter into heaven for the final time every sin which you have ever committed will have been forgiven and forgotten because you asked for forgiveness when the sin was committed.

No works. . .

Most *"born again"* believers will do very little along the "good works" line God talks about in **Ephesians 2:10a "For we are his workmanship created in Christ Jesus unto good works."** because they have never been taught what to do. No one has ever really told them they should to go to church to thank God for His forgiveness. They have no one to teach them how to read His Book. They do not participate in any activities of the community or church. They figured they were saved and now they will just wait to pass on into heaven. The reality is they are saved. They do not have to do any "good works" here on earth at all. So when they enter into heaven God is not going to say anything to these people because they did nothing while here on earth to help reconcile men and women back to God, but they will still be welcomed into heaven.

Then there are "good works."

Those who have helped people find God and those who have given of their time and talents will be greeted by God with the phrase *"well done my good and faithful servant."* And those of you who have worked to give to God your time and talents will be in line to receive a crown from God. And after receiving your crown you will become a priest

Revelations 20:6 "Blessed and holy is he that hath part of the first resurrection; on such the second death hath no power, but they shall be priests of God and of Christ, and shall reign with him a thousand years."

Reading the "good" Book. . .

One of the keys to understanding God and His Word is to read it on a daily basis, morning, noon or night it does not matter. The King James Version of the Bible has been around for over 400 years and the original words have not been changed. Why! Because God frowns on those who make changes to His Word, so much so that those who do will not spend eternity with Him in heaven. Unfortunately many of the different versions which are produced today are all changed in one way or another, but I am not the judge. I have trusted the KJV for over 40 years and I have found it to never contradict itself.

Take a look at Webster's definition of the word confidence. *"a state of being certain."*

This book you are reading utilizes scriptures taken from the King James Bible or version. This version was published by King James of England around 1614. It was the first bible published in English which contained both the Old and New Testament translations taken from the Hebrew, Greek and Aramaic writings. King James researchers took over ten years to compile all the necessary information to produce his version. Prior to the publication of the KJV was the Tyndale Bible circa 1500. This version was credited with being the first English translation to include writings from the Hebrew, Greek and Aramaic texts which are contained in a New Testament but only 9 books of the Old Testament.

There are some who say, *believing in a single version of the Bible when there are so many out there may sound like your putting all your eggs in one basket. Drop the basket and all the eggs will break. Fortunately we are dealing with God's awesome Word which has stood the test of time and has not broken nor will it fail it's reader, you*

His Word. . .

God has not forsaken you concerning His Word. He has made sure you and I have received every word which the writers of the Old Testament originally received through revelation. He wanted His Word to be read and digested and lived. And in return for His many promises He asks you to walk out believing in what He has said. You must trust what God says in His Word if you are to claim those promises and stand firm on what they say. Remember the story of Peter in **Matthew 14:24 "But the ship was now in the midst of the sea, tossed with waves,** for the wind was contrary." 25 "And in the fourth watch*(3 am)* of the night Jesus went into them walking on the sea." 26 "And when the disciples saw him walking on the sea they were troubled saying, It is a spirit*(phantom)* and they cried out for fear." 27 "But straightway Jesus spake unto them saying, Be of good cheer, it is I, be not afraid." 28 "And Peter answered him and said Lord, if it be thou, bid me come unto thee on the water." 29 "And he said Come. And when Peter was come down out of the ship, he walked on the water to go to Jesus."

Peter soon grew afraid of the storm tossed water but he still believed in Jesus. He had confidence in Jesus and what Jesus spoke. When Jesus asked him to step out of the boat and walk on the water, Peter's fear disappeared and he did what Jesus commanded. The key to walking out on the promises of God is to *"get out of the boat"* and have confidence or believe in what He says. Fear eventually came back into the picture and Peter lost sight of our Lord Jesus and he began to sink but in **Matthew 14:31 "And immediately Jesus stretched forth his hand and caught him and said unto him, O thou of little faith***(believing)* **wherefore didst thou doubt.** God will do the same with you. His hand is always there. Moving on. . .

What is it about prophecy. . .

II Peter 1:21 "For the prophecy came not in old time by the will of man; but holy men of God spake as they were moved by the Holy Ghost*(Spirit)."* The scripture is saying all the Word of God is prophecy and spiritual in nature. And prophecy means foretelling about an incident which will take place later in time, whether past, present, or future. All time is relative to the period it is represented in. The Old Testament is historical and is addressed to Israel, the people. The New Testament through history carries many spiritual implications with it. There were two groups of people back in Jesus time. Judeans and Gentiles. The title of Gentile covered everybody who was not Judean even if you were a Muslim or Buddhist the Gentile title stuck.

Over the centuries many Judeans and Gentiles have converted over to Christianity.

Have you ever wondered how the word *"Jew"* came about. The word did not exist until the 18th century when the then current versions of the Bible were revised to include the word Jew. It was inspired by the Latin "Iudaeus" to "Gyu.

Back to prophecy. . .

I talked about this earlier. All the spiritual battles you will fight in your life here on earth will be fought between your ears, in your mind. You live in the world of Satan and he controls this world through his influences. Everything you will interact with in your five senses walk with Jesus Christ in your heart will be affected in one way or another by Satan. Keep this in mind the Earth and the elements which affect it belong to God and He will protect them. The spiritual properties of the world belong to Satan and he will not protect them. He will use everything available to fill his needs. The principalities of the world, its kingdoms and governments sit on top of the earth. Just as God is Spirit so Satan is spirit. Neither can be seen in the physical world.

Speaking about Satan, in John 10:10 he is revealed. . .

In **John 10:10a "The thief cometh not, but for to steal, and to kill, and to destroy."** Satan is not going to steal your TV or kill your dog or destroy your house. Satan wants to *steal* your righteousness, your freedom from guilt of sin which God has given you. Satan actually wants to *kill* your belief in THE God, so you in turn can worship him. And finally he wants to *destroy* your spiritual relationship you have with God. Satan will make every effort he can to make your life difficult or depressing or just plain miserable because he knows you have chosen to walk with Jesus Christ and God. **John 10:10b "I***(Jesus)* **am come that they***(us)***might have life, and that they might have it**

more abundantly." This again is referring to the spiritual abundance and with this abundance you will have a very confident, abundant and peaceful walk.

Biblical references. . .something extra

The first complete sentence of a verse is usually designated with an *"a"* and the second complete sentence is designated with a *"b"* and the third complete sentence is a *"c"* and so on. These lower case alphabet letters do not appear in the Bible but are used as a reference when writing or speaking about a specific section of a verse. Notice also, there is one word *(might)* mentioned twice in the above verse **John10:10b**. These words are there to guide you to operate your free will in making any choice the correct one.

The greatest commandments. . .

Your spiritual Father God has given you a great many weapons to help defeat the works of Satan and these two scriptures here are the most powerful.

Matthew 22:37 "Thou shalt love the Lord thy God with all thy*(your)* **heart***(kardio-Greek)(this is your spiritual heart)* **and with all thy soul***(nephesh chaiyim/breath life)* **and with all thy mind***(nous-Greek) (conscious thoughts).***"**

Matthew 22:39 "And the second is like unto it, thou shalt love*(agape, love of God)* **thy neighbor as thyself."** You are to strive to have the love of God toward one another, but if you could just love in a *"phileo"* manner you will succeed. Phileo is Greek and the root for the word Philadelphia, the city of brotherly love.

Did you know you were created before the foundations of the universe?. . .

God created a spiritual heart and soul in you. **Ephesians 1:4 "According as he***(God)* **hath chosen us in him before the foundation of the world***(universe)* **that we should be holy and without blame before him in love."** God knew in his foreknowledge He would chose you to be a believer, but you still had to take the first step of commitment to His Son Jesus Christ utilizing your *"free will"* and the result is you are now a son or daughter of God and can legally call Him Father.

Not a respecter of persons. . .

There are many people, maybe even you, who feel God will single out very special people to carry out His wonderful works upon earth. And that is true. God has opened spiritual doors throughout history in those special people's lives and they in turn walked through of their own free will. This thinking on your part that you were not chosen is a trick from Satan. You would not be a "born again" person if you had not walked thru the spiritual doors God had opened for you. In **Romans 2:11 "For there is no respect of persons with God."** God is not a respecter of persons. He will not favor one person over another. You are equal in God's eyes with all your brothers and sisters. He gave you *"free will"* and the power to exercise it. The choices you make will come with consequences, good or bad. As I said earlier there are certain people which God has opened spiritual doors for them to walk through and in doing so they have brought forth the story of Jesus and God. These people had characteristics which God needed in order for Him to reveal His Word through revelation to them. We are all different. Some of us have a desire to run in races, others to fix computers and so on . . .

A little bit about arch angels. . .

God is Spirit. In 1943 a Daily Devotional, called *"Manna In The Morning"* was written by Charles Fuller. This particular quote appealed because it gives the reader a visual presentation of how God, who is Spirit, appears to each individual. *"I may see Him in the starry heavens, touch Him with the tips of my fingers in the petal of a lily, hear Him in the song of the nightingale and meadow lark, smell Him in the perfume of a rose, and taste Him in the luscious fruit He made."* This quote is metaphorically speaking of course but in each aspect you are made aware of God's wonderful creations.

Let's talk about spirits, Holy and otherwise. . .

Have you ever had the thought of how God may want to get in touch with you. He might use a "burning bush." It worked before and it could work again. In **Exodus 3:2a "And the angel of the Lord***(God)* **appeared unto him in a flame of fire out of the middle of a bush."** God did not actually appear in the burning bush. It was the voice and image of his archangel Gabriel.

God created three Arch Angels. The first was Lucifer, the angel of light. He was second in command to God and eventually became Satan. Next was Michael, the warrior angel. He fought all of God's battles on earth for Israel. And finally Gabriel, the messenger angel. He brought the message from God to Mary when she was going to have the baby Jesus, our saviour. **Luke 1:28 "And the angel came in unto her and said, Hail, thou that art highly favored, the Lord***(Jesus)* **is with thee, blessed art thou among women.**

Has anyone ever seen God?

John 4:24 "God is *a* Spirit and they that worship him must worship him in the spirit and in truth." God is omnipresent in the universe.

Omnipresent means God is everywhere in the universe at the same time. The wind would be the closest of the four elements on earth which could resemble the effect of God passing by you in an open field. You can sense His presence and feel His warmth or coolness. When you are sometimes down in your personal spirit, you can in your mind's eye sense the touch of God in the wind and His touch can be reassuring.

In **John 4:24** the second word *"spirit"* notice lower case *"s"* actually refers, in this case, to the manifestation of speaking in tongues which is found in **I Corinthians 12:10.** The word *"truth"* refers to all the words in the Bible. When you encounter the word *"spirit"* it is normally referring to your personal spirit. This personal spirit is within you. This personal spirit has nothing to do with God. It is your identifying mark as to who you are and how different you are from other people in the world.

Speaking of old spirits. . .

The King James Bible or version was originally written in the language of Old English which is not spoken anymore. In this scripture we see the word "ghost" which is actually translated into the word *"spirit"*. **Matthew 27:50 "Jesus when he had cried again with a loud voice, yielded up the ghost."** The Old English word for *"spirit"* was *"gast"* which is pronounced *"ghost."* So the KJV translators chose the word *"ghost."* In contrast the context of the verse refers to something very personal Jesus gave up. It was his personal spirit which was his breath life or soul. In Hebrew breath life means *"nephesh chai."* We have breath life or soul so for future reference the correct translation for *"ghost"* is *"spirit."*

Two words for spirit, Spirit and spirit, big difference. . .

Notice the capital *"S"* and the lower case *"s"* in **John 4:24**. When the Word talks about God's Holy Spirit a capital *"S"* is used. When a lower case *"s"* is used it will refer to our personal spirit. Again our personal spirit is what identifies you from me. You are totally different from other people. You may have some similarities but for the most part you are different.

Your personal spirit. . .

Your personal spirit is unique to you. You love God with your spiritual heart not your physical one. You love Him with your soul or your breath life. This breath life or your soul is the same breath God breathed into the lungs of Adam upon his creation, and that very moment became Adam's breath of life. **Genesis 2:7 "And the Lord God formed***(fashioned)* **man of the dust of the ground***(elements of the soil)* **and breathed into his nostrils the breathe of life; and man became a living soul***(spirit of man).*"

How will Jesus recognize you. . .

For many years I have wondered just how is Christ Jesus going to recognize me. I will have passed on before Jesus returns. I am a born again believer. Then I found this verse which explains what will happen. In **Luke 23:46b** "Father, into thy hands I commend my spirit and having said **thus, he gave up the ghost."**

Jesus was commending his *"personal spirit"* into his Fathers hands for safe keeping. When you *"pass on"* you will do the same thing, but it will not be an intentional act on your part. God will take care of it for you. Keep this in mind, your physical body will not ascend to meet Christ Jesus in the clouds only your personal spirit. So if you are alive when Christ Jesus returns, the only thing which will go up into the clouds will be your "personal spirit." The next question which arises as to where will your *"personal spirit"* be kept while you await the return of Christ Jesus. Jesus is the anointed one now, and the answer is, in

Paradise. How do you know this? Let's go to **Luke 23:43b "Today thalt thou be with me in paradise."**

While you are in Paradise awaiting Christ's return there will be no conscious awareness on your part. In **I Thessalonians 4:1 "But I would not have you to be ignorant, brethren concerning them which are asleep,"** When you go to sleep each night you are not aware of anything going on around you until you wake in the morning. God has been training you from the day you were born just how to fall asleep. This is the same experience you will feel when you *"pass on"* very peaceful and with no pain. So do not worry about commending your personal spirit to God like Jesus did, it will be taken care for you. **I Thessalonians 4:14 "For if we believe that Jesus died and rose again, even so them also which sleep in Jesus will God bring with him."** So you are *"born again"* and your personal spirit will go to Paradise to receive your new body. Now comes the waiting for Christ to return. You will not be aware of anything happening while you are waiting because you will be asleep. Your new body will be just like the one Jesus has. When Christ returns to gather together all the believers you will be transported to heaven and eventually be presented to God in your new body. As a *"born again"* believer your name appears in the Lambs book of Life and as a faithful believer you will receive one of five different crowns. Now if you were **not** *"born again"* then your name will not appear in the Lamb's Book of Life. You will be judged by God and will not receive a crown. **Revelations 20:15 "And whosoever was not found on the book of life was cast into the lake of fire."** Satan and all his unholy angel spirits will be waiting for you forever.

How does your free will fit in here. . .

When you made the commitment to follow Jesus Christ, God energized His Holy Spirit in Christ in you. Together they make up the *"hope of glory"* for you. **Colossians 2:27 "To whom God would make known what is the riches of the glory of the mystery among the Gentiles; which is "Christ in you, the hope of glory."**

And what does the *"hope of glory"* really mean? You can believe whole heartedly there will be a return of Christ and all those who are in Paradise will spend eternity with him and his Father God.

I Peter 1:23 "Being born again not of corruptible seed but of incorruptible by the word of God which liveth and abideth forever." You have been chosen by God and now have His Holy Spirit*(pneuma hagion - Greek)* within you. You cannot lose what God has given you.

This is one of those extra facts I found very interesting. . .

When I first started studying the Bible I wondered why Jesus was only in the tomb for three days*(72 hours).*

According to Jewish custom, physical burial must take place within 24 hours after death. However a spiritual burial must take place within three days. The body of Jesus was placed in the tomb within the specified period of time thereby meeting the Jewish requirements for handling of a dead body. But he only stayed in the tomb for three full days. Then God raised him from the dead to eventually be seated at his right hand. Jesus acquired his new body in Paradise within a very short period of time after his resurrection and then came back and was seen by over 500 people in the surrounding areas. His stay was only forty days long and then he ascended *ten days* before Pentecost. The total number of days from resurrection to Pentecost equals 50. The number 50 is called Pentecost *(pentekoste-Greek).*

Our body begins to decay. . .

God, in His magnificent wisdom, designed the human body as well as animal bodies to begin it's decay within 72 hours or three days after death. Had God left his son in the tomb more than three days then his body would also begin to decay . **Matthew 12:40b "so shall the Son of man be three days and three nights in the heart of the earth."**

Remember Lazarus in **John 11:17 "Then when Jesus came he found that he had lain in the grave four days already."** And in **John 11:39 "Jesus said, Take away the stone. Martha, the sister of him that was dead, saith unto him, Lord, by this time he stinketh; for he hath been dead four days."** Jesus still raised Lazarus from the dead and this miracle restored all of Lazarus's bodily functions completely with no smell. Lazarus had been sick for quite some time but Jesus felt he would only be sleeping. He died and was dead spiritually for three days. By the time Jesus was made aware spiritually of Lazarus's death and was able to make his way to Lazarus' home took a total of four days. This action which Jesus took was considered to be one of the four Messianic Miracles proving Jesus was the Messiah. The other three are; The cleansing of Leprosy **Exodus 4:6.** The casting out of the deaf and dumb spirit **Mark 4:9.** And the healing of the man's birth defects **Exodus 34:7b**

Did you know Jesus has two titles. . .

The first is found in the Gospels. Which are considered by many theologians to be part of the Old Testament. Jesus the Christ. The Greek word for Christ is Christos,"the anointed one" The *"os"* ending of the word indicates it came from the south of Greece. The Hebrew word for the same name is Mashiach or Messiah. This means according to the Hebrew faith Jesus was the Messiah. Unfortunately there were many Judeans of old and of new times who still do not believe Jesus was the long awaited Messiah.

Now in the Epistles of the New Testament his name is Christ Jesus. His Father God whose right hand he sits at gave him this new title when Jesus ascended to heaven. See what **Luke 4:18a says, "The Spirit of the Lord is upon me(***Jesus***), because he(***God***) hath anointed me."**

As you begin to read the Bible for content you will find that the writers will have sometimes use the title of *"Christ Jesus"* which normally refers to Jesus after he ascended. And then there will be times when the writers will use the older title *"Jesus Christ"* which normally refers to

Jesus while he was still here on earth. When reading God's Word each scripture has a meaning as well as the context of the paragraph and also where the verse first appeared in the Bible. One of the wonderful facts concerning the Bible is so much of the word is inter-connected. You cannot start down one path of discovery for very long until you uncover another path. Let's get back to prayer.

What makes up prayer. . .

I believe prayer is the greatest act of humility which you can ever give to God.

James 4:10 "Humble yourselves in the sight of the Lord and he shall lift you up."

When you speak to God the walls of your insecurity and shame as well as those of mistrust, doubt and un-forgiveness should come down. You are to open your spiritual heart, your very being*(consciousness)* to God when you pray. You and I should come to Him as a little child, metaphorically speaking. In **Matthew 18:3 "And said, Verily I say unto you, Except ye be converted***(change your mind)* **and become as little children, ye shall not enter into the kingdom of heaven."** Small children do not identify with a conscious agenda. They have no recognizable ego. They are innocent and they come to God quietly. There is a peace in their spiritual hearts and conscious thoughts as they come to rest in His arms. You must try to come to the feet of God with a humble attitude concerning anything which is on your mind.

Look at **Matthew 18:1 "At the same time came the disciples unto Jesus, saying, Who is the greatest in the kingdom of heaven?" 2 "And Jesus called a little child unto him, and set him in the midst of them." 3 "And said, Verily I say unto you, Except ye be converted***(change your mind)* **and become as little children, ye shall not enter into the kingdom of heaven." 4 " Whosoever therefore shall humble himself as this little child, the same is greatest in the kingdom of heaven."**

A quiet place. . . it bears repeating again.

In **John 14:13 "And whatsoever ye shall ask in my name that will I do, the Father may be glorified in the Son."**

Every time you pray you should end your prayer *"in the name of Jesus."* On the other hand you can have an ongoing discussion with God all day long beginning in the morning when you wake up and finally when you are going to sleep you can just end the prayer, *"thank you Jesus."*

Talking with God. . .

As I said earlier, carrying on a conversation throughout your day with the Creator of the universe is exactly what he wants you to do. He is listening to all your complaints and praises and dreams and disappointments. He wants to know what you are thinking because when you begin to understand just what is going on in your life and mind then God will begin to speak to you when you pray. The important part is to be quiet when you are finished praying, so you can hear His answer.

God is your closest friend. He is your spiritual Father and He wants you to talk with Him about everything going on in your life. Does God know your thoughts? God knows everything about you. His Holy Spirit is within you and He can speak to your conscious/spiritual mind if He needs to. He will never take over your mind because your *"free will"* would be negated, therefore when you speak He will listen. Spirit can only speak to spirit and God will communicate with you through your "personal spirit."

Your conscious mind. . .

When He (*God*) knows you are beginning to understand what is going on in your mind(*consciousness*) and heart(*spiritual*) then He will begin to speak specifically to His (*Spirit*) within you. All you have to do is listen.

I know this must sound like a broken record but it is very important for you to remember and apply in your daily walk.

In **Romans 7:25 "I thank God through Jesus Christ our Lord**(*master*). **So then with the mind**(*conscious thought*) **I myself serve the law of God; but with the flesh the law of sin."** The word *"flesh"* refers to the carnal mind, which is the *"sin nature"* you received from Adam, spiritually speaking. Your body does the act, and your mind directs it.

Your spiritual heart. . .

Proverbs 3:5 "Trust in the Lord(*God*) **with all thine heart and lean not unto thine own understanding." 6 "In all thy ways acknowledge him**(*God*) **and he shall direct your paths." Proverbs 4:23 "Keep**(*guard*) **thy heart with all diligence; for out of it are the issues of life."**

Your spiritual heart is where God resides which means He is with you 24/7. Every moment of your day and night, awake or asleep His Holy Spirit is waiting to energized all you have to do is request it. In **Proverbs 3:5 "Trust in the Lord**(*God*) **with all thine heart; and lean not unto thine own understanding."** You are talking about trusting God with your very being. In order to accomplish this you have to give up control of your life, spiritually speaking. **II Corinthians 10:5 "Casting down imaginations and every high thing that exalteth itself against the knowledge of God and bringing into captivity every thought to the obedience of Christ."** In other words give over to God any temptations you have been holding onto. To further confirm what Jesus was doing, in **Ephesians 4:8** Jesus is saying, **"Wherefore he saith, When he ascended up on high, he led captivity captive and gave gifts unto men."** When Jesus ascended he took with him all the temptations you would possibly encounter in this life. The gifts refer to the manifestations in **I Corinthians 12:4-10.**

Being good stewards, didn't think about this one did you. . .

This is where trusting in God comes into play. Everything you own or possess really belongs to God in the first place. He has made you a steward of His possessions. Think this through for a moment. You might be saying, you bought this car not God and this is true. You physically purchased the car but where did the original thought to buy the car come from? Where did the money come from? How well have you taken care of the possessions He has already given you? As you grow in confidence of being a good steward then God may begin to open more doors for you to accept additional responsibility.

In **Proverbs 4:23** He asks us to guard or protect or keep your spiritual hearts for they contain His Words which is His Will for you. You have free will to chose whether you will use God's Word or those thoughts in your conscious mind to solve any problems.

Earlier we talked about *"trusting God"* in **Proverbs 3:5.** Well these two scriptures which have been mentioned before in the New Testament will lead you to the accuracy of the truth of God's matchless Word. And from this accuracy you can sense the feeling of trust in what you are reading.

II Peter 1:20 "Knowing this first, that no prophecy of the scriptures is of any private interpretation." 21 "For the prophecy came not in old time by the will of man, but holy men of God spake as they were moved by the Holy Ghost *(Spirit).***"**

Private interpretation means the words and phrases could have been made up out of the imaginations of these old holy men, but these words were not made up. God through revelation spoke to each of these men and gave them the words to speak. These men then wrote and spoke these same words in their own syntax or speech style. Since all scripture is prophecy these words were foretold long before you arrived on the scene.

In **Revelation 22:18 "For I testify unto every man that heareth the words of prophecy of this book, If any man shall add unto these** things, God shall add unto him the plagues that are written in this book.**" There are at least fifty different versions of the Bible.

II Timothy 3:16 "All scripture is given by inspiration*(revelation)* **of God and is profitable for doctrine, for reproof, for correction, for instruction in righteousness."**

The first five books of the New Testament are Matthew, Mark, Luke and John followed by Acts.

Next you can start with *Romans* which is the first of the epistles Paul wrote. It is considered the Doctrine for Right Believing. *I and II Corinthians* are for Reproof. *Galatians* is for Correction. The next three are *Ephesians* for Right Believing. Then *Philippians* for Reproof. And then *Colossians* for Correction. The final three books are *I and II Thessalonians* for Right Believing and *I and II Timothy* for Reproof and then *Titus* for Correction. These nine books correspond to above scripture.

Paul wrote these letters to various groups of believers because they were all struggling with either incorrect believing or being reproved for incorrect beliefs and then being corrected in an effort to bring their thoughts back into alignment and harmony with God's Word.

And this leads you to how your present and future sins will be forgiven.

Occasionally there will come a time where you step out of fellowship with your heavenly Father and follow through on one of those worldly temptations. You will sin. It is a given.

Should you realize what you have done and humbly come to your Father and ask him for forgiveness, He being a just father will forgive you of your sin and forget all about it. **I John 1:9 "If we confess our sins, he is faithful and just to forgive us our sins and cleanse us from all unrighteousness."** Nothing complicated, just do it.

Negative confessions. . .

These are some examples of negative confessions or putdowns of a person; gossip, heresy, false stories and lies. Are these all sins? **Yes.** Any unkind word you utter is looked upon as a sin. How many times have you said something which was not true? When you brag about what you have done or thought you had done in this world then bragging falls into Pride and you are guilty of yet another sin. Pride is one of Satan's favorite vices and it is the easiest to commit.

However, here is the real blessing. When you begin to stop making negative statements about others you may begin making less negative statements about yourself. It is only when you put voice to your thoughts can Satan hear them. ***Satan cannot read your thoughts.*** If you are speaking negatively about a friends personal qualities then Satan can hear you and may act accordingly should he chose to do so through some of his unholy angel spirits. The solution is not to talk about your friends faults openly. Those words fall into the category of *gossip*.

Did you know you are always protected when you are praying to the Father.

God knows your thoughts and heart and mind but Satan knows none of what you are thinking until you put your voice to it. However in your daily prayer mode when you speak out loud you are especially protected by God from anything Satan can throw at you.

The Lord's Prayer. . .

The disciples did not know how to pray to God so Jesus showed them with this prayer. This prayer is the prime example for a new believer to follow when beginning their walk with God.

In **Matthew 6:9 "After this manner***(example)*** therefore pray ye; Our Father which art in heaven, Hallowed be thy name." 10 "Thy**

**kingdom come. Thy will be done in earth, as it is in heaven."
11 "Give us this day our daily bread." 12 "And forgive us our
debts***(sins)*** as we forgive our debtors." 13 "And lead***(allow)*** us not
into temptation, but deliver us from evil; For thine is the kingdom,
and the power, and the glory, forever. Amen."**

"Our Father which art in heaven." God is our spiritual Father and
He has adopted you and I as His sons and daughters. This adoption
is called *"Sonship."* As his sons and daughters you now have *fellowship*
with Him. God dwells in heaven and heaven is anywhere God is and
since God is Spirit, His Spirit and heaven encompasses the Universe.

"Hallowed be thy name." Holy is the name of God and it is greater
than any other name in the Universe **"Thy kingdom come."** There will
be a time in the future when the kingdom of God will come to pass and
Christ Jesus will be Lord of Lords and King of Kings of the new heaven
and the new earth. **Revelations 21:1 "And I saw a new heaven and a
new earth; for the first heaven and the first earth were passed away;
and there was no more sea."** The seas will not be necessary because
we will have spiritual bodies which do not need earthly food, fish, etc.

"Thy will be done in earth as it is in heaven." God's will is for His
children to stand boldly on this earth and in this world and proclaim
His truth to those who do not know His heart or His Word.

"Give us this day our daily bread." God supplied Israel in their
40 years of travel with manna, which is a bread like food they baked
each day. It purposely spoiled in twenty four hours so Israel would have
to depend on God for their food each day. On occasion He also gave
them some quail.

"And forgive us our debts." Your debts are your sins and God is a
just and fair God who will forgive your sins when you confess them to
him. **"As we forgive our debtors."** As God forgives your sins you must
in turn forgive your fellow brothers and sisters when they transgress
against you. You should also ask for forgiveness from anyone you have
transgressed against.

**Ephesians 4:32 "And be ye kind one to another, tenderhearted,
forgiving on another even as God for Christ's sake hath forgiven you."**

"And lead us not into temptation, but deliver us from evil." Temptations come from Satan through his worldly*(spiritual)* unholy angel spirit influences. Satan already knows your weakness because you told him what they were over all those years you were not a Christian. This is a mental battle we all fight between our ears. All our action and conversations are food for the unholy angel spirits which is why we must endeavor to study God's word to begin replacing those negative confessions with positive confessions.

II Timothy 2:15 "Study to show thyself approved unto God, a workman that needeth not to be ashamed rightly dividing thy word of truth."

And finally **"For thine is the kingdom and the power and the glory forever."** This phrase means exactly what it says.

Speaking in Tongues is another form of prayer.

Now let me share with you another form of prayer which was given to the disciples by God in the upper room. Before Jesus ascended into heaven he told the disciples to tarry in Bethlehem so they could receive the "Comforter" and then . . .

Acts 2:3 "And there appeared unto them cloven tongues like as a fire and it sat upon each of them." 4 "And they were filled*(within)*** with the Holy Ghost***(Spirit)***and began to speak in tongues as the Spirit gave them utterance."**

Just as Jesus had promised the disciples in

John 14:16 "And I will pray the Father and he shall give you another comforter that he*(it)*** may abide with you forever."**

The **Comforter** is God's Holy Spirit.

In the next few days the twelve disciples and one hundred and twenty other followers were able to speak to a great multitude of men, women and children. Greek, Hebrew and Aramaic were the major languages of the time. The number of people the disciples spoke to is not known but the number who believed and came to Jesus were about three thousand <u>men.</u> **Acts 2:41 "Then they that gladly received his word were baptized; and the same day there were added unto them about three thousand souls."** The number of women and children who also came to the Lord is not known. You could figure if half of the men were married there would be a total of forty five hundred and if each family had one child who also believed then there would be six thousand people involved. The wonderful part of this whole experience was each person understood exactly what was being spoken by Peter **or the disciples or those who were with the disciples in the upper room.** How did this miracle happen? When the disciples received God's Holy Spirit in the upper room God was able to energize His Holy Spirit within each of these people to the point when they spoke in various tongues He was supplying the correct words.

It was said earlier, God has given each of you the same important gift.

When you commit your life to God and Christ Jesus, God's Holy Spirit will be *energized* within your spiritual heart. God does not just select a few people and give them His Holy Spirit as many religions adhere to. God chose each of you before the foundations of the earth. Let's look at **Ephesians 1:4 "According as he** *(God)* **hath chosen us in Him before the foundation of the world***(universe)* **that we should be holy and without blame before him in love."** God's Holy Spirit was within you the day you were born into this world. How do you know this fact. Read on.

What about speaking in tongues. . .

Your being chosen by God as His son or daughter allows the Comforter*(Holy Spirit)* to reside within you and it is this comforter which gives you the ability to speak in tongues through your believing. In **I Corinthians 12:10e "To another divers***(different)*** kinds of tongue."** Then in **I Corinthians 13:a "Though I speak with the tongues of men and of angels,"** Tongues is a language and as such to become proficient you must practice speaking it.

For the first time in **Acts 2:3,4** God has placed his Holy Spirit *within* man. In times past His Holy Spirit was *upon* those holy men in the form of revelation. **II Peter 1:21b "but holy men of God spake***(spoke)***as they were moved***(revelation)*** by the Holy Ghost(Spirit)."**The revelation concerned their speaking and eventually writing words which became part of the Old Testament. There is another example which was prior to the disciples receiving God's Holy Spirit. In **Luke 1:41 "And it came to pass, that Elisabeth heard the salutation of Mary, the babe leaped in her womb; and Elisabeth was filled with the Holy Spirit."** Elisabeth was filled with God's Holy Spirit as well as the baby John through Elisabeth's blood. **Luke 1:15b "and he shall be filled with the Holy Spirit even from his mother's womb."** Her son would later become John the Baptist who in turn would baptize Jesus.

The ability to speak in tongues first comes from your believing the word of God where He tells us in **I Corinthians 12:7 "But the manifestation of the Spirit***(God)***is given to everyman to profit withal."** You have to be a believer in order to profit from the use of these manifestations. An unbeliever will not understand what the tongue is or how to use it. There have been unbelievers who when hearing tongues being spoken have decided to become a believer.

Operation of tongues. . .

The basic operation of speaking in tongues utilizes the fundamentals of speech. You move your tongue, your lips, your mouth, your teeth and most importantly your breathing. Bringing these elements together in the five senses world will cause you to begin forming words which you can understand. Now when you speak in tongues out loud you will form and speak words just like you normally do *but you will not* understand these words, only the Holy Spirit will. The act of speaking in tongues does not require you to utilize your mind or conscious thought patterns to form the words, the Holy Spirit will take care of this action. *For you to simply relax and allow the Holy Spirit which is in you to bring forth sounds from your mouth which will make no sense at all and yet as you continue to speak the sounds will eventually form words, not of your understanding. God, however will understand everything you are speaking.*

When unbelieving or believing people hear you speak these words they will not understand them. Unbelievers will think you are speaking foolishly. Believers who are in a believers meeting know you will interrupt what you have spoken. Now there is the possibility someone in the known world might be the person who will understand the language you are speaking but not to worry, God will understand what you are saying and that is what counts. **I Corinthians 13:1a "Though I speak with the tongues of men and of angels,"**

The important part of speaking in tongues is God will understand what you are saying because it comes from your spiritual heart to His heart and He will act accordingly. Tongues is direct communication with the creator of the universe. You will not have to end your speaking in tongues *"in the name of Jesus"* because you are talking directly with God. Speaking in tongues is the external manifestation of the internal reality and presence of the Holy Spirit within you. **So if the question ever occurs to you as to whether you born again or not when you begin to speak in tongues you will know without a shadow of doubt the Holy Spirit is residing within you.**

Once you become comfortable with your newly acquired skill and are practicing it on a daily basis in your private prayer life you will begin to sense the presence of the Holy Spirit even more.

Did you know Christ Jesus your Saviour is also your spiritual step brother. . .

It is difficult to think of Christ Jesus as your step brother when all of the Christian world worship him as God thanks to Emperor Constantine at the Council of Nicea, Turkey in 325 AD. People will admit he is the Son of God and then turn around and pray *to* him rather than *through* him for whatever is going on in their lives. You must keep this in mind when you pray, Christ Jesus besides being our Saviour is our representative to his Father. Christ Jesus is your advocate to present your petitions before his Father for consideration. Christ Jesus does not answer your prayers, his Father does.

When you gave your life to Jesus Christ and his Father God, you received some wonderful blessings. The most important blessing is being able to glorify the Father. The next blessing is being saved for eternity and of course becoming a son or daughter of God. He has adopted you to be his son or daughter. Which means again He chose you before the foundation of the universe to belong to His family and since His Son is Jesus, by birth, this would then make Christ Jesus your step brother. In **Ephesians 1:11 "In whom also we have obtained an inheritance, being predestinated according to the purpose of him who worketh all things after the counsel of his own will."** When you finally meet Christ in the clouds you will have a body like his. A spiritual body which can go anywhere and pass thru anything. This time though when you meet Christ he will be King of Kings and Lord of Lords and deserves all the praise and worship due him.

Your new sins. . .

I talked earlier about how your present sins will be forgiven since all your past sins were forgiven when you gave your life to Jesus.

If there is a question in your mind concerning what sins were covered by Jesus Christ giving up his life on the cross look at **Romans 3:25 "Whom God hath set forth to be a propitiation through faith in his blood, to declare his righteousness for the remission of sins that are *past.* through the forbearance of God."**

This is a very important verse of scripture. God has given permission to His Son Jesus to pay the price for all the sins of mankind committed *prior or "past"* to his death on the cross, you as a" *born again"* Christian are <u>grandfathered</u> into this verse because you died spiritually with Jesus on the cross. For all of your *past* sins to be covered by this scripture, you have to believe Jesus' blood was the price. Jesus was declared to be righteous so your sins could be forgiven by remission through the gift from God.

If you do not believe in God or Jesus Christ you sins will not be forgiven and this will not go well in your favor at the "bema."

Jesus was given all power while here on earth. . .temporarily

Here is an interesting note, when you begin to study God's word in earnest He will open up the details so His word becomes even richer. In **Matthew 28:18 "And Jesus came and spake unto them***(the disciples)* **saying, All power is given unto me in heaven and in earth."** Which means Jesus could forgive anyone's sins while he was here on earth. Let's look a little deeper with this scripture. In **I Corinthians 15:27 " For he***(God)* **hath put all things under his feet. But when he saith all things are put under him it is manifest that he is expected, which did put all things under him." 28 "And when all things shall be subdued unto him***(God)* **then shall the Son also himself be subject unto him that put all things under him, that God may be all in all."** Now Christ is ascended and is seated at the right hand of his Father. God has resumed forgiving all the sins committed by you.

And since you are on the subject of sinning. . .

A situation has arisen here in your life where you have given into Satan and you have sinned. **Psalms 34:17"The righteous cry and the Lord***(God)* **heareth, and delivereth them out of all their troubles."** You can go to your heavenly Father and humbly confess your sin and thank Him for His forgiveness and you will be cleansed. **I John 1:9 "If we confess our sins, he***(God)* **is faithful and just to forgive us our sins and will cleanse us from all unrighteousness."** Note, in this last scripture the first word is *"If."* This is a conditional word which God has put here on purpose. He is saying if you want to exercise your *"free will"* and not ask for forgiveness then you do not have to. Of course you will not be forgiven and then you will probably not receive any answers to your prayers. Should you continue this type of behavior situations may not go well for you on the judgment day, so why take the chance. Just ask for forgiveness. Read on. . .

When God forgives your sins He will not remember them ever again. In **Psalm 103:12 "As far as the east is from the west, so far hath he removeth our transgressions from us."** You will however have to make every effort possible not to repeat the sin you were just forgiven of. And this will prove to be a very difficult task to do, but you must keep on trying. There is an expression *"to repent"* of one's sins is what you are going to have to do.

Here is an interesting note. Some people when questioning the word will ask, " Why in the above scripture is the phrase *"east is from the west"* rather than *"north is from the south."* The answer is, *"north is from the south"* have endings. The North Pole is at the top of the earth and the South Pole is at the bottom of the earth. The direction of east to west is continuous around the earth. There is no starting or stopping point.

Now repent. . .

Repent literally means "to change one's mind *(thought)* or consciousness 180 degree's, a complete change of direction of your walk with God. So to change your mind about committing a sin seems to be the easiest thing to do and yet it will require great fortitude on your part to not be lulled into Satan's trap of repeating the sin again. However, you are greatly blessed. You have a heavenly Father you can go to again and again and repent of the same sin and he will lovingly forgive you. He is a glorious Father of second and third and fourth chances and so on.

Neural Pathways. . .

What does *"neural pathway"* mean. Your brain consists of billions upon billions of neural pathways which you have formed over your lifetime and are continuing to form new pathways every time you learn something new. These pathways are for guiding the signals your body sends to your brain. When you want to make a particular motion or speak a certain word you are thinking about it in *"nanoseconds."* Walking or talking or breathing require neural pathways. The more you do the same thing the greater the size of your neural pathway. Thinking negative thoughts about yourself or another person will generate a neural pathway. The more you consider these thoughts the greater the size of the pathway and the greater are your chances of not overcoming the use of this pathway without some serious renewing of your mind. Thinking positive thoughts also requires a neural pathway. The more positive thoughts you think the larger the pathway will grow. So if you begin to think about your walk with God and it is your first steps with Him you are beginning to set up a neural pathway for God. The more you read and pray and talk with God the more neural pathways you are setting up and soon it will become very easy to spend more time with God. Those of you who have been studying God's word for a while have already developed neural pathways telling you to put off your old behavior. In **Ephesians 4:22a "That ye put off concerning the former conversations."** The word **"conversations"** means *behavior.* Doing this act is the beginning of putting on the new mind and putting off the old mind. It will take time to replace your old thoughts with God's new thoughts. It will happen when you do not give up the practice.

More about prayer. . .

In **I John 5:14 "And this is the confidence that we have in him, that if we ask anything according to his will he heareth us." 15 "And if we know that he hear us, whatsoever we ask, we know that we have**

the petitions that we desired of him." Note the words *"if"* used again in these scriptures, another condition for our *"free will."*

This is important to remember you have a vertical alignment with God. . .

In your walk with God in this life there is a vertical alignment between God and you at all times. It is very important you keep this alignment in harmony with Him through His Word. The rest of your family and work and school and church are on a horizontal basis and are prayed for on a daily basis accordingly. In other words you are *first* in your prayers to God then everyone else follows. Some old timers in the Word believe you should never pray for yourself because it is *selfish.* This is a trick of Satan. As the *spiritual leader* in your family you have to maintain your spiritual strength so you can minister to your family. In **Ephesians 5:23a "For the husband is the head of the wife."**

Let's talk briefly about this expression. *"To deny oneself."*

God says in **Matthew 16:24 "Then said Jesus unto his disciples, If any man will come after me, let him deny himself and take up his cross and follow me."** There is a phrase, *"you all have a cross to bear."* which means you all have a burden to bear throughout your walk here on earth. Where do your burdens come from? The answer is the decision making process you used. Remember *"free will."* Most likely your answer was not based on the Word of God.

Take a look at how Webster's Dictionary defines **"deny," "** *to restrain oneself from gratification of desires."* In other words stop being so **selfish** and start giving of yourself to help others.

This next area of concern is about receiving answers to your prayers. . . forgiveness on your part

Mark 11:25 "And when ye stand praying, forgive, if ye have ought against any; that your Father also which is in heaven may forgive your trespasses."

To *"stand"* is to be firm and planted in your belief in God's Word and the truth it speaks. Should you have a grievance against anyone, just as your Father in heaven forgave you when you committed your life to His son, then you should forgive those people for whatever they did against you and then forget about what they did to you. Not mentioned very often but just as necessary, if you have wronged someone then you must seek their forgiveness. Now if they chose not to forgive you then your Father in heaven will still honor your effort and you will be forgiven.

When Jesus Christ gave up his life for your *past* sins you were not even born yet. God in his infinite foreknowledge knew before you had even arrived you would be full of sin nature. God also knew Adam would let him down and take the spiritual bite so to speak. Adam had the same *"free will"* you have, he just was not strong enough in his faith to stand. What is wonderful, God never forsook Adam. He forgave Adam and continued to teach him for over nine hundred years and Adam continued to teach all his offspring including Lamech, who was the father of Noah. Think how awesome it would have been to sit at your fathers feet knowing he had been taught personally by Adam the first man on earth.

Past sins. . .and new ones

In the above paragraph I said **past** sins because it was necessary for you to start your walk with God and his Son with a clean slate.

Every sin you ever committed before you gave your life to Jesus Christ was forgiven the moment you made your commitment.

Now what will happen when you commit a new sin?

Just a quick clarification as to what is a sin. A sin, no matter the complexity, is any action taken by you of your own free will that is against anything which God says in His word you should not commit, however. . . **I John 1:9 "If we confess our sins, he***(God)* **is faithful and just to forgive us our sins***(new)* **and cleanse us from all unrighteousness."** Jesus Christ cannot be sacrificed again. His crucifixion was a one-time situation. So what do you do now?

This information bears repeating again. You now have a heavenly Father you can go to and humbly ask for forgiveness. In order for God to forgive your transgressions you must in turn forgive those who have wronged you and also ask for forgiveness from those you have wronged. The person you are going to forgive in most cases does not even know what he or she did.

It bears repeating again. Concerning those you have wronged. It may be that those individuals are not here anymore. If you cannot reach the specific person involved then you go to the Father and confess and ask for forgiveness and He will grant it. He knows your heart

The longer you continue to hang onto your pride, ego, vanity or anger Satan will continue to have control over you. Vanity and pride are two of Satan's favorite vices. He will do everything in his spiritual power to impede your progress of forgiving anyone because he knows the power you will receive from God when you have finally forgiven those people. Once you have completed the action of forgiving the people involved then the burden of holding onto your past hurts will be lifted away forever.

The action to forgive is simple.

Remember *"deny yourself."* You must endeavor to become unselfish. This means you must put aside **again** all of your ego, pride, anger, envious feelings, vanity and frustrations concerning any situation which is keeping you from receiving the promises of God.

You must stop thinking about yourself. *Do you see yourself as more important than God?* It is very important for you to put aside the *old man, your past hurts,* and put on the new man. Paul speaks to this in **Philippians 3:13 "Brethren***(this is us)* **I count not myself to have apprehended***(comprehended);* **but this one thing I do, forgetting those things which are behind and reaching forth unto things which are before."** The Word says to forget about your past. Beginning this action is one of the most liberating actions you can take because of your action a great spiritual burden will be lifted from your shoulders, a burden which you have been carrying for many years.

God sees you as precious in His eyes. You are more important to God alive than dead. Dead you cannot affect anyone's life. Alive you can become the hands and feet and mouth of God in bringing back to Him those who are lost. **Psalms 116:15 "Precious in the sight of the Lord***(God)* **is the death of his saints."**

Summation of forgiveness.

So here is what God says in **Matthew 6:14 "For if we forgive men***(and women)* **their trespasses, your heavenly Father will also forgive you;" 15 "But if ye forgive not men their trespasses neither will your Father forgive your trespasses."**

Prayer is very important. Prayer is your link with God. Without prayer you will just wander through this life with no real direction.

God has a *path* for you to walk and it is through many prayer's you will begin to understand what He wants for you. There are many people who believe God has a *"plan"* for them. In many of the various versions of the Bible which are available the scripture **Jeremiah 29:11** is commonly used to speak to the plan God has for your life. In the KJV the same verse reads **"For I***(God)* **know the thoughts that I think toward you, saith the Lord***(God)*, **thoughts of peace and not of evil, to give you an expected end."**

Did you know the word *"plan"* does not appear in the KJV of the Bible. Why! because it was added by men to change the meaning of the scripture to fit their own doctrines or religions. However, the word *"path"* does.

Should God have a *"plan"* for you would make God a respecter of persons, **Romans 2:11 "For there is no respect of persons with God,"** but He does have a *"path"* for you to follow and through daily prayer to God He will begin to show you the path.

This is another important aspect of prayer. . . believing: positive or negative.

Let me try to make this as simple as possible. Believing is a verb and therefore requires an action to take place on your part. You have control of your mind and the thoughts you put up there. When you gave your life over to Jesus Christ, God's Holy Spirit within you was energized. The spiritual energy you received from God enabled you to read His word and believe that what you were reading was the truth.

Here are three simple rules to help with believing.

One: To believe means you must have trust in whatever it is you want to believe in.

Matthew 8:13 "And Jesus said unto the centurion, Go thy way; and as thou has believed, so be it done unto thee and his servant was healed in the self same hour."

Two: To trust in something or someone you must have confidence in the something or the person.

Three: To have confidence is to put your whole heart and soul into believing.

You already know God inspired holy men of old times through revelation to write His Words in their own style of speech. What they wrote was the Word of truth. You can **believe** what they wrote because God says they did and you can **trust** in the Word because it is God's Holy Word and you can have **confidence** in the Word because it does not fail to answer the questions you have.

II Peter 1:20 "Knowing this first, that no prophecy of the scripture is of any private interpretation." 21 "For the prophecy came not in old time by the will of man; but holy men of God spake as they were moved by the Holy Ghost *(Spirit)."*

Let us look at some more examples of positive believing in the Bible.

I Thessalonians 2:13 "For this cause also thanking we God without ceasing because when ye received the word of God which ye heard of us ye received it not as the word of men but as it is in truth, the word of God, which effectually worketh also in you that believe."

Mark 11:23 "For verily I say unto you, That whosoever shall say unto this mountain, be thou removed and be cast in to the sea and shall not doubt in his heart, but shall believe that those things which he saith shall come to pass he shall have whatsoever he saith." 24 "Therefore I say unto you What things so ever ye desire, when ye pray, believe that ye receive and ye shall have."

This thought came to me. . .

God will continue to give you examples of His promises. The question is asked,*"How do you know what is a promise or not?"*

The most common answer which covers many scriptures is when the words *shall* or *will* or *shalt* or *wilt* are being used then the scripture is an absolute promise from God. Look at **Matthew 21:22 "And all things whatsoever ye shall ask in prayer, believing, ye shall receive."** The word *"things"* refers to eating, drinking and clothes. This verse of scripture says, *"believe and you shall receive."* when you ask for it in prayer and the answer will come in His timing not yours, but He will never be late.

Now for a few examples of negative believing.

Negative believing is exactly what it says. You believe the outcome of a circumstance will have a negative result on the subject concerned. Medical situations are usually surrounded by negative thinking because you or me, who like control, have none when it comes to the human body being in distress. Negative thinking is based in fear. Fear will always defeat a believer and Satan knows this. Fear is one of Satan's greatest weapons against a believer. To be afraid is to be fearful. In **II Timothy 1:7 "For God hath not given us the spirit of fear, but of power and of love and a sound mind."** Satan gladly gives you the spirit of fear through his worldly influences. Why? Because he knows you will eventually take your eyes off of God and begin placing your believing in him and Satan knows this because you have already invited him into your life long ago when you did not know the truth of God's Word. The world is full of millions of people who are inviting Satan into their lives on a daily basis.

Check out the Third Commandment in **Exodus 20:3 "Thou shalt have no other gods before me."** This is a commandment from God. To break His commandments is a sin. But did you know that Satan is a god to all those who believe in him. So if you are a follower of Satan's ways then you are worshiping him and not the true God. And to be a follower of Satan is easy. Just have fear in your life and you are on your way.

Here is an interesting fact. You cannot believe in God, the true God if you have fear in your heart. Why? Fear will cause doubt in your believing. Does Satan know this fact? To get a handle on fear is to try to understand where the fear is coming from. Usually you will lack an understanding of the fear or do not have all the facts concerning the situation or you are trying to hide something. This is when fear will begin creeping into your conscious thoughts. So in order to dismiss fear you must have all the facts concerning what is causing the fear so you can counter it with God's Word. In **John 20:19 "Then the same day at evening being the first day of the week when the doors were shut**

where the disciples were assembled for fear of the Jews, came Jesus and stood in the midst and saith unto them, Peace be unto you."

You see the disciples behind locked doors for fear of what the Jews would say or do to them. Peter, the rock, has denied Jesus at least three times maybe more. **Luke 22:57 "And he denied him, saying Woman I know him not."** What did Peter have? Fear! Keep this in mind, the Judean population was under the law. It governed everything they did.

The Law. . .

Let me touch briefly concerning the "law." God told Moses after Israel had crossed the Red Sea and had spent the last forty years wandering in the wilderness they were in need of some divine guidance. So God gave to Moses ten commandments which were to help get Israel back on track of worshiping God and not idols. Well when Moses, after forty days with God, came down from Mount Sinai with the ten commandments written by God he found Israel had made a gold idol and were worshipping it. Moses became so angry he broke the tablets. Now Moses had to go back up the mount and spend another 40 days with God. This time God decided Israel needed more help than just the Ten Commandments. So He wrote 611 laws for Israel to follow. He wrote them on clay tablets and Moses brought them back down. Later the first two commandments from the Ten Commandments were added to the original 611 arriving at the common number of 613. Moses gave the responsibility of administering these laws to the tribe of Levi. Now reading the laws gave you knowledge of what was a sin in God's eyes. The problem was most of the Israelites could not follow all the laws because they kept breaking them and that led to a great amount of sin being committed. When Jesus came and died on the cross his death fulfilled all those laws that God had given to Israel. What remained were the original Ten Commandments. These commandments are what we as born again believers should endeavor to follow in our daily walk.

Many years ago I heard this quote *"Fear is the sand in the machinery of life."* Interesting.

UNBELIEF = DOUBT / ANSWER IS CONFIDENCE
UNBELIEF = WORRY / ANSWER IS TRUST
UNBELIEF = FEAR / ANSWER IS FAITH/BELIEVING
Where does spiritual darkness come from? Answer: Satan
What is spiritual darkness filled with? Answer: Fear
What dispels spiritual darkness? Answer: Light
Who is light? Answer: God in **I John 5b "God is light, and in him is no darkness at all."**

Since God is light then his word must be light. When you read His Word and retain it *(here's those neural pathways again)* then you will begin to dispel the darkness within your mind. You know now God will never forsake you. He is there always waiting for you to call upon him. Remember God will always give you a path to escape upon because he will never give you more than you can handle.

I Corinthians 10:13 "There hath no temptation taken you but such as is common to man; but God is faithful, who will not suffer*(allow)* **you to be tempted above that ye are able, but will with temptation also make a way to escape, that ye may be able to bear it."**

Let us summarize what you have received from God so far.

You have accepted Jesus Christ as your Lord and Savior.
You have received and energized God's Holy Spirit within yourself.
You will spend eternity with God and Christ Jesus.
You are joint heirs with Christ Jesus in the inheritance God has for you.
All your past sins are forgiven.
You have a heavenly Father who will forgive all your future sins, one at a time, when you humble yourselves and repent.
You have a new brother in Christ Jesus.
You have a new Holy Father in God.
You have learned believing can be positive or negative, your choice.

You have the spiritual power to do everything Jesus Christ did and more, you just have to believe you can do it. **John 14:12 "Verily, verily, I say unto you, He that believeth on me, the works that I do shall he do also; and greater works than these shall he do;"**

You can now pray to your Holy Father, the creator of the universe thru His son Jesus Christ and know He*(God)* hears your petitions. The term *"greater works"* will be talked about later. **John 14:13 "And whatsoever ye shall ask in my name, that will I do that the Father may be glorified in the Son.**

Is it available. . .is what available.

Now let's take a look at what is available from God. In order to tap the resources of the power of God you must know first of all what is and what is not available from God. It is useless to pray to God for something you want if it is not available.

So, what is available?

First: All the promises in His Word. There are thousands in His Word. All of God's promises are a commitment to you He will provide for all*(without distinction)* your needs.

Second: How do you receive these promises? You must believe God's Word, then to claim these promises you must thank Him for them. You do not have to beg or plead for them. They are yours for the asking. Then all you have to do is walk out on the promises you desire, believing you will receive them. Doing this one will require practice. Start small and work your way up.

Matthew 14:29 And he*(Jesus)* **said, come. And when Peter was come down out of the ship, he walked on the water, to go to Jesus."**

Third: What to do with these promises once you have received them. Let's take an easy one, **Philippians 4:13 "I can do all things through Christ which strengthen me."**

Do you believe this verse of scripture, **Philippians 4:13**? What is being said in this scripture applies to all spiritual situations which will affect you. There is nothing in the physical world which applies to this scripture. In other words you cannot jump off a building and expect to land without an injury. OK! You are in a spiritual battle with Satan. Having the knowledge of God's Word in your heart and mind will allow you to do all things spiritually **through** Christ and receive the strength from God.

Satan would be very happy to see you *not take advantage* of what is available from God whether it be His gifts or abundance or peace or strength. The following scripture is so powerful when you apply it to your daily walk. **John 10:10 "The thief cometh not but for to steal, and kill and to destroy. I am come that they might have life and that they might have it more than abundantly."**

You know who the thief is, Satan. Satan has come to *steal* anything spiritual he can from you. Satan has come to *kill* your spiritual life by causing untruth and lies to enter into your life. And Satan has come to *destroy* what you have gained from believing the Word of God. Jesus Christ has come to give you life and that it will be more than you could ever think or know about.

Part of being able to receive answers to your prayers is you must pray continually, not continuously, for whomever or whatever is on our heart.

In the New Testament, the apostle Paul says in **I Thessalonians 5:17 "Pray without ceasing."** What Paul means is when you are praying for a person or a situation and you want to receive an answer from God one single prayer *will not* suffice. You must endeavor to pray for the same situation *continually* until it comes to a satisfactory conclusion. Mark Batterson in his book *"The Circle Maker"* tells you to pray through the circumstance of receiving the answer to your prayers. When you pray *each day* include any special requests you may have. To receive any answer from God you must continue to pray for any given situation or person daily. When God sees your heart and knows your desire to be willing to put forth the effort He will begin to take action but only in His time.

When you are praying for a person to change their ways you have absolutely no control over them so nothing will happen on your part. You must step back and allow God to take control. You do not have the resources to make the change. Everything depends on the person involved having to change their spiritual heart and mind. With God in control the change will take place in God's timing. During this process God will give you peace in your spiritual heart, but do not stop praying.

Here is some more on what is available from God. . .

III John 2 "Beloved, I wish*(pray)* **above***(concerning)* **all things that thou mayest prosper and be in health***(hogianio-gk),* **even as thy soul***(consciousness)* **prospereth."**

God wants you to have good health. He does not want you to be sick nor does He want you to fail in the pursuit of your heart's desire as long as you are following His will.

Philippians 4:19 "By God shall supply all your need according to his riches in glory by*(thru)* **Christ Jesus."**

All your needs and wants are available to be supplied by God, but those needs and wants have to be in alignment and harmony according to God's word and will. Should your needs and wants meet those requirements then God will supply them in His timing and God is never late.

Your prayers constitute your belief in God that He will provide for you and He will as long as you take believing action and walk out on His promises.

II Corinthians 9:8 "And God is able to make all grace abound toward you, that ye, always having all sufficiency in all things may abound to every good work."

God's promises are available for us to read, remember and claim. Whatever God says in His word He has done or will do. His promise can be taken to the spiritual bank and be deposited.

Matthew 4:4 "But he *(Jesus)* **answered and said, it is written, Man shall not live by bread alone but by every word that proceedeth out of the mouth of God.**"

Interesting note. There is a term used by theologians to give human characteristics to God. In the Greek it is called *"condescensio."* In English it is called *"anthropomorphism."* It literally means *" mouth of God"*.

God talks about eating his word. In **Jeremiah 15:16 "Thy words were found and I did eat them** *(lived by them)* **and thy word was unto me the joy and rejoicing of mine heart; for I am called by thy name, O Lord God of hosts.**"

"Thy words were found" refers to a personal letter of Jeremiah which was found among the Dead Sea scrolls.

"Thy words were found and I did eat them" is what I believe Adam and Eve *"ate"* in the Garden of Eden when they were confronted by Satan. There was no actual fruit, instead it was a metaphor.

God means for you to read and digest or understand His Word. The more you read the more your conscious thoughts will begin to show the knowledge and understanding His Word displays and from knowledge will come God's wisdom for you to apply accordingly. *"Wisdom is knowledge applied."*

For unbelieving singles.

There may be times when you will encounter unbelieving family members who have asked you to pray for them. As believers walking with God it is your responsibility to sow God's Word lovingly without prejudice. An unbeliever who has heard God's Word spoken to them by you through your prayer may have a softening of their hardened heart and want to come into the family of God and your God will know this. You are not responsible for the harvest only the sowing of His seed.

II Corinthians 6:14 **"Be ye not unequally yoked together with unbelievers; for what fellowship hath righteousness with unrighteousness? And what communion hath light with darkness."**

For unbelieving married couples.

I Corinthians 7:14 **"For the unbelieving husband is sanctified** *(set apart)* **by the wife and the unbelieving wife is sanctified by the husband, else were your children unclean; but now they are holy."** Which means your unbelieving wife or husband is covered by your believing. This does not mean they will become believers. It simply means through the marriage covenant with God He will cover these members of your family with the same protection He gives to you.

A Hard hearted individual.

Now a hard hearted individual such as a marriage mate could openly express his or her desire to repent of their sinful life and come to God even if they are on their death bed and God will gladly open His arms and forgive all their sins and accept them into His family forever.

Intercessory Prayer

This is a quote from a devotional called *"Manna In The Morning."* This particular quote was written by Oswald J. Smith in 1943.

"Intercessory Prayer is without a doubt not only the highest form of Christian service, but is also the hardest kind of work. To the person who is not an intercessor such a statement seems absurd. Prayer to most people is looked upon as an easy occupation. Difficulties are unknown. But that is because they know nothing at all of the Ministry of Intercession. Their prayers, for the most part, are centered upon themselves. Their loved ones and their personal interest with the occasional petition for the perishing heathen. To set aside a special hour during the day or to wait before God

half the night never enters their minds. Their prayer life is spasmodic. It is considered a side issue and is readily neglected if other things demand attention. Such persons are in no way affecting the Kingdom of Satan. Hence, prayer, so-called is easy."

"But the Christian who enters upon the ministry of intercession will pass through a very different experience. Satan will do everything in his power to hinder and obstruct this person in their efforts to pray. There will be a conscious realization of his presence and opposition. Interruptions innumerable will come. The telephone will ring, visitors will call, and a hundred other things that never would have bothered otherwise will have to be taken into account. We are living in the 20th century. Never have we known such bustle and rush and hurry. The whole world is forging ahead at a terrific pace. Hours of quietness and retirement are becoming more and more difficult to observe. Thus the work of the intercession becomes hard."

Satan knows full well the less you pray about people's lives your prayer will be powerless and fruitless. Hence if he can keep you busy through his influences then you will not have time to pray and he will have accomplished his purpose. So how do you stay your mind on God. . .by reading the scriptures.

Praying in the scriptures.

This is by far the easiest of all the prayer methods because you only have to go to the Word of God and read the scriptures. In many cases the scriptures like those in Psalms. Written by David as he was fleeing from King Saul he would sing these words to God. You do not have to sing these words unless you want too. They are already prayers in themselves. Find a scripture which will fit your petition or request to God and add a little of your personal life to it. Like who is the Psalm addressed to. Add your name to the verse and you are now *"praying in the scriptures."*

We have already discussed how to listen for an answer to your prayer? Read it again. . .

It will help you to hear from God when you are in a quiet place away from the distractions of the world. You need to be in a prayer mode which means having just finished praying to God. God will answer your prayers in His time and when He answers your prayer, if you are looking for a specific answer concerning a situation the answer may come as your *very first thought*. This thought will come very quickly, very quietly and it will not be repeated. This is why you are told over and over to listen for God to speak after you have prayed.

In conclusion.

To pray you must speak. To speak you must believe. To believe you must be humble. To be humble so you can forgive. And when you forgive then you will hear from God.

Chapter Three

Confronting your unholy angel spirits, these are the bad ones.

You are involved in a major spiritual war today. A war which continues to grow. To give you an idea of what you are up against let me share a quote which I believe will help sum up what you have to be prepared for in this battle. Five hundred years before the birth of Jesus Christ a Chinese general named Sun Tzu wrote a book called "The Art of War." At that time in Chinese history there were warring tribes or clans of families who were constantly fighting each other for power and territory. Sun Tzu became very successful in the battles he fought because he won them all. This is part of what he said in his book, *"If you know the enemy and know yourself, you need not fear the result of a hundred battles. If you know yourself but not the enemy for every victory gained you will also suffer a defeat. If you know neither the enemy nor yourself, you will succumb in every battle. In other words you will win every battle if you know your enemy's strengths, weaknesses and tactics in addition to your own."*

As" *born again*" saints of God you must take a stand against the wiles of the Satan or his war against you will continue to escalate, **Ephesians 6:11a "Put on the whole armour of God, that ye may be able to stand against the wiles of the devil,"** and grip your world. So with this challenge in mind let's move on.

Every day when you leave your home you should endeavor to put on the armour of God. His awesome Word has to be in your spiritual heart and mind. This is the same spiritual heart and mind*(nous - Greek)* or conscious thoughts you received when you became *"born again."* God gave you His Word so you could arrest the wiles (tricks) or works of Satan. God does not say you could defeat Satan only Christ Jesus can and will deal with Satan at the conclusion of your world's existence and the new heaven and new earth are formed.

Ephesians is one of the most comprehensive books of the New Testament in the Bible. In it Paul explains in more detail how you are supposed to withstand the wiles of Satan. In **Ephesians 6:11 "Put on the whole armour of God, that ye may be able to stand against the wiles of the devil." 12 "For we wrestle not against flesh and blood, but against principalities, against powers, against the rulers of the darkness of this world, against spiritual wickedness in high places." 13 "Wherefore take unto you the whole armour of God, that ye may be able to withstand in the evil day and having done all, to stand." 14 "Stand therefore, having your loins girt about with truth and having on the breastplate of righteousness." 15 "And your feet shod with the preparation of the gospel of peace." 16 "Above all taking the shield of faith wherewith ye shall be able to quench all the fiery darts of the wicked." 17 "And take the helmet of salvation, and the sword of the Spirit, which is the word of God." 18 "Praying always with all prayer and supplication in the spirit, and watching thereunto***(every minute)*** with all perseverance and supplication for all saints." 19 "And for me***(Paul)*** that utterance may be given unto me. That I may open my mouth boldly, to make known the mystery of the** gospel."

Here are some positive areas you can take to heart in knowing Satan cannot accomplish;

HE CANNOT CREATE.
HE CANNOT CORRUPT YOUR INCORRUPTIBLE SEED GIVEN TO YOU BY GOD.
HE CANNOT VIOLATE NATURAL LAWS*(God's Law of Nature)*

HE CANNOT VIOLATE THE LAWS GIVEN TO MAN BY GOD. HE CANNOT READ YOUR MIND. **Colossians 1:21 "And you, that were sometime alienated and enemies in your mind by wicked works, and yet now hath he reconciled."** HE CANNOT PREVENT THE RETURN OF CHRIST. . . and HE CANNOT STEAL YOUR ETERNAL LIFE.

The Devil, Lucifer, Satan or The Adversary. . .

These are a few of the many names associated with Lucifer, God's second in command at one time. The words Satan or Devil are used exclusively in the KJV of the Bible, whereas Lucifer is used only sparingly. The word Adversary is a more politically correct name, but does not conjure up as much of a negative feeling as do the words Devil or Satan. The word Adversary is not used in the KJV of the Bible.

So, who was Lucifer?

Sometime long before God created the heavens and earth, He created many spiritual beings called angels. The most important were called Archangels. Michael, the Warrior. He fought for God in all spiritual battles. **Jude 9 "Yet Michael the archangel when contending with the devil he disputed about the body of Moses, durst (dare) not bring against him a railing accusation, but said, The Lord rebuke thee."** Gabriel, the Messenger. He is responsible for all the messages from God to those on earth. Gabriel had at his disposal many angels who were available to help deliver those messages. In **Luke 1:19 "And the angel answering said unto him, I am Gabriel, that stand in the presence of God; and am sent to speak unto thee and to shew thee these glad tidings."** This is the same arch angel who brought the message from God to Zacharias's wife Elizabeth, who gave birth to John the Baptist, Jesus' first cousin. Gabriel personally spoke from the **"burning bush." Exodus 3:2a "And an angel of the Lord appeared** unto him *(Moses)* **in a flame of fire out of the midst of a bush.**" Now this leaves Lucifer the Angel of Light. **Isaiah 14:12 "How art thou fallen from heaven O Lucifer son of the morning! How art thou cut down to the ground which didst weaken** *(revile)* **the nations.**" Lucifer's light was so bright it out shown all the rest of the angels. He was called the Morning Light. He was the most handsome of all the angels and the smartest.

Contrary to popular opinion angels do not have wings. They are spirit beings and can travel anywhere and go through anything. They have the same body as Christ Jesus. The only angels with wings are those depicted in paintings by the old masters.

The Angel/Devil spirits. . .

Revelation 12:4a "And his tail drew the third part of the stars of heaven, and did cast them to the Earth." This is a reference to the constellation *"Draco"* or *"Hydra"* in Greek. The Hydra had seven heads. This constellation is red because of the burning gases which make up the stars within this constellations cluster. The Red Dragon is also called Satan in the heavens.

Did you ever think why did God create evil?

Isaiah 45:7 "I form the light and create the darkness; I make peace and create evil; I the Lord *(God)* **do all these things.**"

God deemed it necessary to create evil because had he not, we would not have been given *"free will"* to chose between good and evil. God would have had to possess each of us and we would have robbed God of what he really wanted. He wants all the individuals on earth to come to Him of their own free will and glorify Him.

So what you have now is Lucifer and a third of all the angels cast out from Heaven. The key phrase is *"in the earth."* **Job 1:7 "And the Lord** *(God)* **said unto Satan, Whence comest thou? Then Satan**

answered the Lord, and said, From going to and fro in the earth and from walking up and down in it." God did not just cast Lucifer out of heaven and to the earth but He cast Lucifer to roam forever beneath the surface of the earth. The angel spirits which came with Lucifer are now unholy angel spirits. They can wander both under, on and above the surface of the earth. Please keep this fact in mind, all these unholy angels are spirits, they have no comely form.

I know I am getting ahead of myself but what is going to happen in the end. . .?

When you die your personal spirit will pass on into Paradise and wait patiently for Christ to return. When he returns this will be known as the "Gathering." You will rise to heaven with your new body. It is there you will stand before the *"bema"* and receive your *"crown."* Christ will return to earth as King of Kings and Lord of Lords along with those of you who stood faithful to the end. You will be coming back as a priest. **Revelation 20:6b "but they*(us)*shall be priests of God and of Christ and shall reign with him a thousand years."** You will be with Christ for one thousand years reconciling men and women back to God. When the thousand years are completed you will go back to heaven and the battle will commence between Satan and his armies and Christ and his armies. **Revelation 20:7 "And when the thousand years are expired Satan shall be loosed out of his prison." Revelation 13:5b "and power was given unto him to continue forty and two months."** This time will be known as the Tribulation. It will last three and one/ half years. The Tribulation is specifically addressed to Israel and its completion. At the end of the Tribulation Satan will lose the battle and he will be cast into the Lake of Fire forever along with anyone else whose name was not in the Lambs Book of Life. Basically it will be those who were not *"born again."*

Did you know Satan has his own bible. . .

Lucifer wanted to be number one. He wanted all the worship God was going to receive. Well God did not disappoint Lucifer. Satan has the undying love and worship from one third of the unholy angel spirits who joined him and these could easily number in the billions. There is also a very large collection of Satan worshipers right here on earth and they are not unholy angel spirits, they are flesh and blood individuals who believe in Satan. Believe it or not you can go to Amazon/ Books and find Satan's own bible.

Moving on. . .

In **Genesis 1:2b "And the Spirit of God moved upon the face of the waters." 3 "And God said, Let there be light; and there was light." 9 "And God said, Let the waters under the heaven be gathered together unto one place, and let the dry land appear; and it was so." 10 "And God called the dry land Earth; and the gathering together of the waters called the Seas; and God saw that it was good."**

Please keep this in mind when reading the scriptures. Everything did not happen as quickly as it would appear when the scriptures follow each other.

God did not violate any of His physical laws when He created the heavens. Whatever length of time was necessary to create a nebula or a planet, the time was allowed for. Miracles were not necessary in the creation of the universe. God took his time because there was no rush. Man was created way down the time line. We are really nothing but a speck of dust waiting to be blown away. In fact, all of mankind occupies only the last two minutes on a twenty-four clock.

In **II Peter 3:8 "But beloved, be not ignorant of this one thing, that one day is with the Lord***(God)* **as a thousand years, and a thousand years as one day."**

Ok! enough of these facts, let's get down to your battle. . .

Back to **Ephesians 6:12 "We wrestle not against flesh and blood but against principalities, against powers, against the rulers of the darkness of this world, against spiritual wickedness in high places."** All of your personal battles are fought between your ears. Your daily thoughts moment by moment are exactly what Satan is setting his sights on. Remember he cannot read your thoughts. His unholy angel spirits know what buttons to push to take you off your objective and cause disbelief and doubts because they know what can influence your thoughts in this world. What is the solution? Begin memorizing a scripture each day. Just one each morning and as the day goes on repeat the scripture to yourself. As you encounter a situation which could be upsetting begin saying your personal scripture to yourself or when you are in a crowd. If you are alone say it out loud. Satan's worldly influences cannot stand up to God's word.

Possession. . .

Have you ever heard the expression *"I wonder what possessed those people to do such a terrible thing."* The key word is ***"possessed."*** It is the process of a devil spirit inhabiting an individual and it is called Demonetization. There are billions of unholy angel spirits following Satan and inhabiting billions of individuals. The people who are inhabited may or may not be Christians. Just because you say you are a Christian does not mean you cannot be tempted by a unholy angel spirit and your giving into the temptation could mean your spirit life would be inhabited. Satan is after those of you who are new to the Word of God or have just given your lives over to Jesus Christ or who have been following Jesus Christ most of your life, in other words most people who believe they are Christians. Satan's unholy angel spirits have now become an army of pure evil.

For example you see in this scripture of **Mark 5:8 " For he***(Jesus)* **said unto him, come out of the man, thou unclean spirit." 9 "And he asked him, what is thy name? And he answered, saying My name is Legion for we are many."** *(around 6,000)."*

Here is God's Word telling you there was a devil spirit by the name of Legion in this man. Legion was responsible for leading six thousand unholy angel spirits which were also in this person. For further study go to this web site *(greatbiblestudy/biblical_demonology.php)*.

Satan rears his ugly head at Jesus.

Let us look at **Matthew 4:1 "Then was Jesus led up of the spirit into the wilderness to be tempted by the devil.** *(Lucifer).***" 2 "And when he had fasted forty days and forty nights he was afterward an hungered." 3 "And when the tempter came to him, he said, If thou be the Son of God command that these stones be made bread." 5 "Then the devil taketh him up into the holy city and setteth him on the pinnacle of the temple." 6 "And saith unto him, If thou be the Son of God cast thyself down; for it is written He shall give his angels charge concerning thee and in their hands shall they bear thee up lest at any time thou dash thy foot against a stone." 8 "Again the sheweth him all the kingdoms of the world and the glory of them." 9 "And saith unto him, All these things will I give thee, if thou wilt fall down and worship me."**

In this situation God allowed Satan to take on a human form to tempt Jesus.

How unholy angel spirit's have an effect on us!

The most popular opening used by an unholy angel spirit is in your conscious and subconscious mind. To get to this opening they utilize your eyes and everything you see, your ears and everything you hear, your mouth and everything you speak. Satan and his unholy angel spirits cannot read your thoughts but when you continually have negative thoughts and voice them about any situation for an extended period of time then these spirits can begin to infiltrate your body in your limbs or internal organs or sight, speech or hearing. It may be in your thought patterns or a specific sickness, whatever those evil spirits feel may be your weakest points. All these thoughts are called *negative thoughts*. In **James 4:7 "Submit***(subject to or addicted-gk hoputasso)* **yourselves therefore to God. Resist***(against)* **the devil***(diabolos-direct)* **and he will flee from you."** Here is a fact concerning unholy angel spirits lodging within your conscious or subconscious thoughts. You had to give them, at one time or another in your life before you were *"born again"* and usually without your knowledge, permission to inhabit you. This may sound a bit crazy but keep this in mind. Anytime you uttered fowl language or anger towards someone you were giving unholy angel spirits permission to come into your thoughts.

In the Garden. . .

Let us go back in time while the earth was still forming and God in this verse said. **Genesis 1:2a "And the earth was***(or became)* **without form and void."**

Sometime after the creation of the earth and before Adam and Eve were created Lucifer and billions of his now unholy angel spirits had already been expelled from heaven to spend eternity in and on the earth. It seemed only fitting that the sneakiest individual in heaven had to be Lucifer. What better spiritual person than he to mess with the minds of Adam and Eve. Down through the ages people stopped calling Lucifer by his heavenly name and chose Satan or in some cases the Devil. Satan knew God had created Adam and Eve so the thought of causing these people to fall from grace just tickled Satan beyond his wildest dreams. Since he could not be number one in the universe he would do whatever he could to bring down God's own personal creation.

Let's go on. . .

The word *"serpent"* in **Genesis 3:1a "Now the serpent was more subtle than any beast of the field, which the Lord God had made."** Satan chose the body of a snake to speak to Eve and Adam. Satan has the ability to influence our thinking with a variety of stimuli. He spoke to Eve through her conscious thoughts.

The emotion of fear did not yet exist so there would be no reason for Eve to be uncomfortable around a serpent. Once Satan planted the idea in Eve's mind to doubt what God told them the rest was easy. Now God comes along after Satan has confronted Eve and tells the serpent in **Genesis 3:14 "And the Lord God said unto the serpent, Because thou hast done this, thou art cursed above all cattle, and above every beast of the field; upon thy belly shalt thou go, and dust shalt thou eat all the days of thy life."** So we have Satan who spoke through the image of a serpent now permanently changed into the same creature. Here is Lucifer the smartest, most beautiful of all the angels changed permanently into a serpent. Many Medieval and Renaissance period artists depicted Satan in a variety of reptilian forms with wings and tails. So the question came up, what happened to Adam not opening his mouth and speaking to Eve.

God said in **Genesis 2:16 "And the Lord God commanded that man, saying Of every tree in the garden thou mayest freely eat."** 17 **"But the tree of the knowledge of good and evil, thou shalt not eat of it; for in the day that thou eatest thereof thou shalt surely die."** Adam had full knowledge of the rules of the Garden., but he chose not to speak. The phrase in verse 17 *"not eat"* is a figure of speech. This phrase is not true to fact. The word fruit is never mentioned in this scripture. The verse talks about eating so we naturally think food is involved when in reality there was no fruit only knowledge. And what is knowledge but words, whose words, God's Words. It is interesting to note all the trees in the Garden had fruit which made them seed bearing (*this goes back to Genesis 1:29*) except the tree of the knowledge of good and evil. And now we come to the end of the verse. The words *"surely die"* does not mean a physical death but instead a spiritual death or the absence of God's Holy Spirit upon and within your daily existence.

Talk about eating. . .

In **Jeremiah 15:16 "Thy words were found and I did eat them, and thy word was unto the joy and rejoicing of mine heart. For I am called by thy name, O Lord, God of hosts."**

"Thy words were found" refers to the Dead Sea scrolls where a letter from Jeremiah was found. Going back to **Genesis 2:16** the phrase *"thou mayest freely eat"* carries the same connotation as, *"and I did eat them,"* in Jeremiah 15:16. This phrase is *"I did eat them"* a figure of speech. The phrase is not true to fact. So we apply an known fact to a spiritual one and though we literally cannot eat the words off the paper we can through our reading of these words apply their knowledge to our walk. This is what Adam and Eve did in their personal walk with God even after they were expelled from the Garden of Eden. So what is being said here is Adam and Eve ate nothing physical of the tree of knowledge of good and evil because there was nothing physical to eat. Though there is no more mention of Eve in the Bible God did not forsake Adam. God continued to teach Adam everything he would need to know for the next 900 years and Adam in turn continued to teach his offspring including Lamech who was the father of Noah.

Here is another tool to deal with Satan's wiles. . .

I John 4:4 "Ye are of God little children and have overcome them, because greater is he that is in you than he that is in the world." You are a child of God who has His Holy Spirit within you. His Holy Spirit was energized when you made the commitment to follow after Jesus Christ. God in Christ in you is greater than Satan who rules the World.

Please understand this, when we talk about the **world** anytime in this book we are referring to Satan's worldly realm which sits on top of the earth. God still controls the physical **earth** and the elements which affect it. The spiritual world Satan controls sits on top of the earth. Check out **Ephesians 6:12 "For we wrestle not against flesh and blood, but** against principalities, against powers, against rulers of the darkness of this world, against spiritual wickedness in high places."

Deny yourself. . .

This is another method Satan employs to bring you down. Your own **selfishness**. A man by the name of Louis Binstock made a very famous quote many years ago. He said *"We are our own worst enemy."* Could he have been anymore correct. Is he talking about how selfish you are in all aspects of your life? The sin nature you are born with is still active in your daily life all thanks to Adam whose name actually means in the Greek language *"of the ground or earth."*

Adam is gone, so what do you do now?

God says this in **Matthew 7:13 "Enter ye** *(you)* **in at the strait gate; for wide is the gate and broad is the way that leadeth to destruction, and many there be which go in thereat." 14 "Because strait is the gate and narrow is the way, which leadeth unto life and few there be that find it. "**

One path is wide and full of destruction. This is the path Satan shows you. An easy path. The other path is narrow and leads to life, eternal life. This is the path God shows you and it is not easy. You will have to pick the one to walk down.

So! You have now picked the path which gets your life lined up with God and His Son so you can walk His narrow path. In **Romans 10:9 "That if thou shalt confess with thy mouth the Lord, Jesus and shalt believe in thine heart that God hath raised him from the dead, thou shalt be saved." 10 "For with the heart man believeth unto righteousness; and with the mouth confession is made unto salvation."** God has made salvation very easy for you as long as you believe.

Going back to the Garden for a moment. . .

This is an interesting thought. Adam was told he could eat of any tree in the Garden except the tree of the knowledge of Good and Evil. What Adam missed was the Tree of Life. **Genesis 3:22 "And the Lord God said, Behold the man is become as one of us, to know good and evil; and now lest he put forth his hand and take also of the tree of life, and eat, and live forever."** Had Adam partaken of its' metaphorical fruit he would have lived forever.

Here is another tool you have to fight off Satan's fiery darts.

To **not** forgive someone who has hurt you goes against everything God continues to teach. Not forgiving others who have wronged you will affect your expectation of answers to your prayers. In other words if you have not forgiven those who have hurt you in your life then God could withhold answers to your prayers until you have completed the action of forgiveness which He asks for. Keep this in mind. Are you bigger than God to not forgive someone considering God has already forgiven you for all your past transgressions.

When you walk with God you are larger than any situation you will encounter. God within you makes a majority of two.

Colossians 3:15 "And let the peace of God rule in your hearts, to the which also ye are called in one body; and be ye thankful."

Thankful is the key. When you allow God's peace to govern in your heart and mind, the very inner part of your body, your mind *(nous-Greek)* will begin to dwell on what God has given you, an abundance of His Word. A daily diet of this wonderful Word will change your thoughts, and in turn will change your behavior to the point when people who know you will begin to remark about seeing something different in your presence. An inner confidence will be radiated out.

You have been called to the one body of the church by Christ. Jesus who is the groom and you are part of the body, the bride as it were.

You will be joined together forever at the Gathering and then what a wedding celebration will there be in Heaven.

Hebrews 3:8 "Harden not your hearts, as in the provocation, in the day of temptation in the wilderness."

A caution from God. Do not allow Satan to cause you to break fellowship with the Father. Please do not turn your heart away from God. Just as Jesus was tempted in the wilderness he did not yield to the Devil. In **Luke 4:1 "And Jesus being full of the Holy Ghost** *(Spirit)* **returned from Jordan and was led by the Spirit into the wilderness." 2 "Being forty days tempted by the devil (the Devil). And in those days he** *(Jesus)* **did not eat nothing; and when they were ended he hungered afterward." 3 " And the Devil said unto him, If thou be the Son of God, command this stone that it be made bread." 4 " Jesus answered him, saying, It is written, "That man shall(absolute promise from** *God)* **not live by bread alone but by every word of God."**

To harden your heart, your spiritual heart, the one you received from God will break the line of communication you have established with Him and could cause future problems with your earthly walk. Part of your hard heart is made up of pride.

What does Pride mean? "Inordinate self esteem."

You know from *Ephesians 6:12* you wrestle not against flesh and blood but against principalities and the powers of this world. The battle takes place where? Between your ears, your conscious mind. The pride you are talking about is not of the accomplishments of others, but *yourself.*

Pride is of this world, Satan's world, therefore pride is of Satan. The picture being painted of the world in the first part of *Ephesians 6:12* is not what God wants you to dwell upon. God wants you to consider everything He has created for you. All the beauty of nature, the oceans, the mountains and the heavens.

What does doubt means "to lack confidence in."

God is asking you not to worry about what you shall eat or drink. There is a tendency to think too much about where your next meal might be coming from. Sort of a survival attitude on your part. And yet all God asks you to do is count on Him for your survival. He has stated He is your sufficiency in all things. In **II Corinthians 9:8 "And God is able to make all grace abound toward you; that ye, always having all sufficiency in all things, may abound to every good work."**

Remember when God talks about the lilies of the field never toiling or the birds going hungry. A doubtful mind is a mind which lacks the confidence in what God says He will do for you. When you continue to allow the influences of Satan's world to enter into your mind(remember the battleground) you will continually have doubts about what is happening in your walk. Once you allow Satan a foothold in your thought processes, conscious thoughts, then you will begin to doubt your very being and why you are here on earth. Those conscious thoughts will become negative thoughts and you know where those will lead you.

Philippians 4:6 "Be careful for nothing, but in everything by prayer and supplication with thanksgiving let your requests be made know unto God."

What is another word for *"careful,"* in Philippians 4:6? It is *"anxious."*

Please read on in **Luke 12:30 "For all these things do the nations of the world seek after, and your Father knoweth that ye have need of these things." 31 "But rather seek ye the kingdom of God and all***(without distinction)* **these things will be added unto you."**

What are the *"things"* God is talking about in Luke 12:30? Could they be food, confidence, clothing, peace of mind and shelter? God is asking you to seek His kingdom first over Satan's world. You are to make His Word a part of your daily life. You are to act upon His Word by believing what He says. God is aware of your needs and wants and He will supply both in abundance when they are in harmony with His word. **John 10:10b "I *(Jesus)*am come that they might have life, and that they might have it more abundantly."**

Here is another tool to deal with Satan. . .

John 14:27a "Peace I leave with you, my peace I give unto you, not as the world giveth, give I unto you."

The peace God gives you is not what the world calls peace. The peace God gives you comes from a mind totally committed to Christ Jesus and God. When you begin to believe God is your sufficiency in all things then you will begin to have an inner stillness you cannot explain. Your sleep will be sounder. Your body will have more energy and your mind and memory will begin to store more information in a greater depth than ever before.

Your past. . .

How do you still bring up worldly situations which were part of your past and not use those incidents as examples of how God has worked in your life. You don't. Instead you continue to drag your past around with you everywhere you go, just like Jacob Marley in the book The Christmas Carol. When he comes into Scrooges bedroom on Christmas eve dragging his chains and ledgers he had forged over his lifetime you can begin to see just what you are carrying with you in this life. You need to make a change now.

Philippians 3:13 "Brethren, I count not myself to have apprehended; but this one thing I do, forgetting those things which are behind (*past*) **and reaching forth unto those things which are before."**

What does God say in this scripture? He says to *"forget the things of your past."* These things are the deceitful lusts, the ugly incidents and the hurts you received. Your past is over with. You cannot go back into your past and resolve anything. Why continue to drag it along with you. Absolutely nothing in your past can be changed. God then tells you to reach forth, to look to your future for this is where the spiritual things you need for your growth will be waiting.

Some people in this world will tell you to deal with the negatives which occurred in your past and resolve them so those incidents will be null and void in this present world and then you can continue to walk on the worldly path Satan has laid out for you.

So you have a choice. You can forget your past and all the hurts and move along. . .*YES!* or you can go back and deal with each incident spiritually and try to understand just what happened and how it affected your life then and just how you can make the necessary changes to those incidents so they will not affect your life today. Of course you will be charged at least $ 150.00 per hour to start the process. . .*NO!* Whatever took place in your past can be used as a teaching tool to not repeat the consequences of your poor decision made the first time. It is your choice.

Here is another tool!

Ephesians 4:25 "Wherefore putting away lying, speak every man truth with his neighbor for we are members one another."

Lying is one of the key characteristics which can destroy marriages, friendships, confidences, confessions or anything else which must rely on trust. You have lied at one point or another in your life. Sometimes you have been caught in the lie and sometimes you get away with it. Once you are caught it is easier to just *"fess"* up. However, should you get away with it then it will become necessary to continue the lie so as you do not get caught again.

Telling a lie usually means you do not have enough information about a particular situation and you do not want to look insecure about the incident so you make up a false hood to cover your lack of confidence or preparedness concerning the same situation.

God is asking you to speak the truth with your brothers and sisters in the Word. When you are with fellow believers there really is no need to lie because you are all equals in God's eyes and lying is not necessary. Satan will always do whatever he can to cause clouds of doubt to fill your conscious thoughts about who you are in Christ.

Ephesians 4:29 "Let no corrupt communication proceed out of your mouth, but that which is good to the use if edifying, that it may minister grace unto the hearers."

Here are some examples of corrupt communication; **gossip** and **heresy.** When you speak, your words are to be edifying and not destructive. Once you speak a word it is out there in space and it never can be taken back.

Hebrews 4:12 "For the word of God is quick, and powerful, and sharper than any two edged sword, piercing even to the dividing asunder of the soul and spirit, and the joints and marrow, and is a discerner of the thoughts and intents of the heart."

So it sounds to me God is telling you exactly how you are to speak and whose words you should be using. Satan continues to influence your life and it is up to you too use wisdom, the wisdom of God, when you speak words to your fellow men and women.

The Unruly Tongue.

Your tongue is probably the greatest tool Satan has to defeat your walk with God and your family. *Your brain must be engaged before you can put your tongue in gear.*

Micah 6:12b "their tongue is deceitful in their mouth."

Jeremiah 9:8 "Their tongue is as an arrow shot out; it speaketh deceit; one speaketh peaceably to his neighbor with his mouth, but in the heart he layeth his wait."

God designed your body to perform wonderful actions and the tongue is one of His most awesome body parts. Besides allowing you to enjoy the sweet or sour taste of His endless gardens, the tongue also provides a transport for this bounty to your stomach for processing. On a more personal note the tongue can provide a certain aspect of sensual excitement. Since you spend more time speaking than you do eating your tongue has taken on a role which carries a responsibility far greater than expected. You can speak sweetness and also sourness. Your words can encourage or destroy.

Remember the old saying *"the pen is mightier than the sword."*

In those old days communication was nothing like it is today so written publications were the only sure way people found out what was happening in the world. Well the same is true with the spoken word and in today's world people will listen to only what they want to hear. Once a word is spoken it is in the air of Satan's world. To repeat, the spoken word can never be retracted.

Satan's unholy angel spirits are forever traveling all over the world listening for any word which is not a blessing. Those spirits can take a word and twist its' meaning so the damage done may never be undone. A lifelong trust can be broken forever. A contract of love can be destroyed, never to be put back together again.

Maybe there are some of you who can relate to what I have just written. Maybe some of you are still hurting from words spoken in haste. However, there is still hope, and the hope lies within God's hands. God is the only one who can forgive you and forget what you said. God is the only one who can put together what Satan has torn apart.

You have a tongue. No matter how long you have been a believer or how committed you are to God or Christ Jesus in a split second of weakness on your part is all the time one of Satan's unholy angel spirits needs to strike because he wants to bring you down. As I said earlier, those who are lost Satan does not care about. You are Satan's primary target. Walk carefully.

Let's talk about the following expression of negatives again. . .

What does *"expression of negatives"* mean?

When you are ill and you speak of your illness to a friend you are sharing a personal aspect of your life to a person you trust. What happens when you speak out loud of your condition, you are allowing one or more of Satan's spirits to overhear what you have said thus making them aware of your negative condition.

Satan cannot listen in on your subconscious thoughts. Those are private thoughts. You can share those thoughts with God. Though God knows the number of hairs on your head, He will not listen to your thoughts unless you ask Him to. For Him to listen to your thoughts without you knowing about it would then put God in a position of possession of your soul and would also make God a respecter of persons which He is not. Remember this, God wants a relationship with you which is honest and truthful. He wants you to be able to come to Him and confess your sins or bad thoughts with a repentant heart joyfully.

I will continually repeat certain concepts concerning our walk with God. . .

Satan can hear your words as well as God when you speak them out loud and Satan can then act upon whatever he or his unholy angel spirits have heard. To utter a negative confession about another individual is considered *"gossip"* and Satan may jump on those kind of words and cause pain to those individuals concerned.

Negative confession in prayer.

To utter a negative confession in the act of prayer quietly in your heart to God is protected by God. In fact all prayer to God is protected whether spoken out loud or said within the confines of your heart. When you are praying God will hear your prayer. **I John 5:14 "And this is the confidence***(boldness)* **that we have in him***(God)* **that, if we ask anything according to his***(God)* **will, ***(God)* **he heareth us."** If you want God to consider positive action upon your prayer requests then you should endeavor to end your prayer as He says in His Word, *"in the name of Jesus."* Jesus is your intercessor with his Father God. **John 14:14 "If ye shall***(absolute promise)* **ask any thing in my name***(Jesus)***, I***(God)* **will do it."**

I have said this before but it bears repeating. In order for God to provide an answer, even in His own timing, you must come with a humble and forgiving heart towards those who have hurt you. Once you have completed these actions of forgiveness then you have met His commandment. So you can expect an answer in God's timing, but you will still have to listen quietly for His response.

Your life and its outcome. . .remember this

God has a path for you to follow while you are here on earth. The key word is *"path."* The word *"plan"* does not appear in the KJV of the Bible. Look at **Jeremiah 29:11 "For I know the thoughts that I think towards you saith the Lord, thoughts of peace and not of evil, to give you an expected end."** Many of the other versions of the Bible have changed the word *"thoughts"* into *"plans."* This particular verse of scripture has caused many people to wonder *"just what is God's plan for me."* Should His plan not be evident in your world then you begin to wonder *"what am I to do while I wait for God to tell me what His plan is for me."* There are many people who have waited and heard nothing so they go and do what they want which is usually against what God wants for them.

Psalms 16:11 "Thou*(God)***wilt shew me the path of life; in thy***(God)***presence is fullness of joy; at thy***(God)***right hand there are pleasures for evermore."**

Proverbs 3:6 " In all thy ways acknowledge him*(God)*** and he shall direct thy paths."**

Does God know what you are going to do with your walk or your life moment by moment?

Logic seems to be, He should know what step you are going to take next and He might want to get your attention if the step was going to be too dangerous. Should He do this He would be overstepping your free will with His action and since God is not a respecter of persons the chances are He will not interfere with your walk or your life. However He may open a door of wisdom for you to consider before you take your next dangerous step. Which would mean you can take a step and believe it is the correct one. And if the step is in alignment and harmony with God's word then you could feel very confident the step was the right one. Base your steps on what His Word says and you will never go wrong.

In light of what God knows about you, let's look at dying for a moment. . .

Does God know when you are going to die or where you are going to die or what you are going to die of? These are questions you may have had in your lifetime but they are not valid in the eyes of God because He has put you here on earth with the sole purpose of glorifying Him and reconciling your fellow brethren back to Him. He has given you a physical body to do this act with and He has given you *"free will"* to accomplish this task. Your knowing about your ultimate end would consume all your waking thoughts and you would lose sight of your spiritual goal for God. You are here to do His will just like His Son did. As long as you are faithful to God and do the best you can to walk in the steps of Christ Jesus then when you finally call it quits you can safely say you did your best for Him. There is an old Hebrew saying, "May the dust of the Rabbi's sandals settle on your sandals." Which means you want to walk as close as you can to the teacher, God.

In conclusion. . .

Satan and his unholy angel spirits are out there watching everyone as they walk through this life here on earth. His unholy angel spirits are reporting back to him about any hesitations you make with your conversation with God. You can defeat the works or influences of his unholy angel spirits simply by humbly coming to your heavenly Father God and thanking Him for His protection.

Remember this scripture, **John 14:14 "If ye**(*you*) **shall**(*absolute promise*)**ask any thing in my name**(*Jesus*) **I**(*God*) **will do it."**

Chapter Four

Becoming a godly man. . .and much more over again.

Let me preface this chapter with a few thoughts. The Bible is a book full of both loving and stern commandments on how to live your life as you walk with Him. God is a loving and forgiving God of second chances. He expects you to do your best and He is always there to guide you down the path He has laid for you.

What does a godly man look like today in this worldly society you live in? I would think he would stand out head and shoulders above a worldly man. What do you think? Do you have any friends who are godly men? Do they live their lives above reproach? Do you see them at the grocery? Are they at work with you? Do they live next door to you?

Here are some easily identifiable characteristics of a godly man:

He is loving to his family and those around him. He has a warm sense of humor. He does not poke fun at people for a laugh. He is a man at peace when all around him are frustrated and depressed. He exhibits an aptitude for patience with his associates. He is gentle with animals and people. There is a goodness to his nature which is evident when he is with those of the world. His meekness shows a strength of respect and is not timid. He shows temperance in all he consumes both of food and drink. Most importantly, he believes in Christ Jesus' return and he believes in God's matchless Word. He does the best he can to reconcile his brothers and sisters back to God and most importantly he glorifies God daily.

Look at **Galatians 5:22 "But the fruit of the Spirit***(God)*** is love, joy, peace, longsuffering, gentleness, goodness, faith***(believing)."*** **23 "Meekness, temperance, against such there is no law."**

These characteristics are available to all men. The only question remaining is how many men are going to claim these attributes of a godly man. Now in order to claim them we must first believe in the Words of God, the Bible.

However, there is a small condition. You will have to give up your worldly ways of thinking and acting. You have to give up all of your selfish ways. And you have to give up control of your spiritual lives and turn to God for your future answers to life's many questions. Have you ever heard the expression *"deny yourself?"* To deny oneself is literally to stop being selfish.

Turning our lives over to God means believing in the unseen. . .

God speaks in His Word, **John 20:29b "blessed are they that have not seen, and yet have***(will)*****believe."**

To *"believe"* is a verb which requires action on your part. To continue to believe God's Word will help build trust in your spiritual heart which in turn will generate confidence in what God says. His Word is true and you can place your dependence upon what He has written.

One of the hardest aspects of believing in someone or something you cannot see is that you are dealing with spiritual entities which can manifest themselves only through your believing. In other words if you do not believe the spirit of Christ Jesus is full of his Fathers Holy Spirit and together they occupy your spiritual heart once you have made the commitment to follow them then most likely your life will not be fulfilled. Then again you would not be reading this book if you were not at least thinking about becoming committed to follow Jesus Christ or have already made the commitment.

Lets continue with our reading. . .

As you read God's Word word you may come across the word *"faith."* You will find this word used many times in the Old Testament more than in the New Testament. Why! Because faith is believing in something unseen as many of the holy men of God can attest to. Faith was necessary because Jesus was yet to be born of woman. Once Jesus appeared in the New Testament and walked this earth and spoke His Fathers Words people's **faith began to change to believing** because they saw and touched and heard him speak.

The New Testament is addressed to all of the Gentiles and you are a Gentile. According to a Greek definition, Gentiles are worse than dogs in the street. This was probably spoken by an angry Judean in Jesus' time.

In the New Testament you start with the four Gospels; Matthew, Mark, Luke and John which tell the story of Jesus Christ's walk here on earth. Then those books are followed by the book of Acts which is a transitional book summarizing the Gospels and laying the outline for the next nine books which were written by the apostle Paul. Paul's writings are the greatest writings concerning the Word of God ever written. Paul had God's Holy Spirit in Christ within his spiritual heart. God was able to speak to Paul directly at anytime during the day or night concerning the Words Paul was to write.

Please believe me when I say you have the same Holy Spirit of God in Christ within you just as Paul had, the only problem may be yours has not been sufficiently energized yet. We will talk about how you can energize His Holy Spirit in you later.

The beginning. . .

You are a worldly man, full of all the insecurities, doubts, suspicions, fears, angers, egos, agendas and regrets and these vices continue to plague you daily. When you finally feel the calling from God to change your worldly ways and become a man of God, you will have to put all of your trust in God. The feeling of being *"called"* is a moment in time when you might be under stress and are becoming frustrated with the situation and there comes over you a wonderful peaceful feeling. This is God's loving way of getting your attention. You may be in moment of great joy or sadness and He will begin to talk to you.

The first area you must cover is your commitment to God. We talked about this in the first two chapters of this book. Should you not be committed, then this is the time to do so. Take a moment and think about what you are going to do. Making a commitment to God is making an unbreakable contract or covenant with God. This is the ultimate promise. A word of warning: Do not make this promise or covenant lightly! **I John 4:15 "Whosoever shall confess that Jesus is the Son of God, God dwelleth in him and he in God."**

Please understand this. God loves you with an unconditional love. This means you can mess up many, many times in your walk through life, and He will still love you. All God is seeking from you is your faithfulness, your complete faithfulness, a never ending faithfulness to worship Him and no other. Follow His commandments, and He will shower down on you more blessings than you could ever hold. **John 10:10b "I am come that they might have life, and that they might have it more abundantly."**

So you must keep this very important thought in mind: When you make a mistake, do not run from God. Instead run to Him. Satan would like you to run from God and run to him where his unholy angel spirits will be waiting for you.

Satan will continue to. . .

Now, Satan will continue to hurl his fiery darts at you as long as you continue to walk with God. The longer you walk with God, the stronger you will become, and Satan's fiery darts will just seem to bounce off your spiritual heart.

God says in **Ephesians 6:11 "Put on the whole armour of God, that ye may be able to stand against the wiles of the devil."** And you ask the question again, " what is *the whole armour*" of God? The answer is His matchless Word.

So how does God's matchless Word protect you? When you read His scriptures, your mind is concentrating on what you are reading. Satan can only influence your thinking with outside stimuli, such as magazines, TV, radio, movies, internet, pictures, paintings, people, and books. When you are thinking about God's Word there is no room for the influences of Satan, hence the armour. His Word is protecting you always.

Romans 8:15 "For ye have not received the spirit of bondage again to fear, but ye have received the Spirit*(God)* of adoption whereby we cry Abba Father."

You and I have been adopted by God. He has chosen each one of us to be part of His family long before there was any structure to our solar system or the universe. You have a Father who loves you without any restrictions.

OK! Again let us look a little deeper into these scriptures. . .

Romans 10:9 "That if thou shalt confess with thy mouth the Lord Jesus, and shalt believe in thine heart that God hath raised him from the dead, thou shalt be saved." 10 "For with the heart man believeth unto righteousness; and with the mouth confession is made unto salvation."

In verse **10:9** *"If thou"* is a situation where God gives you the option to act. Now *"shalt"* is an absolute promise from God. And *"confess"* is an action you have to take of your own free will. And *"with thy mouth"* you can confess out loud or to yourself Jesus will be your Lord and Master. The next *"shalt"* is a promise which you will believe in your spiritual heart. God *"hath"* is past tense, which means God has already accomplished what He said He would do. *"Thou shalt"* means you will be saved from the grave to spend eternity with the angels.

In verse **10:10** with your spiritual heart you believe you are as righteous as Christ Jesus because all your past sins are forgiven, and with your mouth *"confession"* is made unto salvation. You are saved for eternity. So what are you confessing? You are confessing all of your past sins which you committed prior to making your commitment to Jesus Christ. This has got to be one heck of a confession on your part. How do you even begin to remember all the sins you committed in the past? Try to remember just one sin from last week or this morning. Fortunately, God has already thought this through. You are not to remember each specific sin you committed but to consider all the sins grouped together. God will forgive and forget all of them forever.

Wait a minute! Christ gave up his life on the cross and all the blood he shed was for your remission of your past sins! Yes! Then why do you have to confess your sins again if they are already forgiven? Because you are making a commitment to Jesus Christ and God. Jesus will be your Lord and Master and Savior. When you confess *(speak)* of your past sins you are telling God you understand what His Word means and the commitment you are making. You have to take the first step and make the commitment in order for God to forgive all your past sins. Should you never take the first step, then your past sins will not be forgiven.

Possible confusion here. . .

Here is a situation where confusion could happen. When Jesus was here on earth he was given complete authority by his Father to forgive all sins and heal all people and perform miracles as well as have dominion over the wind and the seas. When he ascended to sit next to his Father his authority over mankind was put on hold until the Gathering takes place. Christ Jesus responsibility now is to be your intercessor with his Father God. If you want anything from God, even with God being your sufficiency in all things spiritual, you still have to go through Jesus. This is why you should end your prayers **"in the name of Jesus."**

Here is a question to think about.

Why would God allow His only begotten Son Jesus to give up his life on the cross for all your past sins if you are not going to in return, commit to follow His Son and accept him as your Lord and Savior. God knew in His infinite wisdom there will be some of you out there who would not follow after Jesus. Those people will consider their lives complete in themselves and will not want to follow anyone except themselves.

Those of you who chose to exercise your free will and decide to follow Jesus will reap the benefits of a life of peace, filled with hope and, in the end, eternity with your Savior. Until the time comes let's consider this. . .

Egos. . .

Most of you have egos of one degree or another. The problem occurs when Satan's earthly vices get in the way of God's virtues. This means you will have to get rid of them if your walk with Christ Jesus is to be blessed.

Satan loves egos. He knows as long as your egos are in working order you will never be able to build a lasting relationship with God or, for that matter, another earthly individual.

Webster defines **"egoism" as a "doctrine which individual self interest is the actual motive of all conscious action."** Seems to be the exact opposite of "deny yourself."

Doctrines are disciplines which restrict ones movement in any direction but towards the doctrine itself. The thoughts you generate are yours and no one else's. Your interests are those which govern your outside behavior. No wonder Satan loves egos.

We talked earlier about the phrase " being like a little child."

Matthew 18:4 "Whosoever therefore shall humble himself as this little child, the same is greatest in the kingdom of heaven." *"Whosoever"* means *"who" " so" " ever."* You are the *"who."* The *"so"* and *"ever"* mean anyone who comes along who will humble themselves. *"Therefore"* is past tense, meaning whatever is being talked about has already happened. God has already determined you will follow what this scripture says. *"Shall"* means an absolute promise from the Father. *"Humble himself as this little child."* This is the attitude you are to strive to put on. A little child does not have an ego. Children just do not understand or comprehend just what an *"ego"* is. So a small child is innocent of any intentional wrongdoing which is just as God sees you. Humbling yourself in the eyes of God is the greatest attitude you can ever strive for. You are justified *"just as if you had never sinned"* in His eyes.

God knows you have already humbled yourself. To be humble is to put aside yourself. The old expression of *"deny yourself"* literally means to stop being selfish. Stop trying to take control of everything physically and spiritually.

How many little children have you seen in your life who have exhibited pride or vanity? Pride and Vanity are two of Satan's favorite earthly vices. Little children will not exhibit these vices unless they have been taught by their parents. That means their parents most probably had been taught by their parents and generations before them.

Your past is the problem you will continue to carry everywhere you go. When you finally come to the realization you should get rid of your past, then your walk will change paths.

Read what Paul has written in **Philippians 3:13 "Brethren, I count not myself to have apprehended** *(comprehended)***, but this one thing I do, forgetting***(means to forget your past, all of the negative happenings)* **those things which are behind, and reaching forth unto those things which are born."** Your past did not happen overnight, so it will take some time to forget. First, you can pick and chose what you want to forget. You should endeavor to get rid of the deceitful lusts and all the hurt you have caused other people and the hurt you have felt when someone hurts you. The idea is for you to continue your walk down the path God has shown you by clearing away the debris of your past and moving on. There is nothing wrong with remembering those actions or thoughts which were pleasant,

Forgiveness. . .

There may be an occasion when you will remember something that was unpleasant. Well you can use this occurrence as an example to teach from. All your past sins have been forgiven. You, however have to seek forgiveness from some of those past people you have hurt. These people may still be hurting for what you have caused to them so you will need to seek their forgiveness. Now if these people are not available or have passed on then you can humbly go to your Father and confess and He will forgive you.

Agendas. . .

Now let's take a look at agendas. An agenda is what needs to be accomplished. Meetings have agendas so you know what to prepare for when you attend. Many churches have *"Order of Worship"* so you will know when it is time to sing or leave.

Having an agenda about what will happen in your life is foolish on your part. Why? Because you probably have not left any space for God to be part of your walk. Everything you have scheduled is based on your five senses not listening to God. You are aware that God is Spirit so your five senses are useless in any situation dealing with God. You have to rely on His Holy Spirit working within your personal spirit. Should you have personal agendas about people's lives which means you are trying to control certain aspects of their lives then the agenda will have everything to do with Satan and nothing to do with God. **Ephesians 6:12b "against the rulers of the darkness, against spiritual wickedness in high places."** So where does God or Satan fit into your agenda?

As long as you maintain an agenda, you will not allow anyone to interfere with your walk down the crooked path that you have chosen for yourself and in doing so you will miss the true meaning of this scripture. **Matthew 7:14 "Because strait is the gate and narrow is the way, which leadeth unto life, and few there be that find it."** Chose to lose your agendas about people and you will open the door for God to enter in.

Have you ever changed anyone's mind?

This goes hand in hand with changing your agendas. As a worldly five senses man entering into a relationship with a worldly five senses woman you have nothing to base your relationship's success on except what the world has set up as criteria.

Having an ego or agenda will eventually bring about destruction of your partnership because you are putting all your faith and trust in either yourself or each other and not in God. The reality of the situation is neither of you are strong enough to take on the responsibility of the other partner in all aspects of married life including the spiritual aspects. You may be going into a relationship with an agenda to change your spouse's mind to the way you think and you will fail miserably. You will not be able to change another person's mind against their will. So if you cannot change another person's mind then what do you do. The world will tell you to leave the relationship and find another, 63% do.

So, How do I change my mind?

How do you go about changing your sin nature filled reprobate*(rejected or worthless)* mind from what the world wants you to think to the mind of Jesus?

Look at **Romans 12:2 "And be not conformed to this world; but be ye transformed by the renewing of your mind, that ye may prove what is that good and acceptable, and perfect will of God."**

The word *"conformed"* means *"fashioned,"* and in this case you are being molded after this world, Satan's world. You have spent the better part of your life fashioned after this world, so changing your mind to follow God could be a struggle. Satan will not let go easily. The key phrase of this scripture is *"renewing of your mind."* What are you renewing your mind from or to? Answer: You are renewing your conscious thoughts from the world and submitting any new thoughts to God's Word. When you renew your mind to God's Word you will be transformed spiritually from your earthly, physical thinking to a man of God. This will not happen overnight. You must remember Satan can only influence your thoughts by outside stimuli, nothing inside. Whereas God's Holy Spirit occupies your spiritual heart and mind (*nous*-Greek) and there is now no room for Satan.

Look at this scripture in **Romans 13:14 "But put ye on the Lord Jesus Christ, and make not provision for the flesh, to fulfill the lusts thereof."**

Putting on the mind of your Lord Jesus Christ is to remember God's Word and you will begin to live it. Remember this. You have the mind of Jesus Christ. You received his mind when you gave your life over to him. And another benefit which comes with the mind of Jesus Christ is His Father's Holy Spirit. So now you have God's Holy Spirit within your spiritual heart, and you have the mind of Jesus Christ to guide you. Your conscious thought pattern will change based on the decisions you make upon reading God's Word. The wisdom you gain will begin working within your spiritual heart. With your new mind the temptations of Satan's world will not carry any importance anymore, or at least you believe so.

How to get rid of those worldly thoughts.

II Corinthians 10:5 "Casting down imaginations, and every high thing that exalteth itself against the knowledge of God, and bringing into captivity every thought to the obedience of Christ."

This will take time to accomplish, but it can be done on a day by day, moment by moment happening. Here is how it will work. Satan will provide you with a temptation based upon his influencing your waking conscious thoughts. When this happens you will hopefully recognize what is going on and immediately say, out loud if possible " **Satan I rebuke you and cast your temptation upon the shoulders**

of Christ Jesus." This simple statement will take away the influence or will cause you to recognize how terrible the temptation is, and should help you to begin to back away from it.

Ephesians 4:8 "Wherefore he saith, When he *(Jesus)* **ascended up on high, he led captivity captive, and gave gifts unto men."**

When Satan begins to influence you, you are spiritually taken captive by those conscious thoughts. When Jesus finally ascended to sit at the right hand of his Father he personally took with him all of your past temptations and in the process left the single most powerful **gift** from his Father for you in the manner of the manifestations found in **I Corinthians 12:4-10.** I'll talk about the manifestations later in the book.

Ephesians 4:22 "That ye put off concerning the former conversation the old man, which is corrupt according to the deceitful lusts."

The word *"conversation"* actually translates into *"behavior."* I talked about this earlier. God's Word is saying you should put away or forget about your past behavior or actions because they are part of your *"old man."* This is your past and your behavior is based on the lusts of the flesh or worldly temptations. You cannot change your past, but you can learn from your mistakes. The word *"lusts"* refer to any situation which you **continually** put before beginning your worship to God.

Ephesians 4:24 "And that ye put on the new man which after God is created in righteousness and true holiness."

When you put off or forget about your old man then you will begin to put on the new man. This new man is your renewed thought processes according to God's Word. There are no blessings when you have your old man on in your thoughts. When you begin to remember God's Word in your daily walk, then God will begin to heap blessings upon you. You will become as righteous as Christ Jesus.

Ephesians 4:25 "Wherefore putting away lying, speak every man truth with his neighbor for we are members one of another."

As a new man, the thought of lying to your fellow brother in Christ should not occur. As you continue to put on more of God's Word, you will find telling the truth to your business associates will cause a peace to build in your conscious thoughts and result in a changed behavior for all to see. Christians will see the Christ in you the hope of glory. The rest of the world will see a very pleasant man to deal with.

The Two Greatest Commandments.

Matthew 22:37 "Jesus said unto him(a lawyer)**, Thou shalt love the Lord thy God with all thy heart**(spiritually),** and with all thy soul**(breathe life),** and with all thy mind**(nous-Greek)**"38 " This is the first and great commandment." 39 "And the second is like unto it, Thou shalt love thy neighbor as thyself."**

Sounds pretty easy to follow. What if your neighbor is an unbeliever. He or she will have no inclination about coming to the Lord or believing anything about Him. God's word says you are to love thy(your) neighbor as thyself. What self respecting Christian does not love himself, not in a narcissistic way, but as a son or daughter of God. So if you are to follow what God is commanding you to do, then you have to love your neighbor the best you can. Now this will take time. Small, random acts of kindness may help. Invitations to special events at the church may also help. Remember your job is to sow the seed or speak the word and God will take care of the harvest.

The Mind Of Christ.

Earlier I talked about you having the mind of Christ. How do you go about acquiring the mind of the Son of God? Easy. When you committed your life over to Jesus Christ you gave up your worldly five senses reprobate mind for the mind of Christ. Making this commitment also allowed God's Holy Spirit to dwell within your spiritual heart, so you now have the potential to energize God's Holy Spirit to act upon your life and at the same time you have the ability to receive from God

His revelation of instructions but from **within** your mind and not **upon** your mind as happened to the holy men of the Old Testament.

While Christ was here on earth he received revelation from his Father on a moment by moment basis. Before Jesus ascended to sit at the right hand of his Father he said to his disciples he would send a *"comforter."* The comforter was the Holy Spirit of his Father. So the disciples received God's Holy Spirit. In **Acts 2:4 "And they***(disciples)* **were all filled***(pletho-filledto over flowing)* **with the Holy Ghost***(Spirit-Greek)* **and began to speak in other tongues as the Spirit***(God)* **gave them utterance."**

Beginning your walk as a godly man.

Again here are some of the characteristics of a godly man. **Galatians 5:22 "But the fruit of the Spirit***(God)* **is love, joy, peace, longsuffering, gentleness, goodness, faith***(believing).*** 23 "Meekness, temperance; against such there is no law."**

Let's look a little closer. The **Love** mentioned is not the narcissistic kind of self love similar to eros which is a sexual kind of love. Rather it is a phileo or brotherly type of love. God's agape love for you is a complete love with no strings or conditions attached.

Joy means gladness. **Peace** is a state of tranquility or being quiet. **Longsuffering** means patience. **Gentleness** means mildness or manners of disposition. **Goodness** is the quality or state of being good. **Faith** means believing. **Meekness** is enduring injury with patience and without resentment. And **Temperance** means moderation in all actions, thoughts or feelings.

Do you have any of these qualities? All of these virtues are available from God's Word, and the only thing necessary on your part is to believe you can acquire them. This means you will have to study God's word on a regular basis to gain the depth of understanding necessary. Believing God's Holy Spirit is within your new "born again" heart will energize His Spirit, and this action will become the beginning of your changes.

The first day of your walk with God. . .

Please, start the day by praying to God and thanking Him for all the blessings He has given you. Then begin reading one (1) chapter of the New Testament starting in Acts 1:1*ff.* Tomorrow pray and read Acts 2:1*ff.* The next day pray and read Acts 3:1*ff.* And so on until you have finished the book of Revelation. When you reach this point start over. Remember from day one till you breathe your last breath you must endeavor to pray and read His Word daily.

Note: *"ff"* means *"all the following verses,"* after verse one (1) through till the end of the chapter.

As you read the KJV of the Bible and you come across a word which does not make worldly sense, which will happen more often than not in KJV. Go to your handy concordance and look up the word. Concordances contain all the words specific to your version of the Bible.

Concordances are designed to either contain all the words for the KJV of the Bible or all the words for NIV, NLT, ESV, NASB and other Bible's separately.

Going through this type of look up or research will help you gain a better understanding of the words in the Bible. Try to avoid using *"Google"* only because when you physically take the time to research God's word you are conditioning yourselves to learn how to study.

Anytime you begin to pray please close your eyes and begin to talk (pray) with God about yourself and your health and your walk and any relationships you may have especially if you are married. Then move on to your family, brothers, sisters, your parents and your wife's parents, if this applies, grandparents, aunts, uncles, and your family is covered. Then your boss and your fellow workers. Then the church, pastors, ministries and any special people at the church. Next is the world, Washington and anything else on your heart. Then finish your (talking) prayers by saying *"in the name of Jesus."* Now you can begin reading His Word.

Stickler for forgiveness. . .

Here is one thing which God is a stickler on and we have already mentioned this fact. If there is anybody in your life who has wronged you or visa-versa then you need to forgive them or yourself because until you have a clean slate God could hold up answering all of your petitions. Remember when you first gave your life to Jesus, well all your past sins were forgiven by the Father and you had a clean slate to start with. Now it may have been a few days or weeks or months or years and if you have not confessed any of your new sins to the Father, well. **John 1:9 "If we confess our sins, he is faithful and just to forgive us our sins and cleanse us from all unrighteousness."**

Once you have forgiven those people who have hurt you or been forgiven by those you have hurt, then you can be at rest knowing God in His own time will reconsider answering your prayers.

Let's talk again about learning to pray.

Prayer is simply talking with God in a very personal and humbling way. As you talk God will listen to your heart and the issues it contains rather than the fancy words you may speak. You should endeavor to attain an attitude of being humble as you come to the feet of the Creator. As you start out on your walk it will be difficult at first. Do not give up. Now this next part is very important. I know I have already talked about this before. It is very important. There have been times in your life when you have been wronged or you may have wronged another person. You must take the *"bull by the horns"* so to speak and forgive those who have wronged you. They might not even be aware they did anything to hurt you. Should you be able to remember anyone you have wronged then you must ask for forgiveness from these people. Now if any of these individuals are not alive then beg forgiveness from your Father God, and He will forgive you. Should you go to a particular person and ask for forgiveness and they say no they will not forgive you then do not worry. You took the right steps and asked forgiveness. The person who is refusing to forgive you is now the one who will be responsible to God in the end. This whole procedure may take some time to accomplish, but there is no rush.

In the future when you are tempted and you give in to sin you can come to Father and beg forgiveness and He will forgive you. This is not rocket science just a real simple way to keep your sinful soul free of spiritual dirt.

You have learned in order to come to the Father with your petitions you must take on a child like behavior and be humble with no agenda or ego. You must also remember, you are to go through the Son, Jesus when approaching his Father and you do this by **John 14:13 "And whatsoever ye shall ask in my name, that will I do, that the Father may be glorified in the Son."** ending your prayers *"in the name of Jesus."*

God has given you *"free will"* which means if you do not want to end your prayers *"in the name of Jesus"* you do not have to. Now God has instructed you to follow His Word so if you want to see an answer to your prayers then you should do as He says. I learned how to pray over 40 years ago and I have ended all my prayers as He has instructed and all the prayers which needed to be answered have been answered. Some of my prayers are for people and until they can come to understanding about God the answer will have to wait. Keep in mind all things about your life being equal God will answer your prayers in His time. His time is designed to see if you will remain faithful to your stand and request. Most people will pray once and then forget what they asked for an go on with their lives.

God likes repetition, not the vain kind which has no heart in it. So you start praying on Monday. Then Tuesday comes and you pray again for the same things. You should continue repeating your prayers until they are all answered. This is called *"praying through your prayer."* God also likes for you to be specific about what your needs are. Asking for world peace will not do it, too vague. Asking if a specific senator be given a renewal of good health to do his job would be good.

Another very important part of prayer is listening to God as He speaks to you and He will. Many people just utter a quick, unspecific prayer with an *"amen"* an expect God to answer them and when He doesn't they get all upset and utter words which are not a blessing about God and His lack of interest in their lives

God will speak to you and His Words will come in over quiet waters. When you are alone and peaceful is when it will most often happen, be ready to listen and to take action anytime. This happened quite a few times when I was writing this book. While I was slowly coming out of my sleep period God spoke into my thoughts. At first I would hear His words and I thought ," that's ok, I'll remember them when I get up," wrong! The words were gone but not forever. Once I got back into fellowship with Him He gave me the words I needed to bless you.

Family prayer. . .

One of the most important facts about being a man of God is your family must be part of your prayer life. You are according to **Ephesians 5:23 "For the husband is the head of the wife, even as Christ is the head of the church; and he is the savior of the body."**

Your children should, if possible, be present for all your prayer sessions. As the spiritual head of your family it is your responsibility to lead your family into God's Word and guide their spiritual growth. When you are praying for your family be specific about your wife, calling her by name. Praise her life and her health and her well being. Praise her for being your wife and the mother of your children. Your wife will be doubly blessed to hear you praise her to God and the children will see and hear an example of a godly man and how he is to act. Praise the children as well. In **Ephesians 6:1 "Children obey your parents in the Lord, for this is right."** This verse means the family must be in the Lord. Committed to following Jesus Christ and God. This verse does not pertain to non-believers for they are not in the Lord.

In Genesis 2:24 it says "Therefore shall a man leave his father and his mother and shall cleave unto his wife: and they shall be one flesh." There are three key words in this verse; first *"cleave"* and then *"one flesh."* "Cleave" is a term commonly used by butchers when they cut apart meat. When you cut fresh meat apart with a knife or a cleaver you have two pieces. You cannot put the meat back together. However when you cut apart your skin or flesh accidently you can stitch or tape the skin back together and the flesh will soon renew itself. With *"one flesh"* remember that God took a rib from Adam. God closed the hole where He took the rib from and created woman and Adam called her Eve. The flesh of man was joined with the flesh of woman and they were one. *"One flesh"* also means being of one mind or one thought and that thought is keeping God in your thoughts daily.

Contrary to popular opinion man, because of what God did to create woman, does not have one less rib than woman. Adam lived out his life with one less rib, but God did not mess with Adam's DNA. All of Adams offspring had a full set of ribs. Keeping these facts in mind when you come to a couple getting married. In **Malachi 2:16a "For the Lord the God of Israel saith that he hateth putting away,"** *"Putting away"* is an old English term for separation. This is where the man will put the wife out of their home for breaking the marriage vows with the act of adultery. God is angry with those who get separated because you have not kept God's word concerning marriage. Just as your cut flesh will join together after being separated God wants the same thing to happen to your separated relationship. Once a man and wife are married they are to stick together like cleaved flesh for the duration of the marriage. Some translations will define **"putting away"** with divorce. *"Divorce"* is a poorly translated word from the Hebrew word for *"separated."*

Ephesians 6:2 "Honour thy father and mother; which is the first commandment with promise." The promise is in **Ephesians 6:3 "That it may be well with thee, and thou mayest live long on the earth."** And *"live long"* means up to 120 years. **Genesis 6:3 "And the Lord said, My spirit shall not always strive with man, for that he also is flesh; yet his days shall be an hundred and twenty years."**

What if I am single?

Not a problem. God likes single people as much as married ones, but He knows a single person is more flexible. When you are married you will have more responsibilities. A single person can move about as God inspires him. So concentrate on your walk with God and Jesus and God will provide you with a wonderful **wife** of His choice at the right time, usually when you do not need a wife. When He makes the choice it will be the best for both you and your new mate.

Acts 2:28 "Thou hast made known to me the ways of life; thou shalt(absolute promise from God) **make me full of joy**(gladness) **with thy countenance."**

This subject has been talked about before. Anytime you read the words *"shalt"* or *"wilt"* or *"shall"* or *"will"* these are absolute promises from God for you to apply to your lives. Of course it goes without saying you must believe what God has written in His Word for these promises to apply in your life.

Awesome promise. . .

Philippians 4:13 "I can do all things through Christ which strengtheneth me."

This is probably one of the most familiar scriptures you will have heard in your life. The first time I heard it, I thought God was giving me the strength to tackle anything in the world, and I would have the strength to finish it. I was close. This scripture does say you can do anything **through** Christ, but it is not referring to a physical action but a spiritual action. The scripture is very specific that you have to go **through** Jesus Christ to gain the Father's ear. Jesus is your representative to his Father. No one can come to the Father without first going through the Son. The word *"which"* refers to God. Yes, you can do anything spiritual when you go through Jesus and then he goes to his Father, who in turn will answer your request with the strength you need. You are dealing with spiritual needs here and since God is spirit who better than to be able to provide you with the necessary strength.

Continuing with your first steps.

Keep this scripture in mind, **II Timothy 3:17 "That the man of God may be perfect, throughly furnished unto all good works."** The word *"throughly"* means perfected three times.

As you are reading the word you may come across a scripture asking you to forget your past. This subject has also been talked about before. **Philippians 3:13 "Brethren, I count not myself to have apprehended** *(comprehended);* **but this one thing I do, forgetting those things which are behind and reaching forth unto those things which are before."** Everything which possibly could hurt you, you are to forget about it. You are to put it aside. All the bad decisions. All the guilt from relationships gone bad from those who did not like you and all the hurt you caused to others. In other words you are to put off*(forget)* the *"old man"* nature now.

This action on your part will not happen overnight. Maybe not even the next day or week or month. The important thing is you begin to forget your past. You cannot return to the past. You can only learn from the past and try not to make the same mistakes twice.

In the book "The Christmas Carol," the story is about Ebenezer Scrooge, I liked this book because of its message. On Christmas Eve he is getting ready for bed, and he hears the rattling of chains in the hallway. He starts to go toward the bedroom door to open it when the ghost of Jacob Marley, his old business partner, comes thru the door dragging behind him the chains and balls and ledgers he forged in his lifetime. Well, this is exactly what each of you carry as you walk through this life now. So, the longer you are studying the Word and making it part of your daily walk, the more of the *"old man baggage"* you can get rid of so. . . The next time you are in a room filled with people, imagine each of them dragging behind them the chains they have forged with all the ugliness of their pasts.

Let's recap just where you are right now.

You gave your life to Jesus Christ.
You believe God raised His Son Jesus from the grave.
You believe you will spend eternity with God and Christ Jesus.
You believe Jesus gave up his life for your past sins.
You believe the stripes which Jesus bore are for your physical healing.
You believe Jesus was a flesh and blood person so he could take death away from Satan.
You are working through the destruction of your egos.
You are working through the destruction of your agendas.
You are continually working to renew your thoughts to God's Word.
You are validated by God as a man.
You are putting off your past and remembering it no more.
You have learned to put God's Word on first in your life.
You have learned you have the characteristics of a godly man.
You have learned in order to receive anything from God, you must be as humble as a child.
You have learned you must forgive those who have hurt you and those that you have hurt in order to receive answers to your prayers.

Your walk through life.

You have begun a walk today which will change your life. This walk will affect the lives of those you know, especially the close ones in your family as well as the new people you meet.

As you continue believing God's Word and studying the same on a daily basis, you will grow stronger in the confidence and knowledge of His Word. Keep this in mind as you read His Word. What you are reading is the truth. What you are reading will never have to be defended.

Satan and his unholy angel spirits are in the world just waiting for you to walk out without the armour of God on. Look at it: **Ephesians 6:11 "Put on the whole armour of God that ye may be able to stand** against the wiles of the devil*(Satan)."* **12 "For we wrestle not against flesh and blood, but against principalities, against powers, against the rulers of the darkness of this world, against spiritual wickedness in high places." 13 "Wherefore take unto you the whole armour of God, that ye may be able to withstand in the evil day and having done all, to stand." 14 "Stand therefore having your loins girt about with truth and having on the breastplate of righteousness." 15 "And your feet shod with the preparation of the gospel of peace." 16 "Above all, taking the shield of faith, wherewith ye shall be able to quench all the fiery darts of the wicked." 17 "And take the helmet of salvation, and the sword of the Spirit, which is the word of God." 18 "Praying always with all prayer and supplication in the spirit and watching thereunto with all perseverance and supplication for all saints."**

Summing this up is simple. Satan is waiting for you. He is making plans to *"mess"* with you because you are now more of a threat to him and his goals than you were as a non believer. Do not fear. God is still here and He will never leave you. So. . .

Let's win a few points with her. . .

You are walking the walk. Now a few hints to help you along the way. Simple acts of kindness will go along way with your wife. Hold open a door, any door, just hold it open whether going in or out. Do this consistently. How about making the bed in the morning or getting the bed ready at night? What about cleaning up the bathroom mess in the morning and wiping down the wash basin. Maybe you could even clean the toilet. Does washing the windows sound too drastic a chore? Don't forget to mow the grass. This one always gets a few points, fill up her gas tank or have her car washed. Maybe you could bring in a surprise dinner or maybe even cook a surprise dinner. Never under estimate the power of flowers for a non-special event, why, just because.

No chocolates. Try a date night for fun, but not a surprise. Give her a chance to dress up. Say comforting words to your wife. Encourage her to step out of the box with a particular event she is undertaking. Above all, do not try to solve your wife's problems. Listen quietly and if she asks for a comment then very carefully repeat what you heard so you can speak to the situation accurately.

As the spiritual head of the family, it is your responsibility to show your wife in God's Word where He provides the answers to her problems, which will greatly encourage her to trust you and the Word more. When you look at your wife see her as the woman in **Proverbs 31:10-31.** These particular scriptures refer to the *"virtuous woman."*

In **Proverbs 15:1** God's word says, **"A soft answer turneth away wrath; but grievous words stir up anger."**

When speaking with your wife the tone of your voice should be of a counselor, not an attacker. Should there be a situation concerning both of you and a decision has to be made, God says the husband is to make the decision. **Ephesians 5:23 "For the husband is the head of the wife, even as Christ is the head of the church; and he is the savior of the body."**

All these actions on your part are based on the one simple fact: you must **"deny yourself."** This particular expression is very old. Early Bible preachers used this phrase to put the fear of God in unbelievers. The phrase means, *"stop being so selfish."* Stop putting yourself before others in your family or your work place or with your friends. You love to hang onto the past for some unexplainable reason. I do not know why, it is like there is some kind of hidden power there you can call up at will. Well you are right. There is a hidden power there, and you can indeed call it up at will, but what you are calling up is totally of Satan and he knows it and relishes the fact you are doing this now.

All the heartaches you went through as a child were just that, heartaches. Something you went through as a child should have no bearing or consequence on how you conduct yourself today.

Did you just say you should forget about all the abuse you took as a child or teenager and move on with your life? If you did not say it before then you should be saying it now. Move on with your life. This subject has been talked about before and it cannot be emphasized enough.

Ephesians 4:22 "That ye put off concerning the former*(your past)***conversation***(behavior)* **the old man which is corrupt according to the deceitful lusts." 23 "And be renewed in the spirit***(God's spirit in you)* **of your mind***(consciousness).*** **24 "And that ye put on the new man, which after God is created in righteousness and true holiness."**

The answer is to forget about what happened to you as a child or teenager or adult. Replace those thoughts with that of God's word and keep running those scriptures over and over again until you can't remember what happened back then.

A beginning. . .

When you give your life to God and His Son Christ Jesus you should endeavor each day to walk like Jesus and to think the Words his Father gave to him.

Will your walk be successful each day? What a wonderful question. There are some days when you will have no problems at all and then there will be some days when you will have many problems. God is within you as you walk through this life. He will not forsake you. He loves you like no other father could ever love you.

My life. . .

In the beginning, it was hard to put off my *"old man"* nature and put on my *"new man"* nature. I was in my early 20's when I accepted God into my life, but I never really made the complete commitment until I was 40 years old. By then there was a lot of *"old man"* to get rid of. Gradually though it is still happening. I never went to a counselor to deal with my past, only my present. I found it much easier to just forget about all the issues I had growing up. Doing it God's way was the most liberating feeling I have ever had. When you begin to live your life according to

God's Word and not what society dictates, you will find an inner peace surrounding your walk.

So do you want to become a godly man, respected by your peers, admired by women and loved by children? Then all you have to do is forget all the past hurts, put on God's awesome Word in your mind and heart, step out and walk like the man of God He knows you will be. Does it sound too easy? Should it be a little harder? Well, God does not want this walk to be hard. Satan and his world will want you to struggle. Satan and society actually are one in the same. The spiritual world, which sits on top of the earth, belongs to Satan. The physical earth with all its elements belongs to God. Satan, who is darkness, will do everything to bring you down, and God, who is light, will do everything to lift you up. **I John 1:5b "God is light and in him is no darkness." 6 "If we say that we have fellowship with him** *(God)* **and walk in darkness, we lie, and do not the truth." 7 "But, if we walk in the light as he is** *(in the light - not in the original texts)* **light, we have fellowship one with another, and the blood of Jesus Christ his son cleanseth us all from sin."**

Some of what you have heard here may sound redundant, and maybe you should have heard some of these scriptures over again. The more you hear a scripture, the greater the opportunity there is to remember it. Repetition, repetition, repetition.

This whole occurrence of putting God on in your mind is not rocket science. Please do not over think this process. Take your time with the change. It is a moment-by-moment, thought-by-thought process.

Common courtesy. . .

This was mentioned earlier but it's always nice to have a little review.

How many men open a door, any door, for their other half or, for that matter, just anyone who is going to walk through a door?

How many men pull out a chair, any chair, anywhere for their other half?

Think about all the ways there are to bless your other half. You only know what you have been taught. If your father or mother or friend did not teach you any of these courtesies then how could you know about them? Check out Emily Post at the old fashioned library or go online.

Now let's talk a little bit about your validation.

Validation as a man.

Many men today have come to manhood without being validated as a man by their fathers. For whatever reason their fathers were never involved in their childhood, events, such as football or baseball games or going hunting or fishing or maybe building a dog house or painting a room just never happened. So maybe you learned to sew or cook or draw or paint pictures. You might have hung out with the girls because there was no one else available. You still like being a male, but there was no one available to teach you the manly characteristics.

What if your mother took over the role of being a father to try to teach you how to act as a man? Of course, you learned some valuable tips on what pleased a woman and since you were going to be married someday, these tips would come in handy, but you still never had a adult man speak words of affirmation into your life

The end result...

I am here to say you have the most awesome Father in all of the universe. His name is God. He has been with you from day one of your life because He is everywhere. He is Spirit and as such is within and without everything in the universe. He has never left your side. His arms have been around you in times of trouble and joy. He is your heavenly Father and He has validated you like no man on earth could ever do. Your heavenly Father has made available eternal life for you to chose. What has your earthly father done. God loves you with a love which transcends all understanding.

About the Holy Spirit. . .

The Holy Spirit will be mentioned several times in this book. As lovingly as I can say this, one important thing about God and His Word as it appears in the KJV of His Bible, is that it is not a mystery. He did not want His Word to be confusing so He made sure the holy men He chose to transcribe His Word would present it as He said it. God does not want you ignorant of His word. He delights in showing you the deeper meanings of His Word when you show Him you want to know more. So when I say His Holy Spirit resides in you from birth and will not become energized until you make the free will choice to accept Jesus Christ as your Savior and Lord and Master, that is what I mean. For God to withhold His Holy Spirit for only certain special people would make God a respecter of persons, and you know He is not. The KJV does not contradict itself. Its words fit together like a hand in a glove. God is Spirit. **John 4:24a "God is Spirit."** No man has seen Him.

Chapter Five

Christ's last words and more

Jesus was in the Garden of Gethsemane with the disciples. **Matthew 26:36 "Then cometh Jesus with them***(disciples)* **unto a place called Gethsemane, and saith unto the disciples, Sit ye here, while I go and pray yonder."** Jesus brought eleven of the disciples with him. Judas was not part of this group as he was off betraying Jesus. Jesus moved to another area of the garden to pray by himself and asked his three most trusted disciples to keep watch for him; Peter, James and John, what happened? They fell asleep. Some kind of watchmen they turned out to be. **Matthew 26:39 "And he***(Jesus)* **went a little farther and fell on his face, and prayed saying, O my father, if it be possible, let this cup***(crucifixion)* **pass from me, nevertheless nor as I will, but as thou wilt."** Jesus prayed to his Father two more times to let this cup *"or responsibility"* pass from him but Jesus knew it was not possible. He was here to do his Father's will, not his. Then in **Matthew 26:53 "Thinkest thou that I cannot pray to my Father, and he shall presently give me more than twelve legions of angels."** Twelve legions of angels would amount to 72,000 spiritual warriors. Interesting note, in **Matthew 26:42,44** Jesus went away a second time to pray and the disciples fell asleep again, and then Jesus went away a **third** time and the disciples fell asleep again.

In the world of numbers three means complete.

Now during the festival time in Jerusalem one prisoner annually would be freed based on the crowds requests. This time the towns people chose Barabbas not Jesus.

In **Matthew 27:26 "Then released he**(*Pilate*) **Barabbas unto them**(*the crowd*)**; and when he had scourged Jesus, he delivered him to be crucified."**

Scourging was part of the legal punishment. During this period of time it was 40 lashes. One person would apply the lashing while another counted the number. The person applying the lashing would only provide 39 lashes to Jesus or anyone's back. The reason being if the person who was counting the lashes missed a lash and 41 were actually applied then the person who administered the lashes would in turn receive 40 lashes.

The whip consisted of thongs of leather inner woven with pieces of glass and bits of metal. As the thong hit his body the metal and glass would embed themselves into his flesh, then as the thong was pulled off, bits of his flesh would come with it. Absolute pain.

In **Matthew 27:27 "Then the soldiers of the governor took Jesus into a common hall and gathered unto him the whole band of soldiers." 28 "And they stripped him and put on him a scarlet robe." 29a "And when they had platted a crown of thorns, they put it upon his head."**

A common hall was where the soldiers would gather to fellowship and swap war stories. Also common in those times with criminals was a form of punishment where a cloth bag was placed over the head so the victim could not see anything happening outside. The soldiers would take turns striking the head and face with their fists or objects, whatever was available. The result after many individuals beating upon Jesus' face was severe swelling which would cause the eyes to close and the tissue around the mouth and nose to swell beyond it's normal appearance.

After the whipping and the beating came the crown of thorns which was reserved for Jesus only. It was not a custom for the soldiers to place a crown on those who were going to be crucified. This was special for Jesus. These thorns were about one to two inches long. The stems were woven together and a crown was made. This crown was then placed on the head of Jesus and the thorns were pushed down into his flesh. The crown could only be pushed down until the bone of his skull began breaking off the tips of the thorns.

Jesus' hands were then tied to a cross beam which in turn would eventually be nailed to the top of a stripped tree stump. The stripped tree stump was given to a person named Simon from Cyrene to carry up to the top of Golgotha. The name Golgotha means *"the place of the skull."* Jesus was marched through the streets to the sound of screaming and jeering of the crowd. When he finally reached the top of the hill he lay upon the ground. His hands were untied from the cross beam. The cross beam was nailed to the trunk of the tree and the joined pieces were placed in an already dug hole. The cross was ready. A rope was then placed around Jesus chest and under his arms to make a sling. He was then hoisted up to the cross beam. His arms again were tied to the beam and then his **wrists, not his hands,** were nailed to the beam. His feet were nailed to the bottom of the tree trunk. One of the Roman soldiers put a ladder up to the cross beam and removed the sling from his body and then cut the ropes which held his arms secured to the beam. His body fell with a dull thud as its full weight was supported by his wrists.

In **Matthew 27:37 "And set up over his head his accusation written; This is Jesus The King of the Jews."**

In **Matthew 27:46 "And about the ninth hour***(3pm)* **Jesus cried with a loud voice saying***(in Aramaic)* **Eli, Eli, Lamana Shabakthani, My God, my God for this I was spared."**

This New Testament translation of verse 27:46 in Aramaic is from the Peshitta, the authorized Bible of the Church of the East by George M. Lamsa, Copyright 1933 by the A.J.Holman Co. In this translation of **Matthew 27:46,** the logic of God's Word comes into play here exactly as it should be. God would or could not forsake His only begotten son whom He had freely given to be the price for all the sin in the world.

Eli, Eli means; **My God, My God**
Lamana means; **For This**
Shabakthani means; **I Was Spared or Kept**

We can search a little farther for additional usages of the word *"spared."*

In **I Kings 19:18** "Yet I have *left me* seven thousand in Israel, all the knees which have not bowed unto Baal and every mouth which hath not kissed him." The word *"left me"* in Aramaic means *"spared."*

In **Romans11:4a** "But what saith the answer of God unto him? I have *reserved* to myself seven thousand men who have not bowed the knee to the image of Baal." The word *"reserved"* in Aramaic means *"remaining."*

Look at **Mark 14:36** "And he *(Jesus)* said "Abba Father, all things are possible unto thee; takeaway this cup *(crucifixion)* from me; nevertheless not what I will, but what thou wilt."

Jesus was there to do his Father's will. God's Word fits together so perfectly it seems very odd Jesus, who spoke both Aramaic and Hebrew, would make a cry from the cross which would be privately interpreted incorrectly as *"My God, My God why has thou forsaken me."* What loving Father could ever forsake their own flesh and blood. Jesus actually spoke *"My God, My God for this purposed was I spared."*

How many times have you read in God's Word He will not forsake you, sinners you are. It is not logical for God to say He will not forsake you and then forsake His own Son.

Jesus did not die. . .he freely gave up his life for you and me.

Yes! It is true Jesus was nailed to the cross to pay the price for all the sins of the world He was the last sacrifice, but he did not die. More importantly he gave up *(free will)* his life for you. Every sin you ever committed prior to accepting Jesus as your Lord and Savior he paid the price for.

Here is something else few people are aware of. Jesus had to be born of a woman. He had to be flesh and blood just like you and me. He could not be a spiritual being and accomplish his Father's will. His sacrifice would take away the control Satan had over all death. His death was in the most gruesome way, on a cross. The cross was used for the worst of criminal offenders. Jesus took away the power Satan had over death and he took away all the sins you had committed before coming to Jesus and claiming Him as your Lord and Master.

When you are again tricked by Satan to sin, because you are human, you can now go to your heavenly Father and humbly ask for forgiveness and He being the awesome Father He is, He will forgive you of your sin and forget all about it

Psalms 103:12 "As far as the easy is from the west, so far hath he removed our transgressions from us."

Remember when you committed your life to God and Jesus Christ you were given eternal life and all your past sins were forgiven.

Our last breath. . .

Luke 23:46 "And when Jesus had cried with a loud voice, he said, Father, into thy hands I commend my spirit; and having said thus, he gave up the ghost*(spirit)."*

This scripture is so profound a statement because it tells you exactly what is going to happen when you breathe your last breath.

Your *personal spirit* will be taken to Paradise for safe keeping until Christ's return. This awesome revelation will appear later on. **I Thessalonians 4:16 "For the Lord** *(Christ)***himself shall descend from heaven with a shout, with the voice of the archangel and with the trump of God, and the dead "in Christ" shall rise first."** It does not say where the dead in Christ will be located. The word *"paradise"* is seen only three places in the Bible and they are all in the New Testament. First in **Luke 23:43b "Today thou shalt be with me in paradise."** Jesus is saying when you(the malefactor) die today you will be with me in paradise. Why are they both going to paradise? The most logical answer is to receive their new spiritual bodies. The malefactor will wait in paradise until Jesus returns. Jesus will receive his new body and return to spend the next 40 days walking among the people and with the disciples and then ascend to be with his Father. When Christ finally returns he will not come to earth. He will be in the clouds waiting to receive you. It is then Christ will collect all those *personal spirits* belonging to the believers who have already died and take them with him into heaven. Now all those believers who are alive at the time of Jesus' return will also be taken up, but only their *personal spirits*, no flesh. The second place we see *paradise* is in **II Corinthians 12:4a "How that he(Paul) was caught up into paradise,"** Paul was actually having a vision of what paradise would look like before he died. And the third usage is in **Revelations 2:7b "To him that overcometh will I give to eat of the tree of life which is in the midst of the paradise of God."** Which means when you arrive in paradise you who overcame the wiles of the adversary in this world, you will eat of the tree of life mentioned in **Genesis 3:22** and live forever.

Chapter Six

The Beginning. . .

Remember all the Bible stories you heard as a child about God creating the entire universe, all the animals, plants, fish, birds, earth, man, woman, planets, stars and the Sun in just six days.

Well we seem to have a conundrum which is a confusing or difficult question. Did God create the universe in six of His days or did it really take a lot longer or maybe **both?**

Let's explore what God's Word says about the situation. In **Genesis 1:1 "In the beginning God created the heaven and the earth."** You will notice the word *"heaven"* is singular in nature. It so happens that this heaven encompasses the entire universe and at this point in the act of creation there was nothing in space. It was very dark and cold and empty and then. . .the heavens were created 13.8 billion years ago and still expanding. The Earth was created 4.6 billion years ago. And Adam showed up around 4,400 B.C.

Genesis 1:2 "And the earth was without form and void;" This does not sound like a planet ready to receive any kind of life. It was a burning hot mass of magma and was void of any life. **"and darkness was upon the face of the deep, And the Spirit of God moved upon the face of the waters."** The subject of the *"deep"* is very interesting and requires a more lengthy study. The word *"face"* means the front or outer surface in this context of the waters. And then we have the word *"waters."* We will talk at length about these special words in Chapter 9 "The Deep."

Genesis 1:3 "And God said, Let there be light; and there was light." 4 "And God saw the light, that it was good; and God divided the light from the darkness." 5 "And God called the light Day, and the darkness he called Night. And the evening and the morning were the *first day."*

Let's summarize where you are now. God has spoken. He opened His spiritual mouth and began speaking everything into creation. Does this give you any indication how powerful the spoken word can be. He spoke and the space for heaven was created. Now He speaks and the Earth is created but it is without form and is void of any life. What is really interesting about this whole process of creation is the introduction of water. It is as if the universe is a baby who is surrounded by water in the womb. In verse **1:2** God who is Spirit is moving upon the face or front of the waters which cover the entire expanse of the universe. At this point now He has spoken light into the mix. What light we do not know yet but He is indicating it could be the Sun, Moon or stars. **Genesis 1:6 "And God said, Let there be a firmament in the midst of the waters, and let it divide the waters from the waters."** God is saying let the heaven divide the waters which are above the firmament from the waters below the firmament.

Genesis 1:7 "And God made the firmament, and divided the waters which were under the firmament from the waters which were above the firmament; and it was so." So now the universe is in the midst of the waters above and below. Have you begun to get an idea of how immense the universe is.

Genesis 1:8 "And God called the firmament Heaven. And the evening and the morning were the *second day.*"** We now have Heaven or the firmament between the waters.

Genesis 1:9 "And God said, Let the waters under the heaven be gathered together unto one place, and let the dry land appear; and it was so." Traces of water began to appear around *4,404,000,000 B.C.**

Genesis 1:10 "And God called the dry land Earth; and the gathering together of the waters called he Seas; and God saw that it was good." In **Genesis 1:2** In this verse God had not named the existence of the Earth yet, it was a boiling mass of magma with no real shape. And again it would take several billion years before the Earth would be cool enough so plant and animal life could exist. The word *"Seas"* or *"yam"* in Hebrew means a lake or pool. The word "ocean" or very large body of water does not appear in the King James Version of the Bible during the creation experience. The ocean's non-existence is proved when Noah was building the ark. God told Noah it would rain for forty days and forty nights. **Genesis 7:12 "And the rain was upon the earth forty days and forty nights."** The appearance of rain was a new concept. **Genesis 2:5b "For the Lord God had not caused it to rain upon the earth, and there was not a man to till the ground." Genesis 2:6 "But there went up a mist from the earth, and watered the whole face of the ground."** Logically for the rain to appear there would have to be oceans present to provide the water, but they were not.

Genesis 1:11 "And God said, Let the earth bring forth grass, the herb yielding seed, and the fruit tree yielding fruit after his(its) kind, whose seed is in itself, upon the earth; and it was so." *"whose seed is in itself"* means it carried the seeds for reproduction within itself. Like an apple or an orange or a pomegranate. By now several billion years have passed since God spoke the Earth into being.

This is the key to understanding the creation of the universe and everything within it. God did indeed create the universe and everything within it in six of His days. The act of creation does not mean completion within itself. For that to happen God would have to negate all the scientific principles He had established.

Genesis 1:12 "And the earth brought forth grass and herb yielding seed after his kind and the tree yielding fruit, whose seed was in itself, after his kind; and God saw that it was good."

Have you noticed the scriptures are repeating themselves. In God's Holy Word when verses begin to repeat themselves this is God's way of making sure the reader understands how important these verses are. Verses which repeat themselves at least two times are established or permanent in God's Word.

Genesis 1:13 "And the evening and the morning were the *third day*.**"** Now we have the lights in the firmament or heaven and more.

Genesis 1:14 "And God said, Let there be lights in the firmament of the heaven to divide the day from the night; and let them be for signs, and for seasons, and for days and years."

What would be in the heavens that might be a sign on the earth? Could it be the constellations? We rotate around the Sun for the seasons and the rising and setting of the Sun for the days and years.

** en.wikipedia.org/wiki/timeline_of_the_evolutionary_history_of_life*

Genesis 1:15 "And let them be for lights in the firmament of the heaven to give light upon the earth; and it was so." The constellations were finally beginning to form along with the planets. The Word of God can now be seen in the evening sky.

Genesis 1:16 "And God made two great lights; the greater light to rule the day and the lesser light to rule the night; he made the stars also." We have the Sun and the Moon as well as all the *"wandering stars."* In Greek the word *"planet"* means *"wandering star."*

Genesis 1:17 "And God set them in the firmament of the heaven to give light upon the earth."

Genesis 1:18 "And to rule over the day and over the night, and to divide the light from the darkness; and God saw that it was good."

Genesis 1:19 "And the evening and the morning were the *fourth day*.

Genesis 1:20 "And God said, Let the waters bring forth abundantly the moving creature that hath life. and fowl that may fly above the earth in the open firmament of heaven." God is telling you He is going to create moving creatures that the waters are going bring forth. And the birds which fly above the earth.

Genesis 1:21 "And God created great whales (*or sea monsters***) and every living creature that moveth which the waters brought forth**

abundantly, after their kind, and every winged fowl after his kind; and God saw that it was good.”

Genesis 1:22 “And God blessed them, saying, Be fruitful, and multiply, and fill the waters in the seas, and let fowl multiply in the earth.” Remember earlier, in the creation process there where no infants of any live creatures. Everything created which had life including fauna and trees was an adult version of its kind. How could it replicate itself without being a mature creature or plant. Also notice in some of the verses the phrase *“after his kind”* is spoken. The male of the species carried the seed for reproduction.

Genesis 1:24 “And God said, Let the earth bring forth the living creature after his kind, cattle, and creeping thing, and beast of the earth after his kind; and it was so.” Here is where God will repeat the verse to establish it.

Genesis 1:25 “And God made the beast of the earth after his kind, and cattle after their kind, and everything that creepeth upon the earth after his kind; and God saw that it was good.”

This is where you will come in. . .

Genesis 1:26 “And God said, Let us make man in our image, after our likeness; and let them have dominion over the fish of the sea, and over the fowl of the air, and over the cattle, and over all the earth and over every creeping thing that creepeth upon the earth.” There are several words in this scripture which are plural, *“our* and *them.”* God is definitely talking about more than one person being present. Here is something you can remember, the Old Testament conceals what the New Testament speaks. God could very well be referencing the presence of Christ Jesus when He is speaking about *“our.”* And then the word *“them”* refers to you and me as well as Adam and Eve and what we are to have dominion over. God tells us in **Ephesians 1:4a “According as he hath chosen us in him before the foundation of the world,”** we were with Him before the foundation of the Earth, spiritually speaking. Since God is Spirit, to make man in

His image means His Holy Spirit will be in each of us before we are born into this world.

Genesis 1:27 "So God created man in his own image, in the image of God created he him; male and female created he them." Again you know God is Spirit so His Holy Spirit is within you just waiting to be energized.

Genesis 1:28 "And God blessed them, and God said unto them, be fruitful, and multiply, and replenish the earth, and subdue it; and have dominion over the fish of the sea, and over the fowl of the air, and over every living thing that moveth upon the earth."

Genesis 1:29 "And God said, Behold I have given you every herb bearing seed, which is upon the face of all the earth, and every tree in which is the fruit of a tree yielding seed; to you it shall be for meat." This verse tells us exactly what God has given to all of us who are believers. God uses the word *"meat"* to be a suggestion for what we should eat. God says nothing about eating any flesh yet. So we are going to eat vegetables and fruit instead and they will be our *"meat."*

Genesis 1:30 "And to every beast of the earth, and to every fowl of the air, and to everything that creepeth upon the earth, wherein there is life, I have given every green herb for meat; and it was so."

Genesis 1:31 "And God saw everything that he had made, and behold, it was very good. And the evening and the morning were the *sixth day."*

Genesis 2:1 "Thus the heavens *(plural) remember in Genesis 1:1 there was only one element in the sky and it was the earth. Now all the planets and stars and constellations and everything in space has been completed.* **and the earth were finished, and all the host of them."** *The creation has been completed. However it will take several billion years for everything to be completely formed.*

Genesis 2:2 "And on the seventh day God ended his work which he had made; and he rested on the *seventh day* **from all** his work which he had made."

Genesis 2:3 "And God blessed the seventh day, and sanctified it; because that in it he had rested from all his work which God created and made." God is telling you to rest on the seventh day, in this case it would be our Sunday. Should you be Jewish then Saturday would be your day of rest.He does not want you to do any *"work."* Your time should be spent reading and studying the Word of God. This is the day where you will put on the *"armour"* of God to do battle with the world you live in.

Now it is time for man to appear on the earth, fully formed and ready to procreate his species. The year is circa 4,000 B.C. **Genesis 2:7 "And the Lord God formed(***fashioned***) man** *of* **the dust of the ground and breathed into his nostrils the breath of life; and man became a living soul."** Now we go over to. . . **Genesis 2:21 "And the Lord God caused a deep sleep to fall upon Adam, and he slept; and he took one of his ribs, and closed up the flesh instead thereof;"** God took one of Adam's ribs and formed woman. Adam lived out the rest of his life with one less rib than Eve. God took the rib but did not alter Adam's DNA. All of Adam's offspring had a full set of ribs. Remember there are spaces of time between scriptures.

Genesis 2:22 And the rib, which the Lord God had taken from man, made he a woman, and brought her unto man."

Genesis 2:23 And Adam said, This is now bone of my bones and flesh of my flesh; she shall be called Woman, because she was taken out of man."

The key to understanding what God is saying in His Word is to read each scripture with your eyes then your mind and then with your knowledge. Think through what you know about a subject. God's Word is not rocket science. It is logical, full of knowledge and wisdom. It is your play book for life here on earth until it is time to go. . .

The conclusion is God indeed created the universe and everything in it in six of his days but those days did not follow each other consecutively. The key word here is *"generations"* in **Genesis2:4 "These are the**

generations of the heavens and the earth when they were created in the day of the Lord God made the earth and the heavens." There were several billion years in between each act of creation and each act was not to completion of whatever was being created only the start of its generation. It would take billions of years to finally end up with mature plants or animals that could reproduce their kind the way God wanted them to. Notice man and woman are way down on the list of creation. Many billions of years would be necessary for the earth to become habitable for both man and plant and animal.

Chapter Seven

Holy Spirit . . .

In looking back through the Old Testament, God's method of communication with man or woman was upon them through revelation. Now for the very first time in the New testament God places His Holy Spirit **within** a human being. How much of His Holy Spirit did He place in each human being. Each person received the exact same amount. God is not a respecter of persons.

Now it was Elisabeth, Mary's cousin. In **Luke 1:41b "and Elisabeth was filled with the Holy Ghost***(Spirit.)***"** Elisabeth was pregnant with John. John would eventually go on to be called John the Baptist and baptize Jesus in the Jordan River. John through Elisabeth's blood was also able to receive God's Holy Spirit. In **Luke 1:15 "For he***(John)* **shall be great in the sight of the Lord, and shall drink neither wine nor strong drink; and***(but)* **he shall be filled with the Holy Ghost***(Spirit)* **even from his mother's womb."**

In **John 14:16** Jesus is talking to the disciples and he says, **"And I pray the Father, and he shall give you another Comforter that he may abide with you forever."** Jesus was the first comforter. The second Comforter is the Holy Spirit.

Then in **Acts 2:4** the twelve disciples were in the upper room along with 120 other disciples and they all received God's Holy Spirit. This time instead of His Holy Spirit being **upon** these people His Holy Spirit was **within** their spiritual hearts. **"And they were all filled with the Holy Ghost** *(Spirit)* **and began to speak with other tongues as the**

Spirit*(God)* **gave them utterance."** Speaking in tongues has nothing to do with salvation and everything to do with confirming God's Holy Spirit is within your spiritual heart.

There is only one Holy Spirit, God. In Greek His Spirit is called *"pneuma hagion,"* or Spirit Holy.

Remember in **Ephesians 1:4 "According as he(God) hath chosen us in him before the foundation of the world, that we would be holy and without blame before him in love."** From a spiritual standpoint this is when you received God's Holy Spirit. His gift to you will remain inactive until you have made the commitment to follow His Son Jesus. At that point in time His Holy Spirit will become active within you.

The men of the Old Testament wrote God's Word and His Holy Spirit was **upon** them in the form of revelation. The men of the New Testament wrote God's Word and His Holy Spirit was **within** their spiritual hearts. Keep in mind the men of the New Testament did not begin writing the New Testament until almost 25 years after Christ ascended. God would talk with them and they would write what He spoke. In this manner He was sure no one would try to change the words He had spoken. Woe be to the man who changes God's Word. **Revelations 22:19 "And if any man shall take away from the words of the book of this prophecy, God shall take away his part out of the book of life, and out of the holy city and from the things which are written in this book.**

How to recognize the difference between "spirit" and "Spirit."

I mentioned earlier how to identify the word spirit in the Bible and who it refers to. When the word *"spirit"* is in a lower case **"s"** it means it is the gift from God such as your breath life. When the word *"Spirit"* is in upper case **"S"** it refers to God Himself. The word Holy will usually precede the word Spirit when speaking directly of God.

Image of God. . .

When man(Adam) was created there are many who say he and all those who followed were formed in the image of God which in this case would give God human characteristics. This particular circumstance is called *"condescensio"* in Latin and in Greek *"anthropomorphization."* Since God is spirit and has not been seen by any man the statement needs to be clarified. **John 1:18 "No man hath seen God at anytime; the only begotten Son, which is in the bosom of the Father, he hath declared**(*spoke of Him*)** him."**

Just as God breathed into the mouth of Adam and gave him life God has given to you a *"soul or breath life."* This breath of life sustains you for all your living days.

To say again. God is Spirit and He placed a small part of Himself within you **before** you were born. God knows there will be some men and women who will not accept Him as their God. Those people who reject God will have to rely on their own judgments about life and this would be a big mistake. Why! Because should they continue to reject God and His Son Jesus they will never spend a day in heaven. Their rejection of God will find their names not in the Lambs Book of Life. In fact they will burn in the Lake of Fire along with Satan forever. Scary thought.

So many people do not realize their *"free will"* is a gift from God. For those who do operate their free will and chose to follow Jesus Christ and God then His Holy Spirit(*the gift*) will be energized within them. In doing so this will now give these men and women the ability to speak with God directly through His son, Jesus or utilizing the manifestation of tongues which bypasses going through the Son and you will speak directly with God.

So when you hear the statement *"we were created in God's image"* you will know God's Holy Spirit is within you waiting for it to be energized. Theologians of the past have used this statement to give God human characteristics. **Genesis 1:27 "So God created man in his own image, the image of God created he him, male and female created he them."** Giving God human characteristics has caused a great amount of confusion.

Chapter Eight

The flood. . .

You know about the flood and Noah and the ark. God told Noah to build an ark to hold the following; **Genesis 7:2 "Of every clean beast,** *no split hooves,* **thou shalt take to thee, by sevens, the male and female; and of the beasts that are not clean by two the male and female."** A pig which has a split hoof is not a clean animal so it cannot be eaten or sacrificed to God and this is according to Jewish standards. The animals who were clean were to be used for food and sacrifices. The unclean were to be used for reproduction. Accompanying the animals were Noah, his wife and their three sons plus their wives. Noah had no idea how long they would be on the ark so in order for all the animals to fit in the ark he did not take any mature animals. By the time they were released from the ark they were sexually mature to reproduce their kind. What is really interesting is Noah did not have to go and collect the animals. They came of their own accord. Animals are known to have special senses concerning danger. It would not have taken much effort on God's part to stimulate the animals to move toward where the ark was being constructed. Noah had about 120 years to accomplish the construction of the ark, so the animals had plenty of time to find the ark. The ark was launched circa 2347 B.C. God told Noah it would rain on the earth for forty days and forty nights. Noah did not know what rain looked like because it had never rained on earth before. The only water to appear on the earth was a dew like substance, not rain. This dew did appear on a daily basis.

All known animal life which existed on the earth before the flood disappeared during the flood leaving nothing alive. Plant life was not affected. Remains of some of those creatures are still being found throughout the earth today. It took the waters over a year to subside. What you have left is our present day salt based oceans and seas. Over time fresh water became available as the salt was filtered by the atmosphere. As the ocean water is absorbed into the atmosphere the salt in the water evaporates. This process causes clouds to form and it rains fresh water.

Think about this, **Genesis 2:5 "And every plant of the field before it was in the earth and every herb of the field before it grew; for the Lord God had not caused it to rain upon the earth and there was not a man to till the ground." 6 "But there went up a mist from the earth, and watered the whole face of the ground."** No rain had ever fallen anywhere on the earth even before Adam and Eve came about.

So where did the water come from? We know scientists have discovered sea shells on Mount Ararat where the ark finally came to its resting place. And sea shells come from salt water. These facts would tend to lead someone to believe the water for the flood had to come from someplace other than the earth. Maybe it could be someplace outside of our atmosphere. Could we talking about the *"deep."* The flood lasted till around 2346 B.C. a little over a year from start to finish. Remember this fact, The years before Christ's birth are noted as B.C.(*Before Christ*). The years after Christ's birth are noted as A.D. Which in Latin is Anno Domini or the year of the Lord. Another fact to keep in mind. When we are talking about the years before Jesus we see B.C. used but as the years continue they will decrease until they come to 1B.C. Once 1 B.C. ends they start over with 1 A.D. and continue to increase until we reach 2019.

Chapter Nine

The deep. . .

In **Genesis 1:7** "**And God made the firmament and divided the waters which were under the firmament from the waters which were above the firmament and it was so.**"

In **Genesis 1:8a** "**And God called the firmament Heaven.**" Everything you can see on a starry night is considered the firmament or Heavens. These heavens are surrounded by water. Which means outer space will have an ending trillions of light years in the future. Ok! So the heavens are surrounded by water. Then there is water under the heavens which means there was water on earth as it was forming as well as on all the other planets but when God created Adam there was no rain on earth. So in **Genesis 2:10** one river starts in the Garden of Eden and then splits into four different rivers going out into the world. There is no mention of any oceans or seas just rivers. And there is definitely not enough water in these rivers to provide a flood or rain.

Why not sit back and close your eyes and think about this idea. Surrounding the universe is a saline or salt water solution. If you are traveling at the speed of light,186,000 miles per second, and you were put into a suspended state so you would not age as you traveled back in time the universe would eventually come to a stopping point trillions of light years from now. There would be a wall for the sake of discussion. On the other side of this wall is a saline solution surrounding all the heavens. When God created the earth He separated the waters under heaven from those above heaven. Keep this in mind. Heaven is not a one dimensional place. The heavens as they are called surround the earth and all the other planets and galaxies and go on and on for what would seem like forever but there is actually a stopping point. There is another explanation which supports this idea. To maintain the vacuum of outer space there has to be a wall of some sort. What the wall is made of is not important. Whatever the substance it has held up for billions of years.

To give you a better picture of what has happened. Take a beach ball into a pool of water. Push the ball down under the water so it is completely covered.

The beach ball's skin contains the Universe. Everything inside the beach ball is what you see at night when you look up at the sky. The water surrounding the ball is what God was dividing from under and above the firmament. Take a look at **Genesis 1:7**. Heaven is not a fixed location. It is just under the skin of the beach ball. The Universe and Heaven are the same and are contained within the beach ball, and the salt water solution(pool water) surrounds it all.

Because space is a vacuum, only the slightest movement requires a minimum of energy to be applied to it, so it would not go against God's laws of physics to cause the salt waters to move through the skin of the wall and travel across the universe/heavens and upon entering the earth's atmosphere turn into a rain storm. It is not important how God energized the water to move. He's God, He can do it anyway He feels, but keep this in mind, God did not have to break any of His physical laws to accomplish moving the salt water to the right place. We do know it rained for forty days and forty nights and the earth became flooded to the point the waters rose to a height exceeding Mount Ararat whose height was 16,124 feet. And there were no oceans on the earth at that time.

Fourteen months later Noah opened the window on the ark and the waters had dried up. Where did the waters go? Could they have became the oceans you have today. Sounds pretty good to me since they never had rain until after the flood and a funny thing about all this, the oceans are made up of salt water.

The deep continued. . .

In **Genesis1:2 "And the earth was without form and void, and darkness was upon the face of the deep. And the Spirit of God moved upon the face of the waters."**

Webster defines *"deep"* as a "vast or immeasurable extent, the extent of surrounding space and time." In Young's Concordance, the word *"deep"* refers to a *"sea."* In Hebrew the word is *"tehom."* The word sea refers to small bodies of water like lakes or pools. Vast bodies of water such as the oceans, Atlantic, Pacific and Indian are not mentioned, probably because they did not exist until after the flood. The economy of early Israel was agriculture, sheep and goat herding and fishing. The Sea of Galilee was more than able to provide all the fish the population needed and there was also the Mediterranean Sea which provided fish too.

Webster defines *"face"* as the *"outer surface."* In Hebrew the word *"face"* is *"panim."*

So it would read *" The outer surface of a vast extent of space."* Which goes hand in hand with the beach ball theory. When the *"deep"*, being outer space, is spoken of in God's Word, God had yet to place the Sun, Moon and Stars in their respective places. Now when God talks about *"the face of the deep"* you know He is referring to what actually surrounds the Universe. **Genesis 1:7 "And God made the firmament***(heavens)* **and divided the waters which were under the firmament from the water which were above the firmament and it was so."**

The more time you spend searching God's Word for its hidden treasures the greater your understanding will be.

Chapter Ten

Believing

There are two forms of believing. The natural everyday type of believing where what we see or hear or smell or touch or taste we believe in. And the Manifestation of Believing which deals with believing in the supernatural happenings of God, things we cannot see, hear, smell, touch or taste.

In this chapter we are going to talk about the natural everyday believing we all exhibit. Natural believing consists of either positive or negative situations which may require an action on your part. I say action because believing is a verb and verbs denote action. So with natural believing you are taking some sort of action. The direction of which is decided by your *"free will."*

Here is a wonderful example of positive believing:

In **Luke 7:2 "And a certain centurions servant who was dear unto him was sick, and ready to die." 3 "And when he heard of Jesus he sent unto him, the elders of the Jews, beseeching him that he would come and heal his servant." 4 "And when he came to Jesus, they besought him instantly, saying, That he was worthy for whom he should do this:" 5 "For he loveth our nation and he hath built us a synagogue." 6 "Then Jesus went with them. And when he was not far from the house, the centurion sent friends to him saying unto him, Lord, trouble not thyself; for I am not worthy that thou shouldest enter under my roof." 7 "Wherefore neither thought I myself worthy to come unto thee; but say in a word and my servant** shall be healed " 8 "For I also am a man set under authority, having under me soldiers, and I say unto one, Go, and he goeth; and to another, Come and he cometh; and to my servant, Do this, and he doeth it." 9 "When Jesus heard these things, he marveled at him, and turned him about, and said unto the people that followed him, I say unto you, I have not found so great faith, no not in Israel." 10 "And they that were sent, returning to the house, found the servant whole that had been sick."

Believing is not rocket science.

The act of believing is not rocket science. It is not complicated. Believing is simply an act of trust on your part.

Webster defines *"believing"* as; "To accept as true, genuine, or real. To consider to be true or honest."

Webster also defines *"trust"* as; "Assured reliance on the character, ability, strength or truth of someone or something."

You trust the person you are dealing with and that they will follow through with whatever they have promised to do for you. When you have dealings with your fellow human beings, Christian or not, you are all part of this world which belongs to Satan. Though Satan is a spirit and bound within the earth his unholy angel spirits who roam about the earth are applying influences throughout this world moment by moment and they are all being controlled by Satan.

Lets' say with your present believing you have decided to ask your friend to perform a certain task for you. You give him a certain time period to complete the task. He has agreed to perform this task within the time limits imposed on him. The time limit comes and goes and your friend has not even begun the task let alone finish it. Now the question arises. Because he is your friend do you cut him some slack in reproving him because he did not even begin the project or do you say to your friend "you are fired." This was an important project and your superiors had put their faith and believing in you to have the project completed by a certain time. Your friend let you down and now you have to do the project and hopefully you will not get fired.

Your believing in your friend to do what he says he will do is now questionable. Having any trust in his abilities is now suspect.

The wonderful part about God's Word is you can trust His Word and can apply everything God says to your life and see it come to a fruitful completion every time. Because you believe His Word you can now trust it even more because it proves what is true to the facts stated. God tells you over and over again how much He loves you and will never forsake you.

Proverbs 3:5 "Trust in the Lord*(God)* **with all thine heart***(spiritual)***; and lean not unto thine own understanding." 6 "In all thy ways acknowledge from him***(God),* **and he shall direct thy paths."**

God tells you all about the strengths He has given you. **Philippians 4:13 "I can do all things, through Christ, which***(God)* **strengtheneth me."**

God has given you thousands of promises in His Word. All you have to do to claim them is *"believe"* and *"trust"* what God says in His word. Here is a key to finding some of those many promises. When you read the Bible look for words like *"shall"* or *"will."* These simple words are definite promises from God to you.

Look at **Acts 1:8a,** this is Jesus talking to the apostles. **"But ye shall receive power after that the Holy Ghost(Spirit) is come upon you;"** The word *"shall"* is an absolute promise from God.

The more you read and begin to understand God's awesome Word the more you will begin to know His Word and Will for you.

Unbelieving example. . .

Matthew 13:54 And when he had come into his own country, he taught them in their synagogue insomuch that they were astonished, and said, Whence hath this man this wisdom and these mighty works?" 55 "Is not this the carpenter's son? Is not his mother called Mary? And his brethren, James and Joses and Simon and Judas." 56

"And his sisters are they not all with us? Whence then hath this man all these things?" 57 "And they were offended in him. But Jesus said unto them, A prophet is not without honour, save in his own country, and in his own house." 58 "And he did not many mighty works there because of their unbelief."

In Jesus own home town there was no one who would believe he could perform miracles.

When Jesus was 12 years old. . .

A fact rarely mentioned concerning Jesus' age. When Mary was pregnant, by God, with Jesus and before she married Joseph the customs of the country stated Mary could be legally put out of her home because she was with child and had no husband. Joseph was advised by an angel, probably Gabriel the messenger arch angel, to keep Mary safe and put aside her embarrassment of being an *"unwed mother."* **Matthew 1:19 "Then Joseph her husband, being a just man and not willing to make her a public example, was minded to put her away privily." 20 "But while he thought on these things, behold the angel of the Lord appeared unto him in a dream***(revelation)* **saying, Joseph, thou son of David, fear not to take unto thee Mary thy wife, for that which is conceived in her is of the Holy Ghost***(Spirit).***"**

Then moving on in Jesus' life. . .

Luke 2:42 "And when he*(Jesus)* **was twelve years old, they***(Mary and Joseph)* **went up to Jerusalem after the custom***(Passover)* **of the feast."** Jesus would be Bar Mitzvah at the age of twelve only because he was considered *"illegitimate"* by the town elders. Thirteen is the traditional age according to Hebrew culture. This new event took place also because Joseph was not Jesus' biological father.

Again, at the age of twelve, Jesus astounded the scholars in the temple when he began to reason with them out of the Torah or scriptures. There are some questions concerning how did Jesus learn the language or the scriptures? The answer is very simple. Every morning Jesus would go off to be alone and talk with his Father. It was at this time His Father taught him the scriptures. The Torah which was inspired by Moses through revelation consists of the first five books of our Bible. **Luke 2:46 "And it came to pass after three days they***(Mary and Joseph)* **found him in the temple sitting in the midst of the doctors, both hearing them and asking them questions." 47 " And all that heard him were astonished at his understanding and answers."**

Among the elders of the temple, when they read from the Torah they did not teach, as a professor would teach a subject, but they would reason and discuss the wording. They had not yet come to the conclusion completely that the words they read were etched in stone or the truth. To this day some Orthodox Rabbi's will continue to debate the words of the Torah.

This is a little side step concerning a very little word "all".

This small word has great meaning when you are asking for something from God. This word has several meanings but in this case there are two specific meanings. The context of the scripture and the chapter and the book will all play a part in how the meaning is obtained. In **Matthew 21:22 "And all things** *(if available)* **whatsoever; ye shall ask in prayer, believing, ye shall receive."** The word *"all"* in this verse means *"with distinction."*

This means if what you are praying for is available for God to provide and your spiritual walk is in line with God's commands then you should receive your answer from God again this is all based on His timing. Should what you are praying for not be available in God's Word then you should not get your hopes up on receiving it.

The question now arises, how are you going to know what is available? Remember when we talked about the words *"shall"* and *"will"* earlier. These are absolute promises from God which means they are available for the claiming and that means you have to walk out on His promise believing you will receive it. Try this for an example. You are beginning to cross a small creek. There is a flat rock available which is your first step, but you do not see the second rock to step on. In your spiritual heart you believe that the second rock is there so you take the step and sure enough located just below the surface of the water lies the stone. When God gives you a promise in His Word it is spiritual in nature not physical. In **Philippians 4:13** we find God giving you all the spiritual strength you need to fight any battle and all the battles take place where? In your mind.

Here is another example of *"all"* with distinction. **Mark 9:23 "Jesus said unto him, If thou canst believe, all things are possible to him that believeth."** Jesus is talking to the father of a son who has been possessed by a dumb and blind spirit and Jesus is saying if you believe all things *(spiritual)* are possible within the context of casting out of devils spirits in his son then the spirits will be cast out. **Mark 9:24 "And straightway the father of the child cried out, and said with tears, Lord I believe; help thou mine unbelief***(with skepticism.)***"** and then it happened in **Mark 9:25 "When Jesus saw that the people came running together, he rebuked the foul spirit, saying unto him, Thou dumb and deaf spirit I charge thee, come out of him and enter no more into him."** Just an added bit of information. This particular verse of scripture is considered one of four verses which prove that Jesus is the Messiah. This verse is considered a Messianic Miracle. Jesus spoke to the devil spirit which lived in the boy. Prophecy said whoever spoke to a devil spirit would be the Messiah. Jesus did.

Now some more believing examples. . .

Mark 11:23 "For verily I say unto you, That whosoever shall say unto this mountain*(personal problem)***, Be thou removed, and be cast into the sea; and shall not doubt in his heart, but shall believe that those things which he saith shall come to pass; he shall have whatsoever he saith."** Remember when you see the word *"shall"* used it means an absolute promise from God has come or will come to pass.

Ephesians 1:19 "And what is the exceeding greatness of his power to us-ward who believe according to the working of his mighty power." Ephesians is a wonderful book which will help with your walk especially if you are married. Though the word *"shall"* or *"will"* is not used it is implied due to the context of the scripture and the chapter.

I Thessalonians 2:13 "For this cause also thank we God without ceasing, because when ye received the word of God which ye heard of us, ye received it not as the word of men, but as it is in truth, the word of God, which effectually worketh also in you that believe." Again, no *"shall"* or *"will"* but the promise is there.

Hebrews 11:1 "Now faith*(believing)*** is the substance of things hoped for, the evidence of things not seen."**

James 1:6 "But let him ask in faith*(believing)*** nothing wavering. For he that wavereth is like a wave of the sea driven with the wind and tossed."**

Believing is very simple action which we all exercise many times a day. It is trust taken to its absolute perfection.

Chapter Eleven

On what day did Jesus die?

Traditionally it is said Jesus died on *"Good Friday"* and was resurrected on Easter Sunday. This information has been promulgated by all the great Christian and Hebrew churches over the last 2,500 years. Who was the first to say Good Friday would be the specific day when Jesus gave up his life? In order to find out the correct answer lets to go back to the period of time when Jesus was born and lived.

Jesus is born.

There are those theologians who believe Jesus was born in the year 1 A.D. *(anno domini - in the year of the Lord)* and died in the year 33 A.D. Should this be the case then the scriptures in **Revelations 12:1-5** would have fallen apart. For a reference point the apostle John wrote the book of Revelations around 89 A.D.

So let's read **Revelations 12:1 thru 5** and see what God says about this situation.

"And there appeared a great wonder*(sign)* in heaven *(zodiac)*; a woman*(Virgo)*, clothed with the sun, and the moon under her feet, and upon her head a crown of twelve *(12 apostles Matthew 10:2)*.**" "And she*(Mary)* being with child cried, traviling in birth, and pained to be delivered."** *(8/27 thru 9/15 Sun clothed the constellation Virgo)*.**" 3 "And there appeared another wonder in heaven; and**

behold a great red dragon*(Satan)* **having seven heads and ten horns. And seven crown upon his heads."** *(The constellation Draco or Hydra has seven heads)."* **4 "And his tail***(dragon-Satan)* **drew the third part of the stars***(angels)* **of heaven, and did cast them to earth; and the dragon stood before the woman which was ready to be delivered, for to devour her child***(Jesus)* **as soon as it was born." 5 "And she brought forth a man child, who was to rule all nations with a rod of iron; and her child was caught up unto God and to his throne."**

The birth of Jesus. . .

In the year **3B.C.,** these two factors were in precise arrangement for less than two hours, as the observation took place in Palestine, on **September 11.** The precise arrangement began about 6:15pm *(sunset, and lasted until 7:45pm.(moonset).* This was the only day in the entire year where this event could have taken place. This day was Tishri One on the Jewish calendar. Tishri One is none other than the Jewish New Year's.

The leaders of the seven dominate churches convened a meeting in the year of 325 A.D.*(some 236 years after John wrote Revelations)* at Nicea, Turkey to establish a common thread of Christianity for the world. This was Emperor Constantine's dream as well as his mothers to unify the churches so all peoples would be in harmony and belief. It was said *"God the Father', God the Son, and God the Holy Ghost"* or *"The Trinity"* was established at this meeting. Some time has passed now and the Roman Emperor Justinian around 529 A.D. felt it would be better if the Christian people would worship the Son of God instead of the god of Sowing, Saturnalia who was the Roman god of Sowing. The specific date of December 25th was chosen as the birth date of Jesus because it was closely related to the Winter Solstice. Interesting how this ties into our celebration of Christmas or Christ's Mass. Forget about the fact the shepherds did not tend their flocks of sheep in the month of December because it was too cold.

Regardless of what man down thru the ages has theorized or conjured up God's Word will stand the test of time which means this. Revelations 12:1-5 states exactly when Jesus was born, it only requires a little deeper study of God's Word and the existing star maps to bring the wonderful story of his birth to our knowledge.

Now let us look at "time of day".

Time of day was very important to the people of Judea and the surrounding countryside. Most of the people were herdsmen who based their lives on the Sun and its rising and setting. There were farmers in the valley raising wheat and barley to make bread. Bread was the staple item to eat. The herdsmen used the rocky hills for the sheep to graze upon. The hills were full of moisture and there was a small green grass which liked to grow between the rocks. The sheep would eat this grass. There were also many fishermen. Fish and bread and vegetables and occasionally meat made up the diet of these people. The times of day along with the seasons told these men when to plant their crops, when to bring the harvest in, when to take the sheep or goats out into the field and when to bring them back in and when to fish.

There are two recognized methods of determining time of day without a time piece. The one we will be utilizing is *"Sunset to Sunset"* reckoning.

Sunset to Sunset.

Sunset to Sunset is considered one day or 24 hours. The custom of the time was to turn toward the east and pray five times during each day, 6:00am, 9:00am, 12:00 noon, 3:00pm and 6:00pm. In **Matthew 27:45 "Now from the sixth hour** *(12 Noon)* **there was darkness over all the land unto the ninth hour** *(3 pm)."* **46a "And about the ninth hour** *(3pm)* **Jesus cried with a loud voice."** Jesus gave up his personal spirit to his Father.

So from Wednesday at 3pm which was three hours before Sunset till Sunset on Thursday is one day. Thursday Sunset till Friday Sunset is two days. Friday Sunset to Saturday Sunset is three days. And sometime between Saturday's Sunset and Sunday's Sunset Jesus was resurrected from the tomb by his Father, God. We see in **Matthew 12:40 "For as Jonas was three days and three nights in the whales belly, so shall the Son of man be three days and three nights in the heart of the earth."** According to Jewish Rabbinic tradition spiritually speaking the true Messiah would be in the grave three days and three nights. This scripture which is prophecy lends more credence to Jesus being the true Messiah.

The question may arise, Matthew who was with Jesus in his early years of teaching already knew what was going to happen because he was there. But it was 29 years later before Matthew wrote about what took place. Go to **II Peter 1:20 "Knowing this first, that no prophecy of the scripture is of any private interpretation." 21 "For the prophecy came not in old time by the will of men but holy men of God spake as they were moved by the Holy Spirit."** God, through divine inspiration, not revelation, revealed to Matthew exactly what to write. This was the same divine inspiration Matthew received along with the other disciples and about 120 other disciples in the upper room in Acts 2:4

In the book of **John,** who wrote about Jesus being the Messiah. In **20:1 "On the first day of the week***(Sunday),* **which in this case was Easter Sunday, early in the morning, while it was yet dark, Mary of Magdala came to the tomb; and she saw that the stone was removed from the tomb."**

The sun had yet to rise and Mary saw the stone was moved away. Jesus had been resurrected by his Father God. He is now the *"anointed one"* hence the new name Christ Jesus. Christ was then seen walking and talking with approximately 500 people during the next **forty** days. In **John 24:51 " And it came to pass, while he***(Jesus)* **blessed them***(the disciples)* **he was parted***(separated)* **from them, and carried up into heaven."** Christ Jesus actually ascended to be seated by his Father's right hand **ten** days before the celebration of Pentecost. On Pentecost the disciples along with 120 other people were in the upper room. There they received the "Comforter" Jesus promised they would receive after he had gone to be with his Father. Remember what we said earlier, just because verses follow each other does not mean the timing is the same.

Jesus gave up his life at the ninth hour *(3:00pm)* which was before Sunset. In the prophecy of **Matthew 12:40b "so shall the Son of man be three days and three nights in the heart***(buried)* **of the earth."**

Interesting note.

When we begin to think how wonderfully God designed and formed our bodies think about this, whether it be animal or human the body will begin to decay in 72 hours or three days.

I Corinthians 6:14 "And God hath both raised up the Lord*(Jesus),* **and will also raise us by his own power."**

What father would leave part of his family to begin to decay if he had the power to change the action taking place. Christ rising from the grave is the prime example which he is setting for each of you who are *"in him."* When you breathe your last breath God will take back His Holy Spirit which He gave to you in the beginning of your life and then your *"personal spirit"* will go to a wonderful place called *"Paradise."* This is the same place Jesus told the malefactor he would go after he died on the cross in **Luke 23:43b "Today shalt thou be with me in paradise."** The question has arisen, did Jesus go to Paradise to receive his new body before he came back to walk and talk with over 500 people? It would seem logical. Your personal spirit will go to Paradise and wait to ascend with Christ when he comes back. Christ was flesh and blood when he gave up his life so he would go to Paradise to receive his new body, just like you will.

Passover.

There are some theologians who believe Jesus had his *"Last Supper"* or *"Passover"* meal with the disciples and immediately went to the Garden and was then arrested. Again keep this fact in mind, there is usually a period of time between scripture verses.

Let's look at what God is saying here. **Matthew 26:17 "Now the first day of the feast of unleavened bread the disciples came to Jesus saying to him, Where wilt thou that we prepare for thee to eat the Passover?" 20 "Now when the even**(*evening*)** was come, he sat down with the twelve."**

Note again there was a passage of time while the disciples located a place for the Passover meal. This is the third Passover since Jesus began his ministry, three years in total. In **John 11:55a "And the Jews Passover was nigh at hand**." In order to gain a better understanding of what God wanted instituted by Israel to commemorate their escape from Egypt let's go back to **Exodus 12:2 "This month shall be unto you the beginning of months; it shall be the first month of the year to you**." This month will be called **"Abib"** or **"Nisan."**We call it April.

Passover began on the 10th of Nisan or *(our April 1st)*. At sunset we shall secure a lamb of one year without blemish. The lamb shall be kept *(12 days)* until the 22nd day of Nisan*(our April 12th)* when it will be eaten. The lamb will be cooked on the 22nd prior to sunset. The whole assembly of our family will help kill the lamb at 3:00pm or the 9th hour on the 22nd of Nisan. Jesus gave up his life on the 9th hour. Now keep in mind there are still three hours before sunset on the day of Passover. These remaining hours before sunset allowed Nicodemus and Joseph of Arimathaea who were with Jesus when he died, to get permission to take his body down from the cross, and wrap him in linen. There was no time to apply traditional ointments for the body. Then they placed him in the tomb owned by Joseph. Joseph was a wealthy man from Arimathaea. All this took place on Wednesday after 3:00pm and before sunset at 6:00pm. Three days later Mary Magdalene, Joanna and Mary the mother of James returned with oils to anoint Jesus ' body. It was Sunday morning, the 15th of April, and he was gone.

Blood on the lentils of the homes. . .

While still in Egypt the Israelites put the blood of an unblemished lamb on the lentils and doorposts of their homes so the angel of death who came to kill all the first born of the Egyptians would *"Passover"* their home and keep their children safe. The lamb was then eaten by the Israelites standing up with their sandals strapped on ready to go. This was the tenth and final plague promised by God.

Jesus was your Passover lamb. His blood was shed so sin and death would Passover you and me.

Jesus Christ's actual birth and death.

Jesus Christ was born on September 11, 3 B.C. and he gave up his life on Wednesday, April12, 30 A.D.

When you study the star maps for the period of time around and during Christ's birthday you will see how the stars and planets and constellations all fit together to herald this most important birth.

Studying the times and how the Israelites lived will help you gain a better understanding of just when Jesus gave up his life.

Jesus began his ministry at the age of 30 according to the book of **Luke 3:23 " And Jesus himself began to be about thirty years of age, being (as was supposed) the son of Joseph. which was the son of Heli."** To further confirm Jesus was 30 years old when he started his ministry look at the book of **John 2:13 and 6:4 and 11:55.** You have a record of three different Passover celebrations surrounding Jesus' ministry life which confirm Jesus was 33 when he gave up his life on the cross.

Concerning the constellations of Jesus' birth. . .

This is a quote from Craig Chester of the Monterey Institute for Research in Astronomy. "On September 3 B.C. Jupiter came into conjunction with Regulus, the Star of Kingship, the brightest Star in the Leo Constellation. Leo was the constellation of Kings and associated with the Lion of Judah So the Royal Planet approached the Royal Star in the Royal Constellation representing Israel. This kind of astrological symbol would definitely arouse the interest of the Magi." The Magi were astronomer's as well as wise men."

You can also check the email site, *bethlehemstar.net* for more visual confirmation.

Chapter Twelve

Doctrine, Reproof and Correction

These are the three complete divisions beginning in the Book of Romans in the New Testament.

We start with Romans (DOCTRINE)
Then I and II Corinthians (REPROOF)
And then Galatians (CORRECTION)
Moving on to Ephesians (DOCTRINE)
Then Philippians (REPROOF)
And ending with Colossians (CORRECTION)
I and II Thessalonians (DOCTRINE)
Then I and II Timothy (REPROOF)
And then Titus (CORRECTION)
DOCTRINE is the true standard for your believing.
REPROOF corrects your practical error in believing.
And CORRECTION corrects your doctrinal error in believing

DOCTRINE

Let us look at **Romans 3:20 "Therefore by the deeds of the law there shall no flesh be justified in his sight; for by the law is the knowledge of sin." 21 "But now the righteousness of God without the law is manifested being witnessed by the law and the prophets."**

22 "Even the righteousness of God which is by faith of Jesus Christ unto all *(and upon all- not in critical Greek text)* them that believe; for there is no difference." 23 "For all have sinned, and come short of the glory of God." 24 "Being justified freely by his grace through the redemption that is in Christ Jesus." 25 "Whom God hath set forth to be a propitiation *(through faith-not in text)* believing in his blood, to declare his righteousness for the remission of sins that are past, through the forbearance of God;"

REPROOF

I Corinthians 1:9 "God is faithful, by whom ye were called unto the fellowship of his sin Jesus Christ, our Lord." 10 "Now I beseech you, brethren by the name of our Lord Jesus Christ, that ye all speak the same thing, and that there be no divisions among you; but that ye be perfectly joined together in the same mind and in the same judgment."

CORRECTION

Galatians 3:22 "But the scripture hath concluded all under sin, that the promise by faith of Jesus Christ might be given to them that believe." 23 "But before faith*(anytime before Pentecost)* came, we were kept under the law, shut up unto the faith which should afterwards be revealed." 24 "Wherefore the law was our schoolmaster unto Christ, that we might be justified by faith." 25 "But after that faith is come we are no longer under a schoolmaster*(law)*." 28 "There is neither Jew nor Greek, there is neither bond nor free, there is neither male nor female; for ye are all one in Christ Jesus."

DOCTRINE

Ephesians 1:4 "According as he *(God)* hath chosen us in him before the foundation of the world, that we should be holy and without blame before him in love." 5 "Having predestinated us unto the adoption of children by Jesus Christ to himself, according to the good pleasure of his will." 6 "To the praise of the glory of his grace, wherein he hath made us accepted in the beloved." 7 "In whom we have redemption through his blood, the forgiveness of sins, according to the riches of his grace."

REPROOF

Philippians 1:10 "That ye may approve things that are excellent; that ye may be sincere and with our offense till the day of Christ." 2:3 "Let nothing be done through strife or vainglory; but in lowliness of mind let each esteem other better than themselves." 1:16 "Holding forth the word of life; that I may rejoice in the day of Christ, that I have not run in vain, neither laboured in vain."

CORRECTION

Colossians 1:27 "To whom God would make known what is the riches of the glory of this mystery among the Gentiles which is Christ in you the hope of glory." 28 "Whom we preach warning every man and teaching every man in all wisdom, that we may present every man perfect in Christ Jesus."

DOCTRINE

I Thessalonians 1:2 "We give thanks to God always for you all, making mention of you in our prayers;" 3 "Remembering without ceasing your work of faith and labour of love and patience of hope in our Lord Jesus Christ, in the sight of God and our Father." 4 "Knowing, brethren beloved your election of God."

REPROOF

I Timothy 2:1 "I exhort therefore , that first of all, supplications, prayers, intercessions and giving of thanks be made for all men;" 5 "For there is one God and one mediator between God and men, the man Christ Jesus." 4:16 "Take heed unto thyself, and unto the doctrine; continue in them; For in doing this thou shalt both save thyself, and them that hear thee."

CORRECTION

Titus 1:9 "Holding fast the faithful word as he hath been taught, that he may be able by sound doctrine both to exhort and to convince the gainsayers." 2:7 "In all things shewing thyself a pattern of good works; in doctrine shewing uncorruptness, gravity, sincerity," 8 "Sound speech, that cannot be condemned; that he that is of the contrary part may be ashamed. Having no evil thing to say of you."

Knowing how these scriptures are constructed can make finding an answer to whatever is bothering you a much easier task.

Should you be having some doubts concerning the Doctrine of your believing walk then select the appropriate verse from; Romans , Ephesians or I / II Thessalonians.

Maybe you need some Reproof for improper thoughts or words which you could have said or even actions you may have taken then go to; I / II Corinthians, Philippians, or I / II Timothy.

Now that you have found the correct path to walk thru the Doctrine chapters and you have been properly reproved thru the Reproof chapter it is time for some verses of Correction. So go Galatians, Colossians and Titus. Try it, you'll like it. Check out **II Timothy 3:16a "All scripture is given by inspiration of God and is profitable for doctrine, for reproof, for correction, for instruction in righteousness.**

Chapter Thirteen

Put off the Old Man.

Webster defines *"put off"* as *"to rid oneself of."* What a wonderful definition for getting rid of your past.

When God commands you in His Word to *"put off"* the old man and put on new man. He means just what He says. Get rid of your past or your *"old man."*

You know you have been given *"free will"* to make a choice in any matter pertaining to your walk with God, but if you are truly going to *"walk the walk"* and *"talk the talk"* then when God gives you a loving command to follow His Word you are to do exactly as it spoken.

In **Ephesians 4:22 "That ye put off concerning the former conversation***(behavior)* **the old man, which is corrupt according to the deceitful lusts***(lusts of the Deceiver).***" 24 "And that ye put on the new man, which after God is created in righteousness and true holiness."**

I know it sounds kind of crazy to get rid of your past which is your old man. How do you go about forgetting all the hurtful situations you were in, the beatings, the molestation and the psychological confrontations. How do you do it? Nike the shoe and clothing giant answered the question. *"Just do it."* This is your life and walk. There is absolutely no blessing for you to keep harboring these ugly happenings in your mind. Every negative situation taking place as you grew up was not of God therefore why would you want to remember all the hurt when God has waiting for you right now the most awesome blessings.

Society, which is where you live physically says you have to go to a psychologist or psychiatrist once a week for as many years as necessary to learn how to deal with the hurt and the cost is at least $150 per hour, you can do the math. And when it is done what do you do now. Go back to the world you live in wondering about your state of mind. Did you really solve or deal with what really happened to you? Did you confront the person who did the damage? And if you did, do you think they really care about what they have done to you. I do not think so otherwise they would not have done what they did to you. Then again they may have been abused when they were your age. They probably thought it was acceptable behavior to wreak havoc wherever they go. Does all this sound like it has been spoken about before?

You must understand the behavior of this individual which is not of love, but is of Satan. Maybe it sounds like a harsh statement, but think about it for a moment. When you think about a person with love you want the best for those people. The idea of any harm coming to them is not even considered. You have lifted these people to God in your daily prayer life for His mighty hands to surround them and protect them. Your words are sweet and kind to them. Your everyday thoughts are for the very best happenings in their lives. Anything less would be a worldly based thought which is of Satan's world. *Satan's world sits on top of God's earth.*

Let's go back to the scripture **Ephesians 4:22.** All of your former conversations which were with the *"old man"* contained deceitful lusts. They were statements based on lies and half truths. To lust is to continually dwell on something not of a Godly nature. To want something once or twice is not lust, but if you wake up each day and continually think about someone or something then you have an example of lust. So before you had God in your hearts you were part of this world, but now you are set apart or sanctified from this world by your acceptance of Jesus Christ as your Savior. When you were part of this world you would react accordingly to whatever the influence was from Satan. You would lie or cheat or hurt and not even give it a consideration. You were taught this way by either your parents or society, again I say, you are now set apart from this world.

The next part of the scripture reads **Ephesians 4:24 "And that ye put on the new man."**

What does *"the new man"* mean?

You are beginning a new walk with God. You are going to have daily conversations with God. To receive the most from your conversations it will help if you have begun to study God's Word on a daily basis. God will be going to talk with you using His Words, not yours. So now you will have to begin to study His Word. His Words become very comforting. They are peaceful words which can heal. They can strengthen and they can rebuke or correct or encourage or chasten you to do better. As you begin this study it will help you see the path He wants for you to follow.

Here is two scriptures which are very popular and I am sure will help you with your walk. They did mine. **Proverbs 3:5 "Trust in the Lord***(God)* **with all thine** *(spiritual)* **heart; and lean not unto thine***(your)* **own understanding." 6 "In all thy ways acknowledge him***(God)* **and he shall direct thy paths."** Remember earlier we talked about the word *"shall"* being an absolute promise from God.

Psalms 119:105 "Thy word is a lamp unto my feet and a light unto my path."

There are those who say God has a plan for your life. Research has found, the word *"plan"* does appear in many of the translations in the market place except the KJV of the Bible. However the word *"path"* appears in several scriptures in KJV. Should God have a plan for you to strive to follow then how does He go about manifesting His plan to you. The answer is simple. He does not have a **plan** for you. To do so would make Him a respecter of persons, which God is not. **Acts 10:34 "Then Peter opened his mouth and said of a truth, I perceive that God is not a respecter of persons."** And in **Romans 2:11 "For there is no respect of persons with God."** God does have a **path** for you to follow and the path is manifested in His Word for you to read and apply to your daily walk. Look at **Proverbs 3:6 "In all thy ways**

acknowledge him and he shall direct thy paths." This is again a popular verse of scripture. **Matthew 7:14 "Because strait is the gate, and narrow is the way**(path)**, which**(God) **leadeth unto life, and few there be that find it."**

God is saying here is His path. His path is narrow and the opening to the path is clear and strait and He will lead you to a life of great blessings and eternity with Him. It is sad to know many people will not find the gate or the path because of their negative believing.

God's loving commands.

In **Ephesians 4:31 "Let all bitterness and wrath and anger, and clamour**(make loud noises)**, and evil speaking, be put away from you with all malice**(desire to do evil).**"**

To follow this scripture would literally clear up all of your evil emotions which in turn would free you up spiritually to really worship God. This is something to strive for.

Let's say you know of an individual you cannot forgive because of what he or she did to you as you were growing up or even now in today's world. As terrible as the deeds were, you are now in a position to put this individual out of your life forever. God tells you to *"put off"* the old man and *"put on"* the new man. God is not telling you to think about doing this act. He is telling you to take this action because He knows you will be stronger for it and at the same time relieve yourself of a great spiritual burden which has been holding you back.

Keep this in mind the person who did these terrible actions is probably not even aware you are struggling with what went on back then. The unholy angel spirits which are contained within this man's or woman's soul could eventually do them in or Satan may still have more for this man or woman to do in his world. Once an unholy angel spirit is entrenched in a person's mind they usually will stay there unless they are rebuked through Christ Jesus or until the host passes on. Where the unholy spirits go to after the host has passed is not known.

Should this person not be part of your present day life then you will have a starting point to begin to forgive them for what they did to you. Forgiveness is very important for your spiritual walk with God with respect to your communication link with Him. God tells you He has forgiven all of the sins you have ever committed prior to your acceptance of Jesus as your Lord and Savior. You must now forgive those who have wronged you and of those you have wronged you are to ask for their forgiveness. Now this may be difficult because the person you have wronged may have passed on. In this case acknowledgment to God of your heart for this matter will suffice for the act of forgiveness to take place. God comes to the point concerning this forgiveness thing. He is commanding you lovingly to forgive because He forgave you and who are you to say you are bigger than God. But here is the clincher. When you pray to God with special requests God will hear you. Now, unless you have a clear slate of forgiving those who have wronged you His answer may not come immediately. Forgiveness is a must in your life. Once you have forgiven those who have hurt you and ask for forgiveness from those you have wronged then your prayers will be answered, but again only when God feels you are ready and in His timing. Now this may sound like God is a respecter of persons telling you to forgive everyone who has hurt you and you them in order to receive an answer to your prayers but this is a commandment from God for every Christian to follow.

Forgetting the past. . .

It may sound easy enough to do. Just forget what has happened in the past. It is very important you heed God's Word about this situation. The problem you have is you like to dwell in your past, in all the glory's as well as all of the failures you had. What does not bless you should be forgotten. Now, you are not the same person you were twenty or thirty or forty years ago. You have given your life to Jesus. You have changed. You do not look backward for your weakness you look forward to the strength of God. So why would you want to continue to dwell in the past which can drag you down from achieving what God has opened doors for you now to walk through.

Your past hurts can bring up anger and frustrations which will slowly chip away at your strengths until you are brought down again.

Here is how this whole procedure will work. You take steps to forget the ugly parts of your past. All the negatives and hurt feelings and damaged pride and busted egos. Please keep the good positive memories. They will provide many warm and fuzzy feelings. Science states for your memory to truly forget an entry may take up to seven years. So what do you do in the meantime when one of those old thoughts raises its ugly head. You immediately or as soon after the fact began, begin to read God's Word and try to remember what you read. The key is to replace those old ugly thoughts with the Word of God.

The old thoughts. . .

This is the visual mentioned before, but it bears repeating again. In the book, "The Christmas Carol" the scene where Scrooge is about to go to bed when he is confronted by the specter of Christmas Present. The hearty and robust gentlemen warns Scrooge he will be visited by three spirits representing Christmas Past, Christmas Future and Christmas Present. It is during the Christmas Past when Scrooge's old business partner's spirit walks thru the door of the bedroom dragging behind him a great length of big chain links and ledgers and balls. These were forged during my lifetime states Jacob Marley's ghost. Well guess what, you have some baggage still following along in your walk. When you *"put off"* your old man you literally cut those cords and chains releasing yourself to walk unfettered into the light of a new life with God.

In conclusion. . .

So in conclusion, when you *"put off"* your old man you are effectively forgetting about all the hurt you have received from whom ever. You still have to forgive these individuals for their actions towards you just like God forgave you for all your past sins. To forgive means you are going to have to let go of a lot of the pride you have harbored over the years. It may be hard at first, but the benefits are awesome.

Again, for anyone who has hurt you and those you cannot get in contact with or who have died, well God knows you are trying to do the right thing so just come to Him and say "I am sorry but I tried and there was no way they could be found." He'll forgive you because your spiritual heart is in the right place.

There will be some things you can forget right away but there others which will take time.

Keep talking with God. He knows your heart, and when you begin to know your own spiritual heart then God will truly begin a wonderful relationship with you.

Chapter Fourteen

God's plan is His path for us to follow.

How many times have you asked yourself what is God's plan for your life? When is God going to show you the plan for your life? How are you going to know when God actually tells you what His plan is for your life? And now the most important question! Did you miss His telling you what His plan was for your life. The confusion comes from the many different religions quoting from many different versions of the Bible. For instance one of the best translations is in **Jeremiah 29:11***(NIV)(written in 1973)* it reads **"For I know the plans I have for you, "declares the Lord***(God)***, "plans to prosper you and not to harm you, plans to give you hope and a future."**

In the Old Testament the word *"Lord"* refers to God, the creator.

Jeremiah sounds very positive about what God has in store for you. The question now arises how do you find out what God wants you to do? He said He has a plan, where is it? Unfortunately for God to have a plan for you would make Him a respecter of persons. This would mean He has had a plan for everybody who ever lived on this planet. Let's take a look at what the verse of scripture says in the *KJV* which was written in 1614. **Jeremiah 29:11 "For I know the thoughts that I think toward you, saith the Lord, thoughts of peace and not of evil, to give you an expected end."** This is a true statement because God does know your thoughts but thoughts are not plans they are purely thoughts. God will not interfere with your free will decisions which come from your thoughts. God will however provide the answer for your life's questions in His Word, the Bible.

God's path for your life is what He has written in His Word. When you follow His Word which He has laid out for you then you will be following His *"path"* for your life and where specifically do you find clues to the *"path"* you are to follow? In His Word.

Please take a look at **Proverbs 3:17 "Her ways are ways of pleasantness and all her paths are peace."** Who is *"Her?"* What are *"her ways?"* What *"paths"* are they talking about? The answers. *"Her"* speaks of wisdom which is what you want to acquire in your life time. How do you acquire wisdom? By gaining knowledge about your intended subject and in this case you are talking about the Word of God. Knowledge of God's Word will lead to a heart filled with wisdom. For what is wisdom, but knowledge applied which means as you speak God's Word you are speaking the truth of God and His truth is His Word and His Word is His will for your life.

"Her ways" are pleasant to the eye and the heart. There is no contention involved with the paths she has spoken of.

The *"paths"* reference her wisdom which is what you are endeavoring to attain in your walk with God. The paths are as softness of the clouds. There are no *"tares"* in her fields of plenty.

Here is another one. **Proverbs 8:20 "I lead in the way of righteousness, in the midst of the paths of judgment."** *"I"* is wisdom again. Wisdom will lead you on the path to the way of righteousness. When you begin to study God's Word for understanding and knowledge and not just for edification a change will take place in you and how you perceive the world you live in. When you have taken His Word into your heart then God will begin to open paths for you to walk down. Any door which God opens is a good door to walk through so it is important to keep your spiritual eyes open. Because you are righteous in God's eyes you are free from guilt and sin. The knowledge you gain will lead to wisdom and eventually will lead to a confidence far beyond what the world offers.

Again, these next verses of scripture are very popular because they lovely command you to take action through your believing. **Proverbs 3:5 "Trust in the Lord with all thine heart; and lean not unto thy own understanding***(five senses)***." 6 "In all thy ways acknowledge him, and he shall direct thy paths."**

Trust is a tough nut to crack sometimes because to trust you have to give up control of your five senses way of life and allow God to guide your new spiritual path. This is really not a hard thing to do, just go ahead and give up control of an area of your lives you never really had control of to begin with. Who really had control of your thoughts through his influences in this world? Satan did. So it is actually a joy to give up this area of your life because it caused you great concern and mistrust. Leaning upon your own five senses understanding in this world will not lead you to correct godly decisions in life. You must endeavor to put all your trust and believing in God so He can show you the correct path to follow.

OK! So what is my first step?

Can you tell the difference between right and wrong? If you can then God has already been talking with you during your walk down His path. Have you ever questioned whether the path is really the right one. Are you satisfied with your present career choice? Would you make a different choice if you had the chance? Would your new choice bless God?

Here is the deal. God wants you to have your spiritual heart's desire. He also wants you to glorify Him in your walk as you help your brothers and sisters to come back to Him. So let's look at how this could take place.

John 15:16 "Ye have not chosen me, but I have chosen you and ordained you that ye should go and bring forth fruit and that your fruit should remain; that whatsoever ye shall ask of the Father in my name, he may give it you."

This is such a wonderful scripture. You did not chose God. He actually chose you before the foundation of the earth. He also ordained you with oil just as the Old Testament Kings were anointed before the congregation. You are to go forth and bring believers*(fruit)* who have strayed away from God back to the Father. With those*(fruit)* who do not believe, your goal is to bring them spiritually to a point where you can plant the seed of a righteous thought*(God's word)* in their minds about coming to God. God will take care of the rest*(harvest)* and if there is anything you need spiritually just ask God thru his Son Christ Jesus and you will have it, in God's timing.

Now!

You are now walking with God. Your present career choice will actually take on a more pleasant feeling. You will now have more confidence to excel at your work tasks and the example you set will be seen as a positive influence on your fellow workers. You will have the desire to perform random acts of kindness. You will become less selfish in many aspects of your work ethic and your personal life at home with your family or friends will change. How will you do this?

First deny yourself.

The funny thing is when you begin to *"deny yourself"* your job performance will increase. Your family life will change for the better. Your children will notice the difference. You will become a more valuable influence within your company. Your supervisor will see the change and a promotion may be in the works, why?

By changing your career path over to God's way of doing life and begin to follow what He has to say you will stop following the *selfish* path of your own mind and your attitude will change. Your confidence will grow stronger because you are asking God to help you and the more you put on*(remember)*of God's Word the stronger you will grow. Your conscious thoughts will be purer and sweeter and so much closer to the mind of Jesus Christ which is what you received from God when you gave your life over to Him.

Jesus Christ walked a path which had all the temptations of life surrounding it and He did not succumb to them. He spoke these Words of His Father, *"it is written."* In your own lives you will walk a path with great temptations and if you are tempted and do not succumb then you can go on to becoming stronger in the knowledge you beat the question Satan continues to ask you. Now if you do give into sin and it probably will happen, you are not perfect like Jesus, so you will have to go to the Father and humbly ask for forgiveness and He being the just Father He is will forgive you and forget about what you have done, again and again and again.

Have you given up being *"selfish"* yet? Have you given up thinking about yourself all the time?

God's Word is your path to follow. God has spelled out exactly what you are supposed to do in this life. He has written it down so you would not forget the words. His Word has been here all along just waiting for you to pick it up and begin your journey.

Your personal walk.

So! What is your personal goal in life? To begin to follow in Christ's footsteps and remembering, his steps are those inspired by his Father God. By reading God's Word each day He will begin to slowly open the word up for your understanding. When Jesus would get up early He would go into the wilderness to talk with his Father. The words he heard were the same as those written in God's book, the Bible. Jesus spoke his Father's words to all who could hear.

God continues to give you free will. Take a look at the words *"free will."* *Free* means no restrictions. *Will* means a desire or choice, which means you have no restrictions on any desire or choice of your path in life. You can chose God's way or the world's way. God gave you a path which is straight and narrow. Satan gave you a superhighway which twists and turns like going up to the top of Pike's Peak. You pick the route you want to follow.

Every truth of God's Word you learn and remember is part of the armour of protection God has given to you to help defeat the works of Satan. You will never defeat Satan personally, only Christ will accomplish this at the end of times, but you can stand in Satan's way when he attacks because of what you have learned from God's Word. Your confidence will continue to grow as you stand boldly with your hearts full of His Word.

Chapter Fifteen

Claiming your Sonship rights and more.

Sonship is a new word in your spiritual vocabulary. Literally it means you are the son or daughter of God. He has adopted you accordingly. In **Galatians 4:5 "To redeem them that were under the law that we might receive the adoption of sons." 6 "And because we are sons** *(and daughters)* **God hath sent forth the Spirit of his Son into your hearts crying "Abba Father."** Abba is Aramaic for Father, so it means Father, Father.

Remember in the chapter dealing with Creation we talked about scriptures repeating themselves. Anytime in God's Word when a word or phrase is mentioned twice in succession it is established.

Your "born again" package rights. . .

God is your Holy Father. Christ Jesus is your Holy step-brother. You have been given the same rights by God your Father as He gave to His Son Christ Jesus. Those rights are: Righteousness, Justification, Sanctification, Redemption and Ministry of Reconciliation. Now couple those rights along with a guarantee for eternity and salvation and you will have true peace of mind.

A quick explanation of salvation is your deliverance from all temptations and sin. Sanctified means you as a citizen of heaven have been set apart from those who are not "born again."

You were given these rights when you chose, by your own free will, to accept Jesus Christ as your Lord and Savior. To accept these rights means you must also believe in them.

Webster defines "rights" as one who is justly entitled to.

Another example of rights you have been given are located in the Constitution of the United States. These rights are the first ten amendments of the Constitution. They are called the *"Bill of Rights."* The Constitution was God inspired so these rights were imbedded in the minds of your founding fathers when they began to write this document.

Your Sonship rights provide you with a legal spiritual position in Christ. Remember Christ is your advocate, **I John 2:1 "My little children these things write I unto you that ye sin not. And if any man sin we have an advocate with the Father, Jesus Christ the righteous."** Christ is your intercessor with his Father God. Christ represents you before his Father in all matters of the flesh and especially when you pray.

Now, how to receive answers to our prayers.

These are a few things you should remember if you want to hear from God concerning answers to your prayers. God asks you in His Word to end your petitions *"in the name of Jesus."* Not in his "wonderful name" or "glorious name," or Amen. Though beautiful to the ear these words lack the necessary power for your purpose. This has been mentioned before. God commands you to have your affairs in order concerning any grievous accounts against you. There must be forgiveness on both sides. If someone has hurt you then you need to forgive them. If you have hurt someone then you must seek their forgiveness. Should they desire not to forgive you then it is not your problem anymore but theirs.

God asks you to be specific with your requests, nothing in general. God also asks you to be continuous with your requests. In other words praying just once for anything from God will not be acceptable. God hears your first request the first time but if He does not hear from you again then most likely He will feel you are not really serious about your prayer request. The apostle Paul set the example for you by praying continually about the Gentile's and their walk with God. He did not just offer up one prayer and walk away. **Colossians 1:3 "We give thanks to God the Father of our Lord Jesus Christ, praying always for you."** What an example to follow.

Let's take a break for a moment and talk about Adam.

Nowhere in the Bible is it mentioned just what kind of fruit Adam was supposed to eat. It could have been, as some theologians feel a pomegranate, not an apple. Actually there was no food involved at all. In **Genesis 2:16 "And the Lord God commanded the man, saying, Of every tree of the garden thou may freely eat;" 17 "But the tree of the Knowledge of Good and Evil, thou shalt not eat of it; for in the day that thou eatest thereof thou shalt surely die."**

God told Adam this before He created Eve. So Adam already knew they were not supposed to eat of this particular tree. It also does not say just what they were supposed to be not eating if indeed they chose to eat from this tree. Because when God says the word *"eat"* you will automatically assume physical food is involved. God is not talking about physical food. He is talking about spiritual food. The tree was a *metaphor(not true to fact)* for the Word of God. The tree was a symbol to mankind. A symbol of the heart and depth of God's Word. *It is illogical to consider a bite out of a piece of fruit would contain all the knowledge of good and evil, so we must be talking about a spiritual apple.* Adam was not ready mentally or spiritually to take on the responsibility of teaching or even living with the depth of this kind of truth. Notice in **Genesis 3:6** the scripture goes into third person tense and speaks as if someone else were watching Eve. **"And when the woman***(Eve)* **saw that the tree was**

good for food and that it was pleasant to the eyes, and a tree to be desired to make one wise, she took of the fruit thereof and did eat, and gave also unto her husband with her; and he did eat."

Satan had this knowledge also. He knew it was going to be very easy for him to persuade Eve to doubt God's Word. She in turn then spoke her doubt to Adam and they both ate, figuratively, of the words. Here is a better explanation of what it means to eat spiritually speaking. **Jeremiah 15:16a "Thy words were found and I did eat them and thy word was unto me the joy and rejoicing of mine heart."** The reason God said *"thou shalt surely die"* is not literal but spiritual. Adam and Eve gave up their spiritual connection with God and died figuratively. Remember as soon as they *"ate"* or listened to the word and made it their own they discovered their nakedness and were in turn banished by God from the Garden. Adam could communicate with God anytime before he ate of the unknown fruit, but after the incident in the Garden the two way internal connection was lost. However, God did not forsake Adam. God continued to speak and teach Adam for over nine hundred years just as He spoke with the holy men who wrote the Bible, through **revelation** which was **upon** and **not within.**

It is almost like the tree of Knowledge of Good and Evil was an enormous secret God was holding back from sharing with Adam. Then who comes along but Satan, God's arch enemy to spring the hidden secret on two unsuspecting people thereby changing their lives and all the future generations from then on. What is even more interesting, the Tree of Knowledge of Good and Evil could not have been a real tree because it produced no seed to reproduce itself. All the other trees in the garden were fruit bearing trees and each generated a seed to reproduce itself .

Adam's sin was the beginning of the *"sin nature"* which you all, carry in your blood spiritually speaking. **II Corinthians 5:21 "For He***(God)* **hath made him***(Jesus)* **to be sin for us , who knew no sin; that we might be made the righteousness of God in him***(Jesus).***"** Here is the interesting part of this whole thing about **"sin nature"** being in your blood. This is not a physical part of your blood. *"Sin nature"* is a metaphor for all the potential evil you are carrying throughout your body in your spiritual blood stream. This evil resides in your thought processes which come from your mind.

Jesus Christ had perfect blood. **Hebrews 2:14 "Forasmuch then as the children are partakers of the flesh and blood, he also himself likewise took part of the same; that through death he might destroy him that had power that is, the devil."** But how did it happen. Where did Jesus' blood come from? From God, who is Spirit, and also His Father. When God impregnated Mary with His sperm or seed, it carried the gene for the blood, as do all male sperm. Since the sperm came from God, the gene was perfect, this meant Jesus would be perfect and as such be the perfect Passover lamb for man's salvation. You can read in *Isaiah 53:1-12* the prophecy concerning the birth of Jesus and its coming to pass. In **Isaiah 53:10 "Yet it pleased the Lord***(God)*** to bruise him. He hath put him to grief; when thou shalt make his soul and offering for sin, he shall see his seed, he shall prolong his days, and the pleasure of the Lord shall prosper in his hand."** The English word for *"soul"* in Hebrew is *"nephesh."* And the English word for breath in Hebrew is *"chai"* or *"moving life."* When you read or see the Word *"soul"* in the Bible it means *"moving life"* or literally *"breath life."* Jesus had *"nephesh chaiyim"* just like you do. Both the blood and the sex of the baby are contained in the DNA of the male sperm. Jesus took the blood from his Father and it was pure and the flesh from Mary's DNA. Keep in mind Joseph, Mary's husband had nothing to do with the birth of Jesus. Mary is of the lineage of the house of David. Coming from the house of David meant a great deal to the leaders of Israel. This lineage goes back thru Noah to Lamech, Noah's father, and then back to Adam.

Now what about the flood.

The question has been asked, "when the flood came wasn't all life wiped out with the exception of Noah and his family?" This is true, all animal and human life. Noah however was able to continue the blood line through his father Lamech which went all the way back to Adam. Here is another interesting fact. Lamech sat at the feet of Adam who was now about nine hundred years old and he listened as Adam recounted all the teachings God had imparted to him. Though Adam was expelled from the Garden, God did not forsake him. In this manner Lamech was able to share with Noah all the information he would need to continue in the ways of God who originally taught Adam.

The book of Romans

Romans is considered by many theologians to be the Book of Doctrine or the Book of Right Believing. This is the book you as a beginning student of the Word should start by reading and studying. There are many scriptures which explain just how you should walk with Jesus and God. Once you begin your walk do not rush and do not become impatient. This is a lifetime walk so take your time and enjoy it.

Now let's see how you can claim your Sonship rights. The word *"claim"* means an affirmation of what God says you have been given.

RIGHTEOUSNESS

The New Bible Dictionary defines righteousness as: *"Those clothed with this righteousness are justly acquitted and accepted as righteous at God's judgment bar."*

In **Romans 3:26 "To declare, I say, at this time his** *(God)* **righteousness; that he might be just, and the justifier** *(God)* **of him which believeth in Jesus."**

In **Romans 5:19 "For as by one man's disobedience many were made sinners, so by the obedience of one shall many be made righteous."**

Who is the *"one man's"* referring to? Adam. Who is the *"one shall"* referring to? Jesus Christ. The word *"shall"* is an absolute promise from God to you. Remember when you see the words shall and will in scriptures you can be sure they are among the many promises God has given to you, **if** you claim them.

Let us look at **Romans 4:3 "For what saith the scripture? Abraham believed God and it was counted unto him for righteousness."** So Abraham believed God and because of his belief he was made righteous, therefore when you believe in God and His Son Jesus Christ then you too will be made righteous in the sight of God.

II Corinthians 5:21 "For He*(God)* **had made him***(Jesus)* **to be sin for us who knew no sin, that we might be made the righteousness of God in him***(Jesus)*.**"** You are as righteous as Jesus Christ when you believe what God is saying to you. There is no guilt to be felt on your part because of what Jesus did for you. Just as God has a path for you to follow, Jesus had his path to follow also. God says in **Romans 8:1 "There is therefore***(past tense)* **now***(means right now)* **no condemnation to them which are in Christ Jesus***(that is us)***, who walk not after the flesh but after the Spirit."**

You are free from any guilt. God is telling you not to condemn yourself when you have sinned. God is asking you to humbly come before Him and confess your sin and ask for forgiveness. God being a very just Father will forgive your sin and cast it as far as the east is from the west, never to be remembered again. You now have the responsibility to try to not repeat the sin and you must endeavor to forgive yourself for what you did.

This is a wonderful scripture to read over and over because there is so much wisdom in it.

I Corinthians 2:14 "But the natural man receiveth not the things of the Spirit of God for they are foolishness unto him*(not talking to us, the believer)***. Neither can he know them because they are spiritually discerned." 15 "But he that is spiritual, judgeth all things yet he himself is judged of no man." 16 "For who hath known the mind of the Lord***(Jesus)* **that he may instruct him, but we have the mind of the Lord***(Jesus)*.**"**

You have been given this awesome right of Righteousness through Christ Jesus and God, His Father.

Romans 3:21 "But now the righteousness of God without the law is manifested being witnessed by the law of the prophets." 22

"Even the righteousness of God which is by faith(*believing*) **of Jesus Christ unto all them**(Jew and Gentile) **that believe for there is no difference."** There is no difference between a Jew or a Gentile(*that's you*).

JUSTIFICATION

The New Bible Dictionary defines justification as a legal term meaning *"acquit."* You have been acquitted in God eyes, as the highest judge, **"just as if we had not sinned."**

Romans 8:33 "Who shall lay(*call into judicial account*) **anything to the charge**(*calling into question*) **of God's elect**(*you and me*)?" It is God who justifies.

When you accepted Jesus Christ into your life as your Lord(*master*) and Savior you became *"justified"* in God's eyes which means any sins you had in your past you were not guilty of. It was as if you had never done any of those fowl deeds.

Now in **Romans 3:20 "Therefore by the deeds of the law there shall no flesh be justified in his**(*God's*) **sight for by the law is the knowledge of sin."** When you have knowledge of all of the 613 laws the Jewish people had to live by you will begin to understand just what sins carried punishment by God. Two additional laws, the first two commandments from the Ten Commandments were added later to the original 611 by the Levi's for a total of 613. Spend some time reading Deuteronomy. It will help if you gain a better insight of the laws.

Now have you ever wondered where those 611 laws came from. In Exodus when Moses went up upon Mount Sinai to receive the original ten commandments from God he was up there forty days. During those moments God talked with Moses but Moses did not see a physical body. God's Holy Spirit wrote down on the blank stone tablets Moses had brought with him. When Moses came down he found Israel had began worshiping a golden calf. Moses lost his cool and broke the tablets. Israel's action really made him mad. They had gone back to their original ways of worship. Now he was going to have to go back up into the mountain and explain to God what happened and hopefully get a new set of commandments. Well Moses is with God for another forty days and this time he comes down with two new tablets again containing God's word concerning the Ten Commandments. But because God was not pleased with Israel He wrote up an additional set of laws. This time God supplied the tablets. This new set contained 611 laws for Israel to follow. The holy priests, **the Levi's,** would be able to explain the laws to the people. In **Exodus 21:1 "Now these are the judgments which thou shalt set before them."**

God gave the Levites the responsibility of administering the laws to the people and tending to the temple. The Levites owned no property and had no income. They became the responsibility of all of Israel to be cared for.

The law was fulfilled by Jesus Christ giving up his life on the cross, but the law was not replaced. You answer to God today through His son Christ Jesus who is your advocate with his Father.

Your walk

Earlier we talked about two additional commandments being added to the original 611. The Levi's added to the original 611 laws are as follows. This is the first commandment. **Exodus 20:3 "Thou shalt have no other god's before me."** And the second commandment is; **Exodus 20:4 "Thou shalt not make unto thee any graven image, or any likeness of anything that is in heaven above, or that is in the earth beneath or that is in the water under the earth."** This is exactly what Israel was doing while Moses was up on the mountain with God.

Romans 3:24 "Being justified freely by his *(God's)* **grace through the redemption that is in Christ Jesus."** Jesus Christ had to be borne by a very special woman of God from the tribe of David. She was a virgin. Jesus' body was flesh and blood just like you. His body had to be of flesh in order for you to be justified freely by God's grace when you accepted Jesus as your Savior. Here is a great acrostic; **"God's Riches At Christ's Expense."** G-R-A-C-E.

Romans 3:28 "Therefore we conclude that a man*(or woman)* **is justified by faith***(believing in the New Testament)* **without the deeds of the law."**

Galatians 2:16 "Knowing that a man*(or woman)* **is not justified by the works of the law but by the faith***(believing)* **of Jesus Christ, even we have believed in Jesus Christ that we might be justified by the faith of Christ and not by the works of the law, for by the works of the law shall no flesh be justified."**

This scripture is addressed to the Church of Grace. You are the church in the Grace administration of God. You are justified by your believing in Christ Jesus. The works you do, carry no weight in the matter of your justification.

REDEMPTION

The New Bible Dictionary defines redemption as *"Deliverance from some evil by payment of a price."*

What kind of price is being discussed here? Is there anyone who comes to mind who could have paid a price so terrible the outcome would be "redemption" in your case. Would Jesus Christ fall into this category of paying the price?

I Corinthians 6:20 "For ye are bought with a price, therefore glorify God in your body, and in your spirit which are God's." Sound familiar!

Ephesians 1:7 "In whom we have redemption through his blood, forgiveness of sins, according to the riches of his*(God's)* **grace."**

You know, by now, Romans 10:9,10 when you commit your life to Jesus Christ and make him Lord and Master in your life and believe God raised His Son from the dead and when you confess, your past sins then God, your new Father, thru adoption can energize His Holy Spirit in Christ in you. With this simple act on your part you have God's energized Holy Spirit in you and you have the conscious thoughts*(mind)* of Christ Jesus. Now you still have some of your carnal thoughts around. As you continue to walk in the steps of Jesus Christ and endeavor to think like he would have, those carnal thoughts will gradually begin to soften and disappear. To achieve this softening will require you to again begin to renew your thought patterns to those of God's Word. Your believing will eventually take over control of your carnal thoughts and they will begin to diminish. The change will take some time and will become a moment by moment action on your part. As you remain faithful to God's Word the change will happen.

The basic fact is this. Jesus gave up his life for all of the sins you had committed prior to your becoming *"born again."* Jesus did not forgive your past sins his Father God did. Jesus had to give up his life for the action of his Father to take place which was his Father forgiving all your past sins. Now, once you confess Jesus is your Lord and Master, which he truly is, then you are saved and his Father forgives and forgets all of your past sins. **Ephesians 4:32b "Forgiving one another, even as God for Christ's sake hath forgiven you."** Because of your believing and your subsequent faithfulness you will spend eternity with God and Christ Jesus.

Now you ask the question," just who is going to forgive the sins you commit **after** you are *"born again?"* As a human being you will continue to fall down and sin. As I said earlier Christ Jesus is seated at the right hand of his Father God and he will not be sacrificed any more. So what is going to happen?

God adopted you as Christ Jesus' brother or sister and He will forgive all your future sins.

Jesus Christ's blood was shed for the remission of your past sins and as the blood spilled on the ground you were released from all the **guilt** of your past sins. **Hebrews 9:22 "And almost all things are by the law purged with blood and without shedding of blood is no remission."**

The word *"remission"* means to *"send back from whence it came"* or to lay aside. Which means all your past sins were laid aside so you could start your new walk with a clean slate.

Sin

The more time you spend studying the Word of God the greater the opportunity He will open up more paths which will strengthen you in your knowledge of His Word. When I first began studying God's Word I was curious about all the people in the Old Testament who had sinned in God's eyes because they did not have knowledge of what sin was. Would these people be forgiven because they lived and died long before Jesus came on the scene. Here is the answer. From Adam to Moses there was no law to govern peoples actions, therefore there was no punishment imputed upon them. In **Romans 5:13 "(For until the law sin was in the world, but sin is not imputed when there is no law."** That is how the verse reads in KJV. Look at NIV and it will read easier. **5:13 "To be sure, sin was in the world before the law was given, but sin is not charged against anyone's account where there is no law."** Once God gave to Moses the Ten Commandments as well as the other 611 laws to govern Israel then mankind was responsible in God's eyes for every sin they personally committed. Remember we just talked about the first two commandments of the Ten Commandments being added to the 611 laws God has given to Israel which brings the total to 613 laws. Living by the law, all 613 of them, as a new believer is not necessary anymore because the law was fulfilled when Jesus Christ gave up his life on the cross. However the Ten Commandants still apply to our lives now.

Fast forward to today. For every sin you commit after being *"born again"* and forgiven by God, that sin will still have an earthly consequence. Lets understand something here. Your consequence is in the physical world but the sin is in the spiritual world. In God's eyes a sin is a sin, there is no degree of difficulty. The severity of the worldly consequence depends on how complex the sin is. A *"white lie"* may be simple in the beginning but as it goes on and gains a life of its' own the consequence could become enormous. Now murder will have far reaching effects on you and those around you especially if you are found guilty by the courts of law and are put to death.

When you come to God humbly and ask for forgiveness God will forgive you for the sin and He will never remember it. Yes, He will forgive us. **Pslams 103:12 "As far as the east is from the west, so far hath he removed our transgressions from us."**This action on God's part is wonderful for you but the sin you committed will continue to have an effect on someone. What effect is unknown. The result may be noticed very quickly or there may be a longer period of time before anything happens.

So what do you do to eliminate these consequences. Just as God lovingly forgave you for the sin you committed you must go to the person your transgression was committed against and ask for their forgiveness. The action is simple, nothing complex, just do it.

Most people do not understand forgiveness. They think it is a sign of weakness. When actually it is a sign of great strength to go to a person you have wronged and humbly ask for their forgiveness for your action. I have seen some strong (physically) men who could not perform this simple act. To accomplish this feat you must be strong spiritually in God's Word. To know His Word and understand who you are and why you are here will give you the strength to accomplish many feats. And you have to be unselfish.

The act of sinning comes from Satan. He provides, through his unholy angel spirits, influences which are sometimes very difficult to overcome. There is an unholy angel spirit for every evil action or thought or influence in the world today. There are some people who have more than one of these unholy angel spirits within their heart. They could be an alcoholic, on "crack", stealing everyday to feed their habit, maybe killing an individual for money, so there was at least four unholy angel spirits mentioned within this one individual's spiritual heart. Now in **Matthew 17:18 "And Jesus rebuked the devil**_(high ranking spirit)_ **and he departed**_(removed)_ **out of him; and the child was cured from that very(immediate) hour."** The disciples of Jesus tried to cast out these same spirits but they lacked the belief they could accomplish the feat. They had an unbelief which lead to skepticism which in turn lead to an attitude of doubt.

A question was asked the other day. If you are *"born again"* can unholy devil spirits still inhabit your spiritual body? They can and most probably do because you originally invited them into your conscious thoughts before you became *"born again."* Can you get rid of these spirits? Yes! Your "born again" nature means you have a new mind set, that of Chris Jesus and God. God's Holy Spirit has been energized within your conscious thoughts. Your thought patterns should begin to change as you follow what God speaks about in His Word. The more you think about God and His Word the less you will think about the unholy angel spirits which are lodged within your mind. There is probably a good chance you do not even remember which unholy angel spirits there are and if you cannot remember them then they are of no influence to you.

Receiving the Holy Spirit

In **John 14:12 "Verily, verily, I say unto you, He that believeth on me the works that I do shall he do also; and greater works than these shall he do; because I go unto my Father."**

Look at **John 14:16 "And I pray the Father and he shall give you another Comforter that it may abide with you forever."**

Jesus knew he was going to be leaving and he wanted to help the disciples with the knowledge of a *"comforter"* which was going to come and would be in the manner of the Holy Spirit which in turn lead to the Manifestation of Speaking in Tongues. In **II Corinthians 12:10d "to another divers kinds of tongues;"** The disciples received God's Holy Spirit permanently in the temple in **Acts 2:2 "And suddenly there came a sound from heaven as of a rushing mighty wind, and it filled all the house**(temple) **where they were sitting." 3 "And there appeared unto them cloven tongues like as a fire, and it sat upon each of them." 4 "And they were all filled with the Holy Ghost**(Spirit) **and began to speak with other tongues, as the Spirit**(God) **gave them utterance."** This comforter is a gift from God for you and as a gift it is considered a manifestation and you have to chose to operate it to reap the benefits it brings. Being able to speak in tongues allows you the opportunity to speak to God directly, one on one without any intermediary such as Christ Jesus. Tongues is part of the nine gifts God has given to you. Remember your *"free will."* Speaking in tongues has nothing to do with salvation. You energized His Holy Spirit when you gave your life to Jesus Christ. Tongues is just another gift God is giving to you to make your life and walk a little easier.

Another thought to keep in mind. You know God is not a respecter of persons. The logic of God's Word dictates He will place in every new born baby His Holy Spirit. Remember John the Baptist. As the baby in his mother's womb, Elisbeth received God's Holy Spirit and so did John thru Elisbeth's blood. If a person chose's not to energize God's Holy Spirit then His Spirit will stay inactive for the life of the person. However, make the commitment and you have energized His Holy Spirit in your spiritual heart and it will be waiting for you to take your first steps.

Renewing your mind is the path to redemption.

How do you go about renewing your mind *(conscious thoughts)?* Very simply when you begin reading God's Word on a regular basis. Every time you read a verse of scripture, you are replacing a negative thought in your conscious thought pattern. Though you may not have purposefully tried to remember the scripture your brain registers the words and they are there for you to recall when you need them.

You were given a spiritual power to energize God's Holy Spirit within you when you needed His help. The problem today is a great many people still do not believe in God or anything about Him so God's Holy Spirit will not be energized within them. I am sure you believe so you will not have to deal with this problem.

As you walk through your life here on earth you must endeavor each day to put on the thoughts Jesus Christ had when he was here. Jesus talked with his Father on a daily basis usually in the morning when it was quiet and the hustle and bustle of the day had not begun yet. As

Jesus went through the day he would continue to think the thoughts his Father had put on his mind each morning. Jesus life was one of being an example to all who knew him or were touched by him. As I said earlier when you gave your life to Jesus you energized his Father's Holy Spirit together with Christ Jesus spirit and the Hope for the Glory of the return.

This is how you renew your mind to God's will and word. The word *"renew"* means *"to make like new."* What are you making like new, your thought patterns. You are exchanging the old man thoughts you grew up with for the new fresh thoughts of Christ Jesus and God's word.

Here is an interesting scientific fact. **"No two objects can occupy the same space in time or place."** Or no two thoughts can occupy the same space in time or place in your mind.

When you are reading God's Word and thinking about what the words say, Satan who is always watching through his unholy angel spirits is looking for an opening where he can influence you away from the word and begin to change your thought patterns back to the old ones you once had.

Here is an interesting fact you need to know. Satan knows God's Word. Satan was there when God began the whole process of Creation. Remember, Satan's name was Lucifer and he was second in command with God

Revelations 12:9 "And the great dragon was cast out, that old serpent called the Devil, and Satan, which deceiveth the whole world; he was cast out into the earth and his angels were cast out with him."

In the very beginning it was necessary for God to create evil in the form of Satan who actually started as Lucifer. He was God's second in command and greater than his brothers Michael, the Warrior Angel and Gabriel, the Messenger Angel.

Lucifer was considered the Angel of Light and to all in heaven who saw him, he was the most beautiful of all the angels.

Should God not have created Lucifer/Satan then there would be no evil and with no evil there would be no need for you to have free will. What would you need it for? You would never have to make a choice because God would be behind anything requiring a decision to be made on your part and any decision would be good not bad.

So now you have evil in the form of Satan and his unholy angel spirits. Considering the number of people in the world today, roughly seven and one/half billion, there are at least one unholy angel spirit for each person of any age. Whether it is active is another question. You can thank Adam for "sin nature " being in your spiritual blood.

So Satan does know God's Word and he knows it as well as God himself.

Romans 12:2 "And be not conformed(*fashioned*) **to this world; but be ye transformed by renewing of your mind that ye may prove what is that good and acceptable and perfect will of God."**

If simply changing your conscious thoughts is all you would have to do then it would be easy, however it takes changing your thought processes over to God's Words. This means you must give up the beloved control you enjoy and turn your lives over to God. **I Peter 5:6 "Humble yourselves therefore under the mighty hand of God that he may exalt you in due time."** *"Due time"* means in God's timing, not yours. In **Luke 18:14b "for everyone that exalteth himself shall be abased**(*humbled*) **and he that humbleth himself shall be exalted."** Did you also say you would have to become *"humble before God."*

Humbling yourself before God in praise(*singing*)and prayers is one of the ways you will begin to receive answers to your prayers. Being humble is the easiest way to hand over control of your spiritual thoughts to God.

Because you have a *"sin nature"* mind(*conscious thoughts*) you are easily drawn off the path God has given you to follow. But because you are his sons and daughters you can just as easily get back on the path by simply returning to His awesome Word and putting it on in your mind and remembering it on a daily basis.

I know I keep going over these same facts but this is a battle we are in here on earth and we need all the help we can get.

Let's try this, **Romans 13:14 "But put ye on the Lord Jesus Christ and make no provision for the flesh to fulfil the lusts thereof."**

This means to remember the words Jesus Christ spoke which were his Fathers words. God gave Jesus the words to speak just as God can give the same to you. Thinking the Words of God will stop Satan from filling your conscious thoughts with his evil ideas.

Ephesians 4:22 "That ye(*you*)** put off concerning the former conversation(behavior) the old man**(*your past*)** which is corrupt according to the deceitful lusts." 23 "And be renewed in the spirit of your mind**(*thoughts*).**"24 "And that ye put on the new man which after God is created in righteousness and true holiness."** The word *"lusts"* in verse 22 means a continual thought pattern 24/7 centered around an image or physical object. You can lust after anything whether physical or spiritual, but to qualify as a lust you must dwell **continually** on the single thought. Looking upon something which may be pleasurable to the eye once or twice or even three times in succession it is not lust, just staring.

So, going back to sin. The act of sinning or not sinning requires a conscious thought or physical action to be taken by you. Should you be tempted and remember the temptation is not a sin. Jesus was tempted, but continued to say *"it is written"* which refers to the Word of his Father. It is when you follow through on those temptations then sin happens. You either recognize the sin and take the necessary action to complete the temptation or you recognize it is a sin and say simply NO! to it. You know it is easier said than done.

When you allow Satan's spirits to influence your thoughts to the point of sinning you are being drawn off the path which God has established for you. **Matthew 7:14 "because strait is the gate and narrow is the way which leadeth unto life and few there be that find it."** This scripture is from God for each of you to walk by.

Here is a wonderful way to conclude being redeemed by the renewing of your mind*(conscious thoughts)*. **Philippians 3:13 " Brethren, I count not myself to be apprehended, but this one thing I do; forgetting those things which are behind and reaching forth unto those things which are before."**

SANCTIFICATION

The New Bible Dictionary defines sanctification as *"the state of growing in divine grace as a result of Christian commitment after baptism or conversion."* or *"set apart."*

John 17:17 "Sanctify them through thy truth; thy word is truth."

"Sanctify" means: to be set apart. *"Them"* means: us. *"Thy"* means: God. And the *"word"* means: Bible.

What or whom are you set apart from? You are set apart from those in the world who do not believe your God is the creator of the Universe, and everything you can either see, hear and touch, smell or taste.

I Corinthians 6:11 "And such were some of you, but ye are washed, but ye are sanctified, but ye are justified in the name of the Lord Jesus and by the Spirit of our God."

Some of you have experienced water baptism just as Jesus did in the Jordan River. I had the awesome opportunity to be baptized in the Jordan River. The water was very cold going in but warm coming out. Water baptism today is an outward expression of your commitment to follow Jesus Christ.

This book is offering a spiritual baptism. The same Holy Spirit which was available to the disciples in **Acts 2:4a "And they were filled with the Holy Ghost***(Spirit),***"**is available to you if you chose to operate your believing and accept Jesus Christ as your Lord and Savior. When you go ahead and accept Jesus then his Father's Holy Spirit, which was already in your body when you were born, is energized within you and you can and will spend eternity with God and Christ Jesus. **Matthew 3:11 "I indeed baptize you with water unto repentance; but he that cometh after me is mightier than I, whose shoes I am not worthy to bear; he shall baptize you with the Holy Ghost***(Spirit)* **and with fire."**

Hebrews 2:11 "For both he that sanctified and they who are sanctified are all of one *(all sons and daughters of one Father God)* **for which cause he***(Jesus)* **is not ashamed to call them brethren."**

Hebrews 10:14 "For by one offering he hath perfected for ever them that are sanctified." The offering is Jesus.

MINISTRY OF RECONCILIATION

The New Bible Dictionary defines reconciliation as *"Doing away with an enmity, the bridging over a quarrel. Sinners are enemies of God."*

Romans 5:10 "For if when we were enemies we were reconciled to God by the death of his Son, much more being reconciled we shall be saved by his life."

The word *"if"* in this verse refers to a condition upon you. You have the choice to exercise your free will and accept Jesus Christ as your Lord and Savior or not. Should you chose not to accept Jesus then God's Holy Spirit will lie dormant and unused.

II Corinthians 5:18 "And all*(with distinction)* **things are of God, who hath***(past tense-it has already happened)* **reconciled us to himself***(God)* **by Jesus Christ and hath given to us the ministry of reconciliation."**

The word **"all"** has two specific meanings depending on the scripture or in the context of the chapter it can mean either; *"With distinction"* or *"Without exception."*

Colossians 1:21 "And you that were sometimes alienated and enemies in your mind by wicked works yet now hath he reconciled."

The word *"you"* means us. The word *"sometimes"* means not all the time or did we have evil thoughts going on. The words *"hath me"* means Jesus Christ.

I Timothy 2:5 "For there is one God and one mediator between God and men, the man*(human)* **Christ Jesus."**

And in conclusion. . .

Hebrews 2:14 "Forasmuch then as the children are partakers of flesh and blood, he also himself likewise took part of the same; that through death he might destroy him that had the power of death, the is, the devil."

This scripture does a pretty good job of answering just who Jesus was and what he accomplished when he gave up his life.

The most wonderful part of this verse is Jesus' death as a human being of flesh and blood. Being flesh and blood and not a spiritual being he was able to take the power of death away from Satan.

Now, because of what Jesus Christ has done you do not need to fear dying or death.

Your ministry, as a believer, is to bring men and women back to the fellowship of God, their Father and glorify your Father God. This is your whole purpose while here on earth. You are to speak His Word to those who do not know. And to walk with those until they can begin to understand His Word. This walking with a person is called under shepherding. Much like a shepherd will guide his flock from feeding ground to feeding ground. This is what God does with you as you gain more of His knowledge and speak it into the lives of people you know.

RIGHTEOUSNESS: free from guilt or sin.
JUSTIFICATION: just as if I had not sinned.
REDEMPTION: we are redeemed from our sin
SANCTIFICATION: set apart from the world.
MINISTRY OF RECONCILIATION: bring back together.

Chapter Sixteen

God's crowns for you. . .

There will come a time when you will die, or pass on. When will the time be you do not know nor do you really want to know.

Heaven and eternity and all the rewards you are going to receive are for those of you who were faithful to God, or in Christ, while you lived here on earth. God has given each of you many opportunities to come to Him and for you to take a humble attitude and repent of your sins and accept His Son Jesus Christ as your Lord and Master and Savior, the only problem is you may have missed some of the doors which were opened unto you. Each of you has free will to make the choices about your path in this life. Should you chose to walk a different way, the wrong way, then God will wait patiently for you to realize you have made a mistake. He will help you see the need to change the direction your life is taking. You will hopefully realize it is He whom you seek and make the change back to Him. Not making the change could affect the outcome of your personal spirit. Whether you realized it or not you have a very personal spirit. Jesus Christ had a personal spirit. As he hung on the cross he commended his personal spirit to His Father, **Luke 23:46 "And when Jesus had cried, with a loud voice, he said, Father, into thy hands I commend my spirit; and having said thus, he gave up the ghost***(spirit).***"**

Looking back. . .

Look back at the Old Testament and see how Israel continued to go against God and His protection. Israel wanted a King so God gave them Saul. God also gave them the prophet Samuel to watch over the King. Nevertheless when Israel walked away from the covering of God this is where their trouble started. When you walk away from the covering of God in your life and you are now relying on the world for your protection and you all know how well that will work out.

All through this book, *"if you do not follow God's way of thinking about how you should live your life then you will not be part of the "gathering" and you will not be spending eternity in Heaven with God and Jesus Christ."* And *"if you want to reap the benefits of being part of God's family then you must follow what God says in His Word."*

Our Father in Heaven is a Father of black and white. There is no gray in God's way of thinking. You have gone over this before. When He says in His Word you have to be *"in Christ"* which means you have given your life over to Jesus Christ and claimed him as your Savior and you believe his Father has raised him from the dead then you will be saved. You also believe all the sins you ever committed up to the point of conversion have been forgiven and forgotten and you will remain faithful to God even when you fall down, you get right back up and stay in the family of God.

Let's say you did nothing in your life here on earth to hurt anyone. The time is drawing near when you will pass on. You were kind to animals and little children but you never accepted Jesus Christ as your Lord and Savior nor did you acknowledge God as your new Father. What about this question? "Should God now accept you when you did not care about Him?" God will not force Himself on anyone. You must take the first step and He will meet you there. Accept Him*(God)* now, why take the chance, you have nothing to lose and everything to gain. Even on your death bed after a life of crime and murder if you accept Jesus as your Lord and Savior you will spend eternity with him, so what is your problem?

Webster defines the word *"judgment "* as *"divine judgment."*

So you have accepted Jesus Christ as your savior. You believe in God the Father of Jesus Christ. You endeavor to follow in the steps of Jesus as best as possible. You may even bring a few people to Jesus for salvation. You confessed all your past sins and they were forgiven. You confessed all your new sins as you committed them and they were forgiven. When you pass on you will spend eternity with God, but because you were faithful there may be a crown for you to wear, of course the decision is God's to make.

Your rewards.

Money will mean nothing in heaven. Acquisition of *"things"* will mean nothing, but because of your commitment here on earth you may receive one of the following crowns.

Crown of Rejoicing **I Thessalonians 2:19**
"For what is our hope, or joy, or crown of rejoicing? Are not even ye in the presence of our Lord Jesus Christ at his coming."

Crown of Righteousness **II Timothy 4:8**
"Henceforth there is laid up for me a crown of righteousness, which the Lord, the righteous judge, shall give me at that day; and not to me only, but unto all them also that love his appearing."

Crown of Life **James 1:12**
"Blessed is the man that endureth temptation; for when he is tried, he shall receive the crown of life, which the Lord hath promised to them that love him."

Crown of Glory **I Peter 5:4**
"And when the chief Shepherd shall appear, ye shall receive a crown of glory that fadeth not away."

Crown of Incorruptible **I Corinthians 9:25**

"And every man that striveth for the mastery, is temperate in all things. Now they do it to obtain a corruptible crown but we an incorruptible."

Which crown you receive will be up to God. Because you are now in Heaven for eternity with Christ Jesus. I do know you will be priests with Christ when he comes back to rule during the millennium, **Revelation 20:6b "but they shall be priests of God and of Christ and shall rule with him a thousand years."** Which is after the "Gathering." So if you have not yet made the decision to join this select growing group think it over. The cost of membership is FREE. The monthly dues are FREE. It is transferrable to anyone you know at no cost to them, it is FREE.

Chapter Seventeen

Does God test you?

This is a question which has been asked for hundreds of years by many prominent theologians and ministers as well as people on the street. Hopefully today this question will be answered.

James 1:13 "Let no man say when he is tempted, I am tempted of God: for God cannot be tempted with evil neither tempteth he any man."

When God created man and woman He gave them *"free will"* to make whatever decision they wanted concerning whatever situation they were in and whatever path they wanted to take in this life.

Every decision you make has a consequence. Whether good or bad there is a result which can be a blessing or a hindrance to your life style.

Some people would call a bad outcome of a situation where you made a free will decision a *"test from God."* Think about this for a minute. God is not a respecter of persons. **Romans 2:11 " For there is no respect of persons with God."**

Romans is the Doctrine on right believing. This means God does not sit up in heaven and look down on the earth and say to himself, *"self"* let me see what trial I can give to little Sally Smith. The reason God does not sit in heaven nor anywhere else for that matter is because He is Spirit and Spirit has no form and as such He encompasses the entire Universe completely at one time. If you are having a little difficulty with this last statement, **"God encompasses the Universe completely at one time."** that's fine.

Little Sally Smith may have been involved in a situation which required her to utilize her *"free will"* decision making process and she made the wrong decision which carries a negative consequence. Her life is now in great turmoil and she has to figure a way out. Who will help her. God will but she will have to call upon Him. How does little Sally call upon God, maybe through prayer, of course through prayer, specific prayer concerning her situation. Now as hard as this sounds Little Sally is going to have to forgive anyone who has wronged her and she in turn has to ask for forgiveness from anyone she has wronged in order for her prayers to be considered for an answer.

Here is another so called test. Mary is very sick. She loves God, she is His child. According to the world who is she going to blame for this terrible illness. Why God of course because God causes all sickness. **WRONG!** God does not cause any sickness to befall His people. He will not test you with a terrible disease and then sit back and see if you call on Him to heal you thru his Son Christ Jesus or just tough it out with maybe terrible results. Those thoughts are all a trick of Satan.

God does not cause sickness.

So then who does cause sickness. The answer is very simple. A *"who"* does not cause sickness. A *"what"* does and what is a *"what?"* It is your body. Your DNA can cause sickness as well as protect you from many of the world's viruses. You carry billions upon billions, actually it is trillions of DNA around in your blood all your life. So physically speaking you are a product of your DNA. You can thank all of your families generations upon generations for your DNA. Now way back in your family's history someone may have contracted cancer but they did not have a name to put to it. He or she may have died from it but in the process that gene may have been transferred to another person through sexual relations or blood transfusions. The sad part is the gene which caused the cancer will continue to get passed around through different generations, sometimes even skipping a generation until your families members and you come along. There is testing in place today which can determine whether you have a specific gene for a specific cancer and if you do then methods can be brought to bear to remedy the situation. Which means, in the long run, maybe nothing will happen. Should something happen on the negative side then you can turn to God and claim healing through His Son Christ Jesus. When God created the earth He set in motion everything we can see today. The sicknesses you have seen in your lifetime started thousands of years ago, they just did not have fancy names. Some of the various viruses existing today came from animals or insects which all stem from their DNA and who knows maybe some of their DNA got mixed up with your DNA, remember it's all in the blood. Here's a point of information. The average female mosquito has 100 million cells which all carry her DNA to cause any number of diseases.

Blood

The blood in your body is very important, without it you will die. With it you can live a very productive life. Remember when Mary was pregnant with Jesus. God, the Father of Jesus Christ, impregnated Mary with His perfect sperm which carries among other things a pure blood type and a sex gene for the baby.

Now thanks to Adam, the first man to sin, actually Eve sinned first because she broke the covenant with God. She doubted His Word and listened to Satan who disguised as a serpent was able to cause Eve to doubt what God had said. Adam was the head of the family. His blood became impure, spiritually speaking. Your blood today is not so clean spiritually speaking. You all now carry the spiritual gene for **"sin nature"**

Over the centuries the continual physical contact of men and women of different races has mixed the *"blood scene"* up considerably. So much so that to find a pure strain of blood on the planet would be very difficult if not impossible.

The sperm or seed contains 22 pairs of chromosomes plus and X/ Y pair on the males part. The female has 22 pairs of chromosomes plus a pair of XX. The sex and blood type of the child will be determined by the sperm. The human body contains 30,000 genes per cell and there are 37.2 trillion cells in the human body which totals 1.11+21 "0's" and it takes only one gene per cell to make a human being.

Mixed marriages have been going on since the beginning of mankind when God gave instructions to forth and populate the world. Interesting to note when God gave this instruction there were only adults in the world at that time. Of course along the way there may have been a defective gene which caused insanity. So this person marries and the insanity gene gets transferred to the baby and now the baby may or may not become insane. The chances for damaged or recessive genes increases to a point which can be magnified trillions of times over. It is interesting to note in the 4th and 5th century of English history among the royals there was so much inter-marriage in order to preserve the blood line of the Kingdom the gene for insanity became very prevalent.

Some would say Satan and his unholy angel spirits have caused the diseases but you have to keep this fact in mind. Satan cannot create anything. He can only manipulate what his influences have on you thru his unholy angel spirits and your environment. You could say Satan influenced those in power to be ignorant about living conditions or medical conditions to a point where careless individuals failed to follow through and you ended up with a lot of deaths caused by diseases which were by your own hands.

So when a tiny helpless baby is born with a disease and dies, God the Father of your Lord and Savior Jesus Christ did not cause the baby to die. In the baby's blood was most likely a damaged gene which resulted in the baby's death. It is very wrong to blame God for anything concerning any death. Consequences of peoples actions over the many years have resulted in many deaths and God did not cause those deaths, people did. And those people were influenced by Satan's unholy angel spirits. Now biblically speaking there are many times when God removed His hand of protection from over Israel as they chose to go to war without God. In the process many thousands of men and women died. Why did God remove His hand because Israel chose to go to battle alone.

Back to the baby. . .

Some people would call the baby dying a test of God. But there are no scriptures in the KJV of the Bible specifically saying God tests those He loves. God has stated it over and over when you exercise your free will power in the decision making process and make the wrong decision there is a consequence to be paid. Fortunately not as great as what Jesus paid. The consequence of your many wrong decisions will result in your going to your Father God and humbly ask for forgiveness over and over again.

Follow God

Your God does not forsake a believer because he or she may have made a free will choice not to follow Him and help bring others back to His loving arms. God gives you choices every day you live. Whether you accept the choice from God is totally up to you. As a young couple just starting out in life to have to deal with a severely handicapped child just might not be the best for their walk or maybe it could be. Should the couple be strong in the Lord they could bond together and form a tight knit team which could beat back the influences of Satan and the child could flourish. I have personally witnessed such a family whose daughter is severally handicapped. She was supposed to die 24 hours after she was born and that was over 30 years ago. God wants you to have your heart's desire for your life. There are times though when the decisions you make are not based on what God says in His Word, but on what the world says is best. Therefore you end up relying on Satan to make the decision for your walk.

In today's society the eventual outcome for the handicapped child we are talking about would be given up to the system. He or she would be cared for and then the couple who gave in would end up blaming each other for the child deformities. Without God in their walk they would probably end up getting a divorce. Each of them would have pangs of guilt about the decision they made for the rest of their lives all because their *"genes"* got in the way.

There has been a question going around about God murdering people. Let me see if this will help with your understanding of the situation. To commit murder such as Cain versus Abel of the Adam and Eve family requires some prior thought. Cain was angry because God had accepted Abel's offering and not his. God does not commit murder. God will, as we said earlier, take His hand of protection off of Israel because they failed to follow the conditions God had set up for them. One condition was their refusing to worship Him and instead began worshipping strange, manmade idols.

When Israel would go to war which they did quite often, they would lose miserably and God allowed this to happen to prove a point to Israel. All God asked for was worship Him and He would provide for all their needs as well as give them victory after victory over those they fought. Israel, however wanted to be in control of their lives and their destiny so God said *"no problem"* go fight your battles without me and they did and lost terribly to the point that they ended up as slaves again. The question now would be were the warriors for Israel murdered or killed by God. To murder involves pre-meditation. To be killed because you wanted to follow your own instructions instead of God's instruction is a consequence of your free will decision. Read **I and II Kings** in the Old Testament for a wonderful story of how God handled those who did not want to believe to worship Him.

Who took the power of death away from Satan?

Jesus Christ, who was a human being at the time, took the control of death away from Satan in order to fulfill the prophecy in **Isaiah 53:11 "He**(*God*)** shall see of the travail of his**(*Jesus*)**soul. and shall be satisfied: by his knowledge shall my righteous servant justify many; for he shall bear their iniquities."** Jesus had to be flesh and blood like you, not a spiritual being which could walk through walls, so he could take control of death away from Satan. Who now has control of it? No person physical or spiritual. Natural death now occurs as the outcome of the human body finally wearing out. Remember God set the whole of the life cycle in motion when He created Adam and Eve. Your heart is a muscle and can only beat just so much in a life time before it stops. Medications can prolong life, but are not necessarily the way to go. Some people feel their days are numbered, they are. All our days are numbered. God set the age limit for all mankind several thousand years ago, at 120 years.

Good and bad can happen to anyone.

Why do bad situations happen to good people. Why do good situations happen to bad people. What is a situation? Webster defines a situation as: *"a relative position or combination of circumstances at a certain moment."* Is it an event which has a negative or positive outcome. Good people or righteous people can make wrong decisions just as well as unrighteous people. The consequences of either decision can cause great pain and maybe death or great happiness.

You must keep your mind focused on God's Word. You have free will to make any choice you want concerning your walk in this life. Therefore any decision you make is your own and the consequences of the decision are solely upon you. There is no one to blame for the outcome except yourself. Should you chose to walk without God in your life then the outcome of each decision you make may not turn out to be the best. God and his Word encourage you to make the correct decision for each situation and the result will bless all concerned except of course Satan.

So what would be the answer to this situation? The answer is very simple. Should you be walking with God and His Son Christ Jesus when a *"bad situation"* happens to you, through no fault of your own or your family then you have the protection of God. You have allowed Him to be the sufficiency in your life. Remember God will never forsake you whatever happens whether you make a bad decision or a good one. So what the world sees as *"bad"* may only be a *"bump"* in the road of life for your family.

Walking through the scriptures in the New Testament especially those in Romans for Doctrine and Ephesians for Correction can be a great equalizer for many of your worldly dilemma's.

You examine yourself because you make bad decisions.

In conclusion, does God test us? The answer is No. Does God periodically take his hand of protection off our heads? Probably. Why, Why not. He took His hand off of Israel so why not you when you get off His path. You have strived to allow God to become your sufficiency in all ways with your walk and you are still striving each day.

The free will decisions you make concerning your walk in this life are your own examinations in themselves. I like the word examination better than test. For God to test us means He is a respecter of persons and you know by now He is not. Is He singling you out for an observation. I do not think so. Good decisions or bad decisions, the examination if any, will come in the form of consequences because of the decisions you make. Should the decision be good then you will be blessed with the outcome and if the decision is bad well the consequence will come and hopefully it will not be to damaging. In **I Corinthians 10:13: "There hath no temptation taken you but such as is common to man; but God is faithful, who will not suffer***(allow)* **you to be tempted above that ye are able; but will with the temptation also make a way to escape, that ye may be able to bear it."**

So your Father God will never forsake you no matter what the situation is or the consequence is of any decision you make, whether good or bad.

Oh! The word *"test"* does not appear in the KJV of the Bible which leads me to believe theologians who translated other versions of the Bible have changed the Word of God to mean what they want it to mean.

The word the translators are calling *"test"* is really *"proof"* as in *"the proof is in the pudding."* This is an old English saying meaning you have to taste the pudding to know how good it is.

You have to taste the Word of God to know how wonderful it is. Literally you have to eat it or in this case study it to make the word your own. The proof is the knowledge you will gain as you continue to speak and read the Word.

Chapter Eighteen

Become a virtuous woman

The Godly woman is not perfect. She is a woman of strength and she will endeavor each day of her walk with God to keep her thoughts on God. She will make every effort to follow in the footsteps of Christ Jesus even though she's human and subject to Satan's ever present temptations. Women are constantly examining their walk in this life.

Over the many centuries men and women have coexisted and it has been found women will think about a particular situation where men will act upon the same situation with little or no thinking. Some women are very introspective. They will spend time reading books which will provide them with the answers to being a better wife, a better executive, a better mother, a better sports person and how to be a better Christian.

In **Genesis 2:20b "but for Adam there was not found an help meet**(*companion*) **for him."**

Adam had just finished naming all the animals with God's help. There were no companions for Adam so God caused a deep sleep to fall upon Adam. During this time asleep God took one of Adam's ribs and created his companion, woman. She was an adult. In **Genesis 2:20b** the question has risen as to just what is a *"help meet."* In Webster's dictionary she is called *"a companion and helper."* Webster agrees with God. Her responsibility is to tend to the home and the children while her husband concentrates on his walk with God and bringing success to the family. We are talking about a spiritual man and woman, not a five senses oriented couple.

As long as the couple remain *"in God"* then their relationship will grow and become stronger and the term *"help meet"* will become an awesome position in their lives together.

God is her Father. She is His daughter. She walks in the footsteps of her stepbrother Christ Jesus. She has been given a role in a God made relationship which is paramount to her being a spiritual *"Mary."* No, she will not give birth to a savior, this has already been done and completed. She will, however, be responsible for the nurture of those who will continue on with the cycle of Christian humans here on earth.

Her special role in the relationship is to be in charge of the home and the rearing of the children in a Godly manner. She will not neglect her own walk with Christ Jesus and God. Her walk is necessary to accompany her husband so together they will be an example for others who will hopefully model themselves after them. Unfortunately this type of relationship began to break down at the turn of the 19th century especially after World War I and then it continued into World War II and so on. . .

One of the major reasons for this breakdown was the loss of a great many of the husbands and potential husbands to the war effort. Women who were left at home, who could not go into the service, went instead into the factories to take their husbands places. Everything the men did the women did and most cases the women did it better because of their personal work ethic. The pride they took in being able to help the war effort was not measurable emotionally but their output for the war effort set records. Now besides their working in the factories they still had to raise the children, take care of their homes and relatives. Their work never ended. They worked from sun to sun.

When the wars were over some of their husbands did not return and these women were faced with raising a family without a husband. The men who did return, whole, went back to their jobs in the factories and continued on with their lives and did not talk about what they had just experienced. The ones who returned less than whole needed to be taken care of which often added to the responsibilities and stress of the wife and sometimes the children.

Now one thing the women did enjoy while there men were away was the freedom to come and go when they wanted to without telling anyone what was going on. Some of the women liked the freedom so much they decided to leave their families and let the father, if there was one, to raise the kids. If there was not a father then the kids would go to relatives or maybe on the streets.

Satan and his unholy angel spirits were doing a wonderful job of influencing these women to follow a path which was not the best and the consequences resulted were even more terrible.

Wives submit.

So here is the question some of the women who were studying the Bible of yesterday and today are asking? What does this scripture mean?

Ephesians 5:22 " Wives submit yourselves unto your own husbands as unto the Lord*(God).***"**

*"Submit"*in the Greek is *"hupotaso"*which means to give yourself***(wives)*** in a loving voluntary manner with a deliberate decision to work with your husband to the end your husband can grow in his walk with God and His Son Christ Jesus. The key to this definition is *"a deliberate decision"* on the woman's part. She uses her free will to make this decision.

Now another thing which is understood here, the husband must be walking with God. He is reading the word daily and leading the family accordingly. **Ephesians 5:27 "That he might present it to himself a glorious church. Not having spot or wrinkle or any such thing; but that it should be holy and without blemish."** This scripture will not work if the husband is not walking with God or the wife is not walking with the God.

Some women seem confused about their role in the family today.

The first part of the 20th century women gained an independence which was both liberating as well as restraining. They suddenly had freedom to do as they pleased but they were not sure how to handle it since there were few role models to give them an example to follow and many still had families. Women were saying they needed this new role to help better define their old role in the family and of course this really threw the husbands for a loss because they were still struggling with their role in the family and they did not know how to act around their independent wives, so what happened? The divorce rate shot up and has continued to go up over 60% nationwide at this writing.

Satan is very happy to see so many marriages fail and as they fail so does the traditional family values many of us were raised with.

Both husband and wife walked farther and farther away from God because they, as children, were either not taught how to worship or they rebelled against the organized religions and began to worship the world, Satan's world. This was not on purpose now, because had they known they were serving another God then their leaving the organized religions probably would not have happened. Satan knew he was able to disguise the whole process of the marriage breakup into something benign. The wives needed some time to be alone or to try to understand themselves. The men needed time alone, for what reason we still do not know.

The Christian marriage was falling by the wayside. Besides heterosexual relationships were failing and there was now a new relationship on the horizon, homosexual, same sex relationships. These were so against God's Word the Christian movement was almost put on hold until these relationships could be figured out. Acceptance is now the watchword of the day. Men and women are still struggling with how this new role will play out in today's society.

So where did this leave the woman of the day. If she was a Christian she might be torn by what God's Word said and what the world's leaders say. Remember you only know what you have been taught and if you have not been instructed in how to read and understand God's Word then the eternal battle between God and Satan will continue in a new and frightening way.

Women's equal rights. . .

Women today feel they deserve to be treated as an equal to men. Equal pay for equal work. Consideration's for promotions based on experience and knowledge of the job at hand, not sex. Women today are not looking for entitlements or handouts, they want to work, to grow, to provide for their broken families or their whole families. The Constitution said you were all equal men and women but there are generations today who will never acknowledge this thought. And why, because this would mean men would have to step down as the leader of the species and allow a female to ascend to her new position as a leader. And who is loving every moment of this confusion, Satan and his unholy angel spirits.

God in his matchless word does not speak of women working outside of the home in the business world. He does address several places in the word for the woman working in the home. **Titus 2:3 "The aged women likewise, that they be in behavior as becometh holiness, not false accusers, not given to much wine, teachers of good things;" 4 " That they may teach the young women to be sober to love their husbands, to love their children."** God does not respect persons. He demands loving obedience for his commandments whether female or male.

In the beginning was Eve.

In the beginning God created woman. She was created from the rib of a man *(Adam)*.

Genesis 2:22 "And the rib which the Lord God had taken from man, made he a woman, and brought her unto the man." 23 "And Adam said, This is bone of my bones and flesh of my flesh; She shall be called Woman, because she was taken out of man."

Genesis 3:30 "And Adam called his wife's name Eve; because she was the mother of all living*(life)***."**

Eve is the name for all womanhood. The first woman to marry. To be seduced, maybe. To taste the word. To establish a family outside of the Garden of Eden. To give birth, in pain.

In **Genesis 3:16 "Unto the woman he**(*God*) **said, I will greatly multiply thy sorrow**(*labor*) **and thy conception; in sorrow**(*labor*) **thou shalt bring forth children; and thy desire**(*self satisfaction*) **shall be to thy husband and he shall rule over thee** (*take care of her sexual needs*)."

God told Eve she would have pain when she gave birth because of her encounter with the serpent Satan and disobeying God's commandment. This explains why women today have pain in child birth. So ladies, stop blaming your husband for causing your birth pain. This is a subtle reminder from God for every mother to remember where the first child came from and what was going to be necessary for her to realize she was responsible for her child coming to God. **Proverbs 31:28 "Her children arise up and call her blessed, her husband also, and he praiseth her." 29 "Many daughters have done virtuously, but thou excellest them all."**

30 "Favour is deceitful and beauty is vain; but a woman that feareth(respect) **the Lord**(*God*)**, she shall be praised." 31 "Give her of the fruit of her hands; and let her own works praise her at the gates."**

Back to Eve. . .

In **Genesis 4:25 "And Adam knew**(*sexual relations*) **his wife again; and she bare a son, and called his name Seth; For God, said she, hath appointed me another seed instead of Able whom Cain slew.**

God must of had compassion for Eve since her first son Able was killed by his brother Cain. So Adam was able to impregnate Eve with another seed and they called him Seth. Seth lived to 105 and fathered a child whom he called *"Enos"* which means *"weak one."* Seth is not mentioned anymore in the Bible.

Now your Godly walk.

First, your walk is always with God. Without God you have nothing spiritually speaking.

A woman is a physical being with doubts and fears and strengths and many questions. She can chose to be a spiritual person whether single or married she can chose to be just a five senses person with nothing spiritual inside. Let's believe for the sake of discussion she chose to be a spiritual person and single. Being single she is perfect for God to work within her because she has little or no entanglements with the world of Satan. God can utilize her to spread his word with accuracy and love. She can be used by God as an example for other women who do not yet have a relationship with the Father. Her walk of spirituality can be seen by all. She is the beginning of the virtuous woman of Proverbs 31:10.

What is required of you as women of God is a commitment on your part to literally be the woman of God, to live out the very essence of what being a child of God means. In order to accomplish this you must give up control of your worldly spiritual life and your conscious thoughts patterns, everything must be given over to God and thru His Son Christ Jesus. Once you have taken this step you will begin to see your new life change in ways you could have never imagined. Your walk begins with reading God's word daily. You can start in the Old Testament which provides a rich tapestry of historical information. The Old Testament is basically addressed to Israel whereas the New Testament is address to the born again believer, such as you. The recommendation would be to start in the New Testament. In the Book of Acts is the best place to begin. Written by Luke, the physician, sometime in the 59th century AD. This is a transitional book which sums up the Gospels and sets up the beginning of the New Testament. The Gospels are considered to be part of the New Testament as well as the Book of Acts so starting in Romans and going all the way through to Titus you have an awesome example of one man's inspired writings from God, the apostle Paul. Should the question ever arise about how the Bible was written by all those many different people both in the Old Testament and the New Testament go to the following verse of scripture in **II Peter 1:20 "Knowing this first, that no prophecy of the scripture is of any private interpretation."** This means all of the Bible is prophecy. Prophecy, quite simply means, according to Webster *"to predict with assurance."* Those men who wrote the Old Testament did not just sit down and think up at random the words which were recorded. God inspired each person, through revelation, to write in their own style or syntax the words God gave to them. Now the men who wrote the New Testament were inspired by God from within their minds. God energized His Holy Spirit in each as they wrote God's words. **II Peter 1:21 "For the prophecy came not in old time by the will of man; but holy men of God spake as they were moved by the Holy Ghost(Spirit - God)."**

This is the beginning of your journey with God's word. Romans is the first book of Doctrine for Right Believing of a new believer. The second two books are I and II Corinthians, these are the books of Reproof which are for a new believer who has strayed off the path God has set for you. *(I and II Corinthians are considered one book of the Bible).* The third book of the trilogy is Galatians, this is the book of Correction for the new believer to utilize in regaining his or her walk with God. The next six books form two sets of trilogies covering Doctrine, Reproof and Correction. **II Timothy 3:16 "All scripture given by inspiration of God and is profitable for doctrine, for reproof, for correction, for instruction in righteousness."**

Start with Romans. Read one chapter per day, no more. Throughout the day endeavor to remember any of the verses or context read. Write down in a Journal as much of what you have read at the end of the day. Repeat the process with the next chapter each day. As the days continue to add up so will your knowledge of the word. Your conscious thoughts patterns will begin to change. Your mind set will soon resemble your Lord, Christ Jesus and soon there will be no room for thoughts of this world, Satan's world.

When you come across a verse of scripture which does not make sense, pause and think, how does this verse fit with the context of the chapter you are reading. If it does not answer your question then go to your concordance and find out where the word or verse of scripture appear **first** in the Bible. Remember this, the Old Testament is the New Testament concealed and the New Testament is the Old Testament revealed. The only element which contradicts the word is your lack of knowledge concerning it. Write down any word which does not make sense. Now if you are reading the KJV of the Bible you will come across many places where an *"old English"* phrase like *"by the by"* which means *"the speaker is introducing a new topic or subject"* is used. When this happens, go to your 21st century machine and *"Google"* the word or verse for a better understanding. Please do not allow the old English words like thee or thine or thy to confuse. They are actually forms of you or we or me.

The word. . .

The virtuous woman will eagerly put on the word of God in her mind(conscious thoughts) which includes her spiritual heart. **Proverbs 4:23 "Keep***(guard)* **thy heart***(mind-nous)* **with all diligence***(day by day action)* **for out of it are the issues of life."** She will gain a confidence five senses women will admire and desire. She will become an ambassador of the word for the world, both Christian and non-Christian. Her husband, should she have one, will look upon her with great pride and love. He will speak of her abilities within their home and how she lovingly cares for their children. In the 21 Century concept her husband would take a bullet for her because of what and whom she represents in this decadent world.

When she puts on God's word she is actually erasing her five senses knowledge and replacing those corrupt thoughts with God's wondrous Word which is knowledge and the acquisition of wisdom. As I said earlier, the daily reading of the word, with understanding, will change her way of thinking concerning how to handle daily situations because she will then be relying on God's word to provide her the answer.

Starting your day with God's word is exactly what Jesus did. He would rise up early before the sun rose and would listen while his Father counseled him on the coming events.

Women may seek you out to talk with them. Your spiritual wisdom will become manifest in the five senses world and you will be able to deal with whatever worldly problem is presented.

The coming temptations. . .

Men's temptations tend toward, greed, power and lust. Women on the other hand are more introspective. They are constantly looking for ways to improved themselves whether physically or spiritually. Women have been known to give into alcohol, drugs, gambling, sex, crimes of all sorts, pretty much the same for men, so no one is outside the realm of Satan's influences in today's world. So how does a women defeat the works of Satan.

Defeat the works, not Satan.

Notice, I said the works of Satan. Satan will be cast into the pit of fire forever in the final days. For now you will concentrate on the *"works,"* those individual influences which Satan and his unholy angel spirits utilize to make your life less than the best. The solution is very simple. You cannot think two different thoughts at the same time. One will be either evil or good and you have the choice. When you chose good and put it on or remember the Word of God or even just begin talking to Him the influences of Satan cannot penetrate your conscious thought patterns. This is an important note. Satan will not directly influence you. Any evil spiritual influence will come from one of his many unholy angel spirits which he brought with him when he was cast out of heaven by God. There are some people, men and women who do not believe there is a devil or Satan.

Lucifer was the Angel of Light. He was the brightest of all the angels and he was very smart. So smart he convinced himself into thinking he would take over Heaven and replace God. Of course we know what happened. God became angered and after a terrible war cast Lucifer and one third of the angels out of heaven. In **Isaiah 14:12 "How art thou fallen from heaven O Lucifer, son of the morning! How art cut down to the ground which didst weaken**(*seduce*)** the nations."**

Man is alone and needs a companion, this was mentioned before.

We do not know how long Satan was cast into the earth before Adam was created. Theologians suggest Adam was created, based on the Hebrew calendar around 5731 B.C. And a rule of thumb now puts Adam's birth around 4004 B.C., but methods of time keeping varied with the existing cultures we have today.

Adam and God had a wonderful time talking about everything God was giving to Adam including naming all the animals on the earth at that time. It was after Adam had finished naming all the animals, God caused a sleep to come over Adam and He removed one of his ribs. From this rib God created Woman. Contrary to popular opinion men do not have one less rib than women. **Genesis 2:23 "And Adam said, This is now bone on my bones, and flesh of my flesh; she shall be called Woman, because she was taken out of man."**

The virtuous woman's family.

This is the story of the virtuous woman. I cannot think of a more perfect example for a woman of today to endeavor to follow in her walk with God. Read on.

Proverbs 31:10 "Who can find a virtuous woman? For her price is far above rubies." 11"The heart of her husband doth safely trust in her so that he shall have no need of spoil." 12 "She will do him good and not evil all the days of her life."

13 "She seeketh wool and flax and worketh willingly with her hands."

14 "She is like the merchants ships; she bringeth her food from afar."

15"She riseth also while it is yet night and giveth meat to her household and a portion to her maidens." 16 " She considereth a field and buyeth it; with the fruit of her hands she planteth a vineyard." 17 " She girdeth her loins with strength and strengthen her arms." 18 " She perceiveth that her merchandise is good, and her candle goeth not out by night." 19 " She layeth her hands to the spindle and her hands hold the distaff." 20 " She stretcheth out her hand to the poor; yes she reacheth forth her hands to the needy." 21 " She is not afraid of the snow for her household; for all her houshold are clothed with scarlet." 22 " She maketh herself coverings of tapestry; her clothing is silk and purple." 23 " Her husband is known in the gates when he sitteth among the elders of the land." 24 " She maketh fine linen, and selleth it; and delivereth girdles unto the merchant." 25 "Strength and honour are her clothing; and she shall rejoice in time to come." 26 " She openeth her mouth with wisdom; and her tongue is the law of kindness." 27 " She looketh well to the ways of her household and eateth not the bread of idleness." 28 " Her children arise up and call her blessed; her husband also, and he praiseth her." 29 " Many daughters have done virtuously. But thou excellest them all." 30 " Favour is deceitful and beauty is vain; but a woman that feareth the Lord, she shall be praised." 31 " Give her of the fruit of her hands; and let her own works praise her in the gates."

Together, you and God will take a walk with each verse and determine how it can be applied to your walk in today's culture. All of God's Words are true and you are indeed very special in His eyes.

The virtuous woman today.

"Who can find a virtuous woman." I would think a virtuous woman of today would be one who is a Christian first. The word *"virtuous"* is defined by Webster as morally excellent, righteous and chaste and where might we find such a woman in today's world. We need to find a woman who is not just a Christian first. One who endeavors to live by God's word every day in every action she takes in her walk. This is not an easy walk because it means she must conform her way of thinking to solve everyday opportunities from what the word says. God will energize His holy spirit within her to provide the necessary answers to all her situations.

"For her price is far above rubies." Those in her day who owned jewels of many kinds placed a value on rubies even greater than diamonds. This phrase means she is worth more than the value of rubies. She cannot be purchased for any amount of money. Her spiritual values are greater than many and she is respected for those values in all the country.

"The heart of her husband doth safely trust in her, so that he shall have no need of spoil." Her husband's spiritual heart is at peace because he can trust her in all her comings and goings. She will never lose her value to him.

"She will do him good and not evil all the days of her life." She will be faithful in her actions toward him and will not be untrustworthy for all her days.

"She seeketh wool and flax, and worketh willingly with her hands." She is industrious and will work with her husband to produce for the family. She is not lazy and will work willingly because she wants to. She may have to think outside the box in her daily walk.

"She is like the merchants ships, she bringeth her food from afar." She will go far to find the best foods for her family and then bring them home. Maybe going to more than one grocery store.

"She riseth also while it is yet night and giveth meat to her household and a portion to her maidens." In order to have the food prepared for her family she would be up before dawn to have it ready. In other words she was not a "sleepy head."

"She considereth a field and buyeth it; with the fruit of her hands she planteth a vineyard." She does not say to her husband that it is his responsibility to make the living, she helps where she can with whatever attributes she has.

"She girdeth her loins with strength, and strengtheneth her arms" We see here hard work makes her strong. She was a vigorous women who did not shirk from heavy loads.

"She perceiveth that her merchandise is good; her candle goeth not out by night."

She produced clothing for her family as well as food and it was good for wealth also. She took care of her family, this was her highest priority.

"She layeth her hands to the spindle, and her hands hold the distaff." She is not lazy. She wove wool into thread to sew the clothing, she had made, together.

"She stretcheth out her hand to the poor; yea, she reacheth forth her hands to the needy." She is not selfish. She helps the needy and the poor. She has a generous heart. She shares of her good fortune.

"She is not afraid of the snow for her household; for all her household are clothed in scarlet." Snow indicates the high altitudes of Palestine so she made sure that her family wore comfortable clothing in the snow. The clothing she made was of the finest material available.

"She maketh herself coverings of tapestry; her clothing is silk and purple." She takes care of herself so her husband can speak proudly of her at the gates of the city. The silk and purple clothing is expensive and is an indicator of God's rich blessings on her family.

"Her husband is known at the gates, where he sitteth among the elders of the land." She made a significant contribution to her husband's well being which afforded him to receive honors from the elders at the gate. A peaceful home leads to a contented husband who can then concentrate on earning an income for the family.

"She maketh fine linen and selleth it; and delivereth girdles unto the merchant." She is seen again making fine clothing to be sold, this of course, is after her household chores are finished. She has time to make specific items for sale. "Fine linen" means righteousness spiritually.

"Strength and honour are her clothing and she shall rejoice in time to come." These words describe the character of the woman who fears the Lord. Her inward spirit exhibits divine wisdom, giving her confidence to face future challenges.

"She openeth her mouth with wisdom; and her tongue is the law of kindness." Her speech conveys wisdom and kindness. She is not a gossip or slanderer. She speaks and it is to help.

"She looketh well to the ways of her household, and eateth not the bread of idleness." She manages her household with wisdom for all. The *"bread of idleness"* literally means *"eyes looking everywhere"* as in the "sluggard" in **Proverbs 6:6: "Go to the ant, thou sluggard; consider her***(wisdom)* **ways***(God's ways)* **and be wise." 9 "How long wilt thou sleep, O sluggard, and gathereth her food in the harvest."**

"Her children arise up, and call her blessed; her husband also, and he praiseth her." Her husband and children see her as being unselfish, loving and with great care she bestows on all them. Everyone is proud of her and they let her know it.

"Many daughters have done virtuously, but thou surpassed them all." Many women are faithful to their husbands, but fall short in some of the areas of responsibility concerning the well being of her family.

"Favour is deceitful, and beauty is vain; but a woman that feareth the Lord, she shall be praised." True holiness and virtue are examples demanding respect, much more than beauty and charm.

"Give her of the fruit of her hands; and let her own works praise her in the gates." Her works speak for themselves. The Lord is pleased with her, because she has done his will where her family is concerned.

In conclusion. . .

The characteristics of a virtuous woman are varied as the flowers in the field, but her walk is with the Lord God. How a woman reads and applies the aspects of a virtuous woman in her life is where her God given *"free will"* will show it's face.

Chapter Nineteen

The Nine Manifestations, I Corinthians 12:1-11

The many gifts which God has given to you are awesome to behold but these Nine Manifestations are the most powerful of all.

These are considered a *single* gift from God. This single gift will provide an abundance of peace to any believers life. And the operation is very simple. All you have to do is trust His Words when you read the Bible. Your basic five senses will not work here because you must operate these manifestations with the super- natural believing God will give to you through His Holy Spirit within you action and revelation.

His Holy Spirit within you will function for the source of power on the Worship and Impartation manifestations. When it comes to operating the Revelation manifestations then His revelation will be the source of power. To receive His revelation only requires you to give up control of your spiritual thinking and allow God into your thoughts. How do give up control of your spiritual thinking? By reading God's Word and keeping it on in your mind. The worlds thoughts, Satan's thoughts cannot occupy the same time and place that God's thought do in your mind.

Now, and this is a possibility, should you decide **not** to believe the Word of God then you will never be able to claim His manifestations nor any of His promises even though you have been given the power of His Holy Spirit through your birth, that power will never be energized.

In I Corinthians 12:7 "But the manifestation of the Spirit *(God)* **is given to every man** *(woman)* **to profit withal."**

Available to all believers.

Since you have started reading this book I have talked about believing as being an act of trust in whatever was needed to be believed whether it was people speaking certain thoughts or physical actions taking place. As long as your five senses, sight, smell, touch, hearing and feeling are in play then you will not have any trouble believing because you have grown up utilizing these senses. The problem may exist when you are asked to believe in something or someone you cannot see.

Look at what God's Word say's, **Romans 10:14 "How then shall they call on him in whom they have not believed? And how shall they believe in him of whom they have not heard? And how shall they hear without a preacher?"**

We are dealing with manifestations which are spiritual and supernatural. Believing in something or someone where your five senses cannot be utilized is very difficult. God has given you His Word so you could begin to understand just who Jesus was and how he lived his life. The more you hear God's Word spoken the easier it will be to visualize Jesus in your mind's eye. Where is the best place to hear God's Word spoken but in a church. Hearing the Words of God spoken or seeing the written word in His Bible will help you to begin to place your trust in the Book and what it says.

Now, back to the promises. . .

In order for the power of each of these manifestations to come to pass you must energize God's Holy Spirit within your spiritual heart through your believing in God. Each of His nine manifestations contain the same spiritual power Jesus Christ received during his brief stay here on earth. This goes to show you how you can utilize this same gift to help those who do not yet believe or are in need of help. Everything concerning these powers and energizing them is spiritual.

We talked earlier about the differences between natural believing and the Manifestation of Believing.

First: Natural believing is when you are presented with a situation in the five senses world and you chose to either deny the existence of the action which takes place in front of you or accept the existence of the action happening before you. This form of believing is the simplest and most common. You have been operating this form of believing all your life.

Second: The Manifestation of Believing, when energized by the Holy Spirit within you through revelation will bring about a spiritual happening which is impossible to discern in the five senses world.

One gift. . .nine parts.

Please understand this important fact. God has given you thousands of promises in His Word all waiting for you to claim them. But when you talk about the manifestations you are speaking of a single gift from God but wrapped in nine awesomely brilliant colors. This gift was not available for believers while Jesus Christ was here on earth.

The apostle Paul received the gift from God to begin his writings of the New Testament around 57 A.D. Inspirit action is God's Holy Spirit working within you. The *"holy men"* of the Old Testament were supplied with all the words by God through revelation which was **upon** them not **within**.

Though the "gift" was not available to believers while Jesus walked here on earth he was able through his Father's revelation to receive the manifestations and operate them. Jesus operated seven of the nine manifestations; prophecy, healing, miracles, believing, word of wisdom, word of knowledge and especially discerning of spirits.

What Jesus did not operate was speaking in tongues and interpretation of tongues. These two manifestations were not available to any believer while Jesus was still walking the earth. They only became available when Jesus ascended.

The *"Comforter"* mentioned in **John 14:16 "And I will pray the Father and he shall give you another Comforter that he may abide with you forever."** Jesus was the first comforter and **now he is going to leave the disciples for awhile and he is now** providing them with his Father's Holy Spirit. The disciples were ordinary people with no special powers or great abilities.

In **Acts 2:2 "And suddenly there came a sound from heaven as of a rushing mighty wind and it filled all the house where they were sitting." 3 " And there appeared unto them cloven tongues like as of fire, and it sat upon each of them." 4 " And they were all filled with the Holy Ghost** *(Spirit)(the word "ghost" in Greek is "pneuma" and translates into Spirit)* **and they began to speak in other tongues as the Spirit***(God)* **gave them utterance."**

What happened in the upper room can happen now. . .

What happened in the upper room can happen right now and right where you are sitting. You have been carrying God's Holy Spirit with you since you were born. You just never knew what it was or how to energize it. And how do you know this is true. Remember when you read that Elisabeth, Mary's first cousin received God's Holy Spirit when she was pregnant with John and he also received God's Holy Spirit through Elisabeth's blood. Well the same action took place you when you were born. Your mother did not receive the Spirit only you. God knew in His foreknowledge you would believe. When you made the commitment to follow Christ and His Father the power was energized in you. Now all you have to do is believe God's awesome Word and act upon it. Without believing, nothing of what God says in His Word will come to pass in your life time. So first you have to start with believing, but this time the believing will be the manifestation of believing not the natural believing. You have been studying God's Word and are slowly beginning to understand what the writers meant especially Paul's writings of the New Testament. The confidence you are gaining you did not have before you began trusting what God's Word speaks to you.

The Manifestation of Believing. . .

I am getting ahead of myself because I believe this manifestation is very important in your walk with God, so let's cover this manifestation now.

This is the first of the Revelation manifestations. To operate the manifestations, all nine of them, will require a mind that understands God's Word. A mind which is confident in who you are, God's son or daughter. Your believing cannot be clouded with worldly thoughts. Because all the manifestations are supernatural in origin you will be operating something which cannot be perceived in the five senses world. The result, however, of your operating these manifestations will be visible in the five senses world.

When it comes to the specific Revelation manifestations His Holy Spirit will give you a little boost in the operation of Healing, Miracles and Believing. Again, the revelation you receive will be the same as the holy men of the Old Testament received when God was giving them His Word to write. God's revelation will come in the form of words, His Words. God because He is Spirit can only talk with spirit, your spirit. Having His Holy Spirit within your spiritual heart gives God an opening to energize you accordingly.

Each person will receive the revelation differently. It may come as a still small voice you hear in your mind. It could come as your very first thought concerning a situation where one of the manifestations would be necessary like healing. Experience dictates that your very first thought concerning any subject will come very fast and you will need to be prepared to hear from God. Only that is if you are considering utilizing one of the manifestations. There will be no loud trumpet sounds, no slap on the back. Everything will be done decent and in order. Because of your *"free will"* if you chose to not act upon this revelation you do not have to. God will not be elated or disappointed with your choice. Remember God is not a respecter of persons so no believer knows when he or she will receive revelation and for whatever reason.

Ok! let's start with the basic beginning manifestation.

Speaking in Tongues. . .

Speaking in tongues is the beginning of all the manifestations. It is the first part of three Worship manifestations. Interpretation of Tongues and Prophecy are the other two. **I Corinthians 12:10d "to another divers**(*many*)**kinds of tongues;"** Speaking in tongues is a language and as such will require you to practice speaking it to become fluent. And how do you become fluent, by speaking in tongues in your private prayer life which should be daily or by just walking alone and speaking to God. Remember in the book of Acts when Peter and the disciples and the 120 additional disciples spoke to the over 3000 people from all around the country side and the people all understood in their own language what the disciples were speaking. Best example I know concerning the power of speaking in tongues.

Speaking in Tongues is a supernatural manifestation utilizing the physical characteristics of your human body. Specifically our lips, tongue, teeth, and breathing. It will be necessary for you to incorporate the usage of these physical organs to bring about the supernatural sounds which God will supply to you. In the beginning the sounds will make no sense at all and this is alright because you will never really understand what you are saying. To an unbeliever these words will sound like nonsense but God will understand every word you utter. Because tongues is a language of men and angels there may be the possibility somewhere in the world there will be a person who understands what you are actually speaking. Another added benefit of speaking in tongues is that it confirms to your spiritual heart and mind the presence of the *"Holy Spirit."* Speaking in tongues is considered *"perfect prayer"* because it goes directly to God. It does not go through Christ Jesus. Speaking in tongues has nothing to do with your salvation. Once you confessed your life to Jesus and God and believed His Father raised him from the dead you were saved for eternity. One unique feature of speaking in tongues is it does not require you to use your mind to form words.

You can actually be speaking in tongues, spiritually speaking to God while you are carrying on a verbal conversation with a friend. One added blessing when you speak in tongues out loud is you are hearing the external manifestation of the internal reality and presence of the Holy Spirit or the presence of God within you. Years ago I came across a wonderful definition of Speaking in Tongues, the specific author is unknown. "*God, Who is the Holy Spirit, energizes the words of perfect praise and prayer within the believing heart of one who decides(via the mechanics of articulation internally or externally) to be edified spiritually by speaking divine secrets in a personally unknown language, thus bringing the gift of holy spirit into tangible and functioning reality within the believer.*"

Interpretation of Tongues. . .

This is the second part of the Worship manifestations and you are again dealing with a supernatural act but this manifestation relies heavily upon your knowledge of God's Word. **I Corinthians 12:10e "to another the interpretation of tongues;"** The interpretation of your tongue will not be an exact translation but a paraphrased explanation. God will give you the words to speak and these words will be acquired from your knowledge of His Word. Whatever scriptures you have retained from your daily studies of His Word may be part of what is used for the translation. When you are in a believers meeting where speaking in tongues and interpretation of tongues and prophecy are a normal circumstance then when asked by the leader of the meeting to speak in tongues you will also be the person interpreting your own tongue. There have been in some believers meetings where someone will be called upon to speak in tongues and then another person in the room will suddenly interpret in the language of the body present what God just gave you to speak. This person will not be providing an interpretation of your tongue but instead a prophecy. God gave you the spiritual right to speak what He has given to you. When you are speaking in tongues in your private prayer life it is not necessary to interpret your own tongue. God knows what you are speaking.

Prophecy. . .

This is the third part of the Worship manifestations. You are going to be dealing with the word ***"prophecy."*** *"the inspired utterance of a prophet, the inspired declaration of divine will and purpose."* **I Corinthians 12:10b "to another prophecy;"** Sometimes you may be giving a prediction which is directly proclaiming the mind of God. When you speak a prophecy to a body of people or to just one person God is providing those words through your spiritual heart. Remember you have God's Holy Spirit as well as the mind of Christ within your spiritual heart. God, who is Spirit, will speak directly into your spiritual mind and in turn you will speak with your mouth His Words.

Though you may not consider yourself as a prophet, in God's eyes you are His mouth and hands and feet. You give God an outward physical presence in your life and to those around you who hear you speak. Knowing you have the ability to operate these three manifestations will give you a greater confidence over any fear you have concerning boldly proclaiming His Word.

The Worship manifestations and are used accordingly in all believers meetings. Interpretation of tongues and Prophecy are not be used outside of a believers meeting unless God feels it is necessary to make a point for Him and then He will advise you accordingly.

Word of Knowledge. . .

Here you have the first part of the Impartation manifestations. You might be in a situation which could require a supernatural answer. **I Corinthians 8:b "to another the word of knowledge by the same Spirit."** You have gone to God seeking such an answer and God will give you a revelation of facts; past, present or future which were not learned through the efforts of your natural mind. **I Corinthians 2:16 " For who hath known the mind of the Lord**(God), **that he may instruct him? But we**(you and me) **have the mind of Christ."** It could be a very dark spiritual situation concerning an individual who is heavily involved with Satan or a person who has taken a wrong turn on their path of life. Your studies and experience with His Word will enable Him to draw from your knowledge of His Word and help you apply it to the situation you are confronting. *For new believers do not worry about receiving any manifestation revelations until you have spent considerable time making God's Word your own.* God will not give you the necessary words to apply to any situation until He feels you are ready to speak with understanding. Be careful you do not fall back on what you feel the words should be, it could be a trick of Satan. Here is a wonderful definition of Word of Knowledge *"Your heavenly Father, Who is the Holy Spirit, energizes and reveals vital information to His gift in you, holy spirit. Then by way of the registering abilities (five spiritual senses) of your inner spiritual nature, He communicates clearly to your cognizant awareness (nous-mind) variables and conditions relative to the unique situation in which you are or will be involved. These essential elements of unveiled truth or fact (above and beyond your functioning knowledge of God's written Word, your previous learning experiences in life, or your vigilant observation) establish your preparation to accomplish the Father's will for yourself, the household of God, and others that may be involved."* author unknown.

Word of Wisdom. . .

This is the second part of the Impartation manifestations. What is wisdom but knowledge applied. **I Corinthians 8a "For to one is given by the Spirit the word of wisdom;"** It stands to reason the more knowledge you have about a certain subject and understand the subject the greater the wisdom you will exhibit when a particular situation arises. In **Luke 12:12 "For the Holy Ghost**(*Spirit*) **shall teach you in the same hour what you ought to say."**Here is a spiritual situation where you will need the right words to speak and God will provide them within the same hour through revelation. Where God will get the words is from your knowledge of His Word. So the more knowledge you have concerning God's Word the greater the chance you will have of speaking God's wisdom into people's lives. For example you may be speaking into a situation of casting out devil spirits or dealing with a death in a family or building confidence with a young married couple. God will lovingly use His Words which are implanted in your mind to speak through you into a five senses situation.

Discerning of spirits. . .

This is the third part of the Impartation manifestations *"The quality of being able to grasp and comprehend what is obscure." "a power to see what is not evident to the average mind." "By this gift the believer is enabled to know immediately what is motivating a person or a situation."* **I Corinthians 12:10c "to another discerning of spirits;"** This is a very powerful spiritual gift which you have been given by God. The above definitions are awesome of an ability or calling which is available to all but seldom utilized by believers. My experience with this manifestation shows itself in women more than men. There is a phrase called "women's intuition" where they walk into a room and become aware of someone who is uncomfortable or struggling with a devil spirit. These women are sure of who they are in God's family. They are sure of the outcome with their life here on earth, eternity with Christ and God. And in addition they are sure of their role in helping reconcile unbelievers back to God. My wife, bless her heart, for the last 40 years together has utilized this gift on many occasions. Having knowledge of God's Word will definitely allow you to operate this gift because you will be speaking from God's will for you from His Word.

Because all nine of these manifestations are a gift from God to you they are all available to be put into operation. However there are some theologians who in their misguided belief feel this particular manifestation can only be operated by a very few select people whom God has called. This is an example of man's knowledge getting in the way of God. When God gives something spiritual to any of us it is His gift for us to utilize for the benefit of all those people who are witness's to it.

The Revelation Manifestations. . .

Now we will look at the Revelation manifestations. As I said earlier God should give you a gentle push when it comes to performing miracles and providing healings but only if in God's thinking the situation requires either manifestation to be performed. God will listen to your heart's desire to perform either of these manifestations and this desire will be taken into deep consideration should the situation arise for their use.

Believing. . .

This is the first part of the revelation manifestations. We covered this manifestation earlier in this chapter and it is still very important because without this form of believing, in things we cannot see in the five senses world, none of us would be operating any of these nine manifestations today. **I Corinthians 12:9a "To another faith***(believing)* **by the same Spirit;"** The holy men who wrote the Old Testament needed God's revelation for inspiration, so do you. Why do I need revelations from God concerning the manifestations of believing, healing and miracles? Let's see if this helps. What is unique about two of these manifestations is they are concerned exclusively with the altering of the flesh of God's creation and in order to bring either of them to pass you will need *believing* in things you cannot see as well as God's revelation.

Here is a quote I received many years ago which describes how the Manifestation of Believing is accomplished. *"Your heavenly Father, Who is the Holy Spirit, initiates this tangible(capable of being touched) energizing of His gift in you, holy spirit, which then catalyzes(bring about vigorous action) your heart as you stay your mind on accomplishing what the Father has unveiled to you by revelation. . . author unknown.*

The manifestation of Believing is necessary within your spiritual heart before you can perform healing or miracles.

Healing . . .

You perform the act of healing thru God's grace and He will bring about the deliverance upon the body or soul by way of the cause *"in the name of Jesus Christ"* **I Corinthians 12:9b "the gifts of healing by the same Spirit."** What is different between healings and miracles is once the healing is complete which is usually immediate there is a period of time which could be days or months for the symptoms of the sickness or disability to diminish and disappear.

Miracles. . .

Miracles are not the same as healings. **I Corinthians 12:10a "To another the working of miracles;"** The action of a miracle is complete the first time out. Again you must speak *"in the name of Jesus Christ."* There are no residual effects from a miracle. Jesus performed miracles throughout his time here on earth with His Father's help through revelation, just like you and me. So in order to perform either of these manifestations you will quite simply need God's help to bring them to pass. Your natural believing is just not strong enough. The disciples in **Matthew 17:20 "And Jesus said unto them, Because of your unbelief, for verily I say unto you, If ye have faith as a grain of mustard seed, ye shall say unto this mountain** *(problem)*, **Remove hence to yonder place, and it shall remove and nothing shall be impossible unto you."** had this same problem when they tried to bring out a devil spirit from an individual and failed. This is why God will give your natural believing a helping hand, spiritually speaking with His revelation just like He did with Jesus.

Some additional spiritual information concerning the manifestations. . .

Jesus Christ, though he was flesh and blood, exhibited the manifestations during his walk among us. God explained to Jesus exactly what was going to happen to him each day including each situation and God would accomplish this action through His revelation. Jesus Christ did not have His Father's Holy Spirit within until he returned from the resurrection to walk among the people for 40 days. Now you might say "well Jesus is the son of God and as such he should be able to take action based on God's Holy Spirit speaking within his spiritual heart. Remember that God is not a respecter of persons so God would not break what He had established. Since Jesus was flesh and blood and as such could not take part in receiving the Holy Spirit until after it became available during Pentecost, but Jesus would ascend ten days before Pentecost would take place. In **Acts 2:4a "And they were all filled with the Holy Ghost(Spirit)."** Pentecost has already past.

In **John 14:12 "Verily, verily I** *(Jesus)* **say unto you, He that believeth on me the works that I do shall he do also; and greater."** *"And greater"* refers to speaking in tongues which was the *"Comforter"* in **John 14:16.** The Comforter was for everyone who believes.

Another example of God's accuracy in His word.

Philippians 4:13 "I can do all things through Christ which strengthens me."

This verse of scripture is probably one of the most famous and much quoted scriptures of all time. But what does it really say. First the word *"which"* means God. How do I know the word *"which"* means God, because Philippians 4:13 is a prayer to God.

You are asking for strength to deal with a particular spiritual situation in your life, and what does God say. You can do all things spiritually. How do you gain the strength you need? You have to go *"through"* Jesus Christ not *"to"* Jesus Christ. The difference between these two words means the outcome of the request. Remember when God taught you in His Word you had to go through His Son Jesus Christ in order to get to him. **John 14:6 "Jesus saith unto him***(Thomas)* **I am the way, the truth and the life; no man cometh unto the Father** *(God)* **but by** *(by* *is another word for through)***me."** So you are praying to God for strength to deal with a certain spiritual situation and God has already confirmed the strength you need is available through this prayer to Him. So who is going to provide this strength for you? God will provide for all your needs when you loving ask for them.

The key to receiving this strength is to believe, first in God's Word and second in a God who is faithful to provide for all you ask for as long as it is in alignment and harmony with His Word. Alignment and harmony are explained in another chapter.

So back to God's special gift. . .

How do you utilize these gifts.

There has been already been an explanation of the manifestations well in worship meetings Speaking in Tongues, Interpretation of Tongues and Prophecy are brought to pass for the benefit of the congregation. **I Corinthians 14:27 "If any man speak in an unknown tongue, let it be by two or at the most three and that by course***(order)* **and let one** *(each)* **interpret."**

Prophecy is never interpreted because it is always delivered in the language of the body present.

John 4:24 "God is a Spirit and they which worship him must worship him in the spirit and in truth." You are worshiping God when you energize His Holy Spirit in you and utilize His gift to you through your *spirit* by speaking in tongues. Reading His Word is a form of worship and His Word is considered *truth. And a very special aspect of worship to God is how you live your life according to His Word.*

Remember Paul in **Acts 6:4 "But we will give ourselves continually to prayer and to the ministry of the world."** Paul is talking about speaking in tongues which you can do continually.

Speaking in tongues is a language of men and angels and as such must be practiced in order to become more fluent. Which means while you are conducting your daily activities you can practice your tongues and what is even more glorious is to practice speaking or singing out loud in your tongue. God is always blessed to carry on a conversation with you in tongues.

Should the question ever arise concerning whether you have part of God's Holy Spirit within your spiritual heart rest assured when you spoke in tongues you have audible proof His Holy Spirit resides within you.

Now let's talk more about Interpretation of Tongues,

1 Corinthians 12:10c "to another the interpretation of tongues."

In a believers meeting there are three separate manifestations uttered and the order of the three will be decided by the leader of the meeting as he or she is inspired by the Holy Spirit.

Let's talk a little more about interpretation of tongues. Usually believers who have studied God's Word and possibly taught some of His Word are the ones who will bring forth this manifestation in a believers meeting. Since it is impossible to understand what you have just brought forth because it sounds like a foreign tongue, God will energize your knowledge and memory of His Word in your mind and inspire you to speak the translation of your tongue, paraphrased, for the body to hear and understand and be blessed.

Now Prophecy, **1 Corinthians 12:10b "to another prophecy;"** does not require any interpretation because it is spoken in the primary language of the body in attendance. Prophecy in some cases will sound similar to the translation of the tongue just given and this is wonderful because it means God is speaking a message to all three of the believers who spoke the manifestations and the message is for all those present in the meeting. God is relying on your knowledge of His Word to provide the prophecy. Keep this in mind all of God's Word in the Bible is prophecy.

1 Corinthians 12:1 " Now concerning spiritual gifts(matters) **brethren, I would not have you ignorant."**

Let's take a look that the remaining manifestations. These are the Impartation manifestations. They are Word of Knowledge, Word of Wisdom and Discerning of Spirits.

Webster defines *"impartation"* as to; *"give, convey or grant"*

Word of Knowledge, what is it? Where would you go today to find spiritual knowledge? Someplace which has been around considerably longer than the Internet and that is the KJV of the Bible. The Bible is your source for all spiritual learning. Starting in 1604 at the request of King James of England and completed around 1614 the KJV Bible is still in print today. **I Corinthians 12:8 "For to one is given by the Spirit***(God)* **to another the word of knowledge."**

The words are spiritual in nature. God thru revelation with the holy men of the Old Testament and inspired within the hearts of the writers of the New Testament wrote His Word. When you are called upon in the five senses world to speak what God has energized within your spiritual heart to those who are suffering both physically and mentally you will be given the necessary information concerning any particular situation by God through the knowledge of God's Word and based upon your believing.

What about *Words of Wisdom*? Have you ever heard the expression *"Wisdom is knowledge applied."*

How does this sound. You have read and committed to memory many biblical facts and scriptures and many of these facts concern specific events which took place thousands of years ago. All these facts are considered an accumulation of knowledge and it is from this knowledge that you will speak forth wisdom concerning any situation you are involved in.

Let's say you are reading **Revelation 12:1-6** which describes the birth of Jesus Christ. These six verses of scripture are separate facts. Individually they are important but collectively they provide a conclusion to the asked question *"when was Jesus born."* The conclusion is considered wisdom because you have applied the knowledge of the scriptures to arrive at an answer.

Now for the last of the Impartation Manifestations. *"Discerning of Spirits."* I said earlier there will be times in your life when you meet a particular person and you just do not feel right about the vibrations you are receiving. You just feel uncomfortable around them. You are not talking about any conversation you have had with them or their appearance. You could sense an unfamiliar *"spirit"* about them. You were sensing their *"spirit."* which is possibly coming from the *"god"* of this world, Satan. On the other hand you may have encountered an individual whose *"spirit"* is very pleasing so much so you feel comfortable around this person and could almost confide a great deal of personal information to them about yourself even though you have never met them. This person's *"spirit"* is from the God and Father of Christ Jesus.

You have to utilize your free will choice, which God gave you, to accurately determine which spirit you are dealing with because sometimes Satan can have his unholy angel spirits adapt themselves to resemble God's Holy Spirit.

So what does *"discerning"* mean? Webster calls it; *"to detect with senses other than vision."*

Discerning of spirits refers to your ability to recognize a *"spirit"* around or in a person or through a person's behavior without ever seeing any spirit.

As with all of the manifestations they are for your personal use in your walk in this world, Satan's world. You can chose to apply these manifestations to situations as they arise if you chose to operate your "free will."

Next we have the Revelation manifestations. These are believing, healing and miracles.

These are the heavy weight manifestations. These by their meanings alone speak volumes about the immense power you have been given by your Father in heaven. Let's recap for a moment.

Jesus Christ operated all the manifestations with the exception of speaking in tongues and interpretation of tongues because they were not available until the disciples were in the Upper Room and it was there that they received God's Holy Spirit into their spiritual hearts and minds just like you did when you gave your life over to Jesus. **Acts 2:4 "And they** *(disciples)***were all filled** *(completely)* **with the holy ghost** *(spirit)* **and began to speak with other tongues as the Spirit** *(God)* **gave them utterance."** The Holy Spirit is the Comforter spoken about in **Matthew 14:16 "And I** *(Jesus)* **pray the Father and he shall give you another Comforter that he** *(it)* **may abide with you forever."** Jesus Christ was the First Comforter.

The Manifestations. . .

In order for you to operate any of the nine manifestations you must believe you can perform what God is asking you to do.

A literal translation of the manifestation of believing is "to bring to pass something which is impossible to do in the five senses realm by your command." You can accomplish this task only by God providing the word of knowledge *(Bible)* or the word of wisdom*(knowledge applied)* or discerning of spirits and where will God retrieve this information from, from what you have stored up based upon your reading and studying of God's Word.

To operate the manifestation of healing, you must first speak *"in the name of Jesus Christ"* and through the manifestation of believing which you have within you, the act of healing according to what God has revealed to you by the word of knowledge, word of wisdom or discerning of spirits will take place within the person you are directing the action toward.

And to operate the manifestation of miracles you must call again upon *"the name of Jesus Christ"* which will bring to pass the operation the manifestation of believing within you. The act of the miracle is according to what God has revealed to you through revelation of the word of knowledge, word of wisdom or discerning of spirits. God is actually going to perform the miracle through you. You are the conduit for the miracle to come to pass in the physical world.

One important aspect about the operation of healing and miracles is the only people in the room or space are to be the person being healed or the person awaiting the miracle and the person operating the manifestation. Non-believers cannot be present including relatives. God activates His gift within your personal spirit when you have given your life over to His Son Jesus Christ. Your operation of the gift depends on the time and effort you give towards your studies of God's Word which is an effort on your part to come to know God's will for you and your fellow believers.

Interesting fact; The number Nine is very interesting because it means *"completely complete"* or completely finished. The number Three means complete. There are three separate groups of three or 3x3. Worship equals Speaking in Tongues, Interpretation of Tongues and Prophecy. Impartation equals Word of Knowledge, Word of Wisdom and Discerning of Spirits. And Revelation equals Believing, Healing and Miracles. These manifestations are completely, completely finished.

Chapter Twenty

How many were crucified with Jesus?

This question has been asked by many over the years and traditionally the answer has been two. Jesus Christ in the middle and one on either side. Three total.

Now the question is, what does God's Word say about this fact. Was it three or could it have been more. In France there is a small church close to Paris and outside the church building stand five crosses.

Why would there be five crosses when all the churches around this little church have three crosses, if they have any. Someone who possibly went to this church did some research on their own and determined from God's Word there are really five crosses which means four other men were with Jesus Christ on Golgotha.

Let's go to the Gospels and see what God has to say about this matter.

Matthew 27:28 "Then were there two thieves crucified with him, one on the right hand and another on the left." The key word in this scripture is *"thieves."* In Greek the word for thieves is translated *"duo lesti."*

In **Mark 15:27 "And with him they crucify two thieves; the one on his right hand and the other on his left."** Again you see the word *"thieves"* which is *"duo lesti."* The word thieves or thief means an individual who commits a theft, but he does it with stealth or cunning. He has taken the time to plan the details of the theft. He knows what he is going to do before he does it. These men were thinkers.

Enter a new word. . .

In **Luke 23:32 "And there were also two other malefactors, led with him to be put to death." 33 "And when they were come to the place, which is called Calvary, there they crucified him and the malefactors, one on the right hand and on the other on the left."**

Now you have a new word introduced here. Instead of the word *"thieves"* you have *"malefactors."* In Greek the *"malefactor"* is translated *"duo cagori."* What is the difference between the two words? A malefactor is an individual who commits a felony whereas a thief commits a robbery where objects stolen have a value less than those of a felony so his term in jail could be considered a misdemeanor. Under the law during Jesus' time if you stole you paid the price with a hand or maybe your life.

Luke was one of the most educated of the disciples so his image of the language could be considered more extensive. Luke was able to recognize the difference between the two men simply because God told him through his inspirit action as he wrote the Gospel.

Whether or not Luke and Mark were there with Jesus does not make any difference. God through His Holy Spirit within these men does make the difference.

Now look at **John 19:18 " Where they crucified him, and two other with him on either side *(one)* and Jesus in the midst."**

The word *"one"* is not in the critical Greek texts and can be eliminated when reading this verse of scripture without sacrificing the true meaning of the word.

Note: In the KJV of the Bible when it was being translated, should one of the translators come upon a phrase in Greek which could be broken down and made easier to read, he would do so. Now understand this, by the addition of a word the translators of the book would put that word in *italics* meaning you could remove the word and not affect the original meaning of the Word. And of course the final editors have loving avoided the scripture in Revelations which says if you alter His Word you will not be in the Lambs Book of Life coming to pass.

The key word now in the above scripture is *"midst."* One person on either side of Jesus place Jesus in the*" middle."* Two people on either side of Jesus place Jesus in the *"midst"*.

Webster's dictionary defines the word *"midst"* as being, *"in the condition of being surrounded."*

This particular verse of scripture confirms there were two thieves on either side of Jesus as well as two malefactors on either side. This would add up to four people not two. Now there may be some of you who would say **"why is this fact so important in the scheme of things in Satan's world today."** And the answer is this. When you begin to dive deeper into God's Word and begin to find these hidden truths your faith or believing in the truth of God's Word begins to strengthen. You begin to form the confidence to face Satan's world head on. Just knowing you have the belt of truth around yourself as it says in **Ephesians 6:14a "stand therefore having your loins girt***(belt)* **about with truth"** is evidence enough.

When you begin to study God's word on a deeper level you will notice a difference between the various versions of the Bible and how they are translated especially the same verse of scripture. I took this verse from **John 19:18** *(in the NIV reads)* **"Here they crucified him, and with two others - one on each side with Jesus in the middle."**

John 19:18 *(in the NLT reads)* **" There they nailed him to the cross, two others were crucified with him, one on either side with Jesus between them."**

We have the words *"between"* written in early 1990 & and *"middle"* written in the 1960

John 19:18 *(in the KJV reads)* **" Where they crucified him, and two other with him on either side and Jesus in the *"midst."* ** This was translated in the early 1600's.

Three different translations written many years apart by three different groups of biblical scholars. Which one do you think stood the test of time?

In conclusion.

The conclusion is again the more you study God's awesome Word the greater the opportunities God will provide for you to gain a more profound understanding of His heart and will for you.

Chapter Twenty One

The Gathering.

Some theologians call the Gathering the Rapture. Call it what you will, what it boils down to is this. Should you chose to not become a *"born again"* individual, then you will have to face the Judgment Seat at the Bema. However, should you be *"born again"* then you will be in line for a reward and this verse of scripture explains just what going to happen after all the peoples of the earth have heard the Word of God.

In **Matthew 24:14 "And this gospel of the kingdom shall be preached in all the world for a witness unto all nations; then shall the end come"**.

In so many words this verse of scripture tells you when all the peoples of the earth have heard the Word of God with understanding then the Gathering will take place. Christ Jesus will come back and collect you with your fellow brothers and sisters who have been waiting in Paradise with their new bodies. Those of you who are *"born again"* and are alive when Christ returns only your *personal spirit* will be collected. Your flesh and blood body will stay here on earth. By the time you arrive in heaven you will have your new body. You will all be escorted to Heaven. How long will you be in heaven before the Millennium takes place I do not know. Christ will return as King of Kings and Lord of Lords along with all those faithful saints including you. You will have the position of a priest who will help Christ rule on the earth for the next ten centuries. **Revelations 5:10 " And hast made us unto God kings and priests and we shall reign on the earth."**

And then we can go to **Revelations 20:6 "Blessed and holy is he that hath part of the first resurrection; on such the second death hath no power, but they(us) shall be priests of God and of Christ and shall reign with him a thousand years."**

In **I Corinthians 16:52 "In a moment, in the twinkling of an eye, at the last trump; for the trumpet shall sound and the dead shall be raised incorruptible, and we shall be changed."**

So if you have just died and are buried in the grave in the cemetery and the trumpet sounds. Remember the moment your physical life ceases your "personal spirit" will ascend to be in Paradise. So the trumpet sounds and Christ returns and lifts up your personal spirit out of Paradise. You then will go to heaven.

Just to repeat, those of you who have not died but are *"born again"* Christians your *"personal spirit"* will also be lifted up into the heavens to be with Christ and God directly without going to Paradise.

However, your earthly bodies will stay here and rot away.

Bad news. . .

Should you not have chosen of your own free will to become a believer and follower of Jesus Christ or God then you may not be joining your families on their trip to heaven this time.

I say this time because we have an awesome God of second chances who still wants all mankind to be reconciled back to Him. So what He is going to do. He is going to give everyone who is left on earth, after the Gathering, the opportunity to join Him and His Son Jesus in Heaven.

Once the Gathering is complete and the thousand year reign is over then Satan will be loosed and have open rule on those remaining humans. There will be quite a few who have not bowed to God or Christ Jesus. Read **Revelations 16:1-21** This period of time is called the Tribulation. It is three and 1/2 years long to be exact. **Revelations 11:2 "But the court which is without the temple, leave out, and measure it not, for it is given unto the Gentiles; and the holy city shall they**

tread under foot forty and two months." Those who remain after the "Gathering" will have to become serious martyrs in order to gain entrance into heaven. Meaning their deaths will be more of a sacrifice than just falling asleep.

This verse of scripture lends itself to a description of what will happen;

II Thessalonians2:7 "For the mystery of iniquity doth already work; only he who now letteth will let, until he be taken out of the way." 8 "And then shall that Wicked be revealed. Whom the Lord shall consume with the spirit(breath) **of his mouth, and shall destroy with the brightness of his coming." 9 "Even him, whose**(antichrist) **coming is after**(according to) **the working of Satan with all**(in every) **power and signs and lying**(falsehoods) **wonders." 10 "And with all deceivableness of unrighteousness in them perish because they received not the love of the truth, that they might be saved."**

This next verse confirms Satan will have but a short time to wreak the havoc he desires and then his end will come in the Lake of Fire along with all his unholy angel spirits and those who chose not to follow Jesus or God.

Revelation 12:10 "And I heard a loud voice saying in heaven, Now is come salvation and strength, and the kingdom of our God, and the power of his Christ; for the accuser of our brethren is cast down, which accused them before our God day and night." 11 "And they overcame him by the blood of the Lamb, and by the word of their testimony; and they loved not their lives unto the death(martyrdom)." 12 "Therefore rejoice ye heavens, and ye that dwell in them. Woe to the inhabiters of the earth and of the sea! For the devil(Satan) **is come down unto you, having great wrath, because he knoweth that he hath but a short time."**

A *"short time"* indicates Satan will have only three and one/half years to wreak his havoc on the inhabitants left on earth. *(see Revelations 11:2b)*

Revelation 20:3 "And cast him into the bottomless pit and shut him up and set a seal upon him that he should deceive the nations

no more till the thousand years should be fulfilled; and after that he must be loosed a little season."

Let's recap what is going to happen when you pass on. Your physical body will be buried in the ground where it will eventually decay and become dust. The moment you pass on or breathe your last breath your *"personal spirit"* will be in Paradise. You will receive your new body as you wait in Paradise until Christ returns. His return will be called the Rapture. When the trumpet sounds Christ will come out of the clouds over the earth, his feet will not touch the earth, and he will collect all those souls in Paradise first. Those born again Christians who are still alive on earth at his coming will die and Christ will then collect their personal spirits. Those who are alive and die will collect their new bodies before they arrive in heaven. They will not go through Paradise. Together you will travel to heaven where you will rejoice with Jesus, King of Kings and Lord of Lords. It will be during your time in Heaven that you receive your reward for being faithful from Christ Jesus.

Once you are all collected in Heaven and have received your rewards you will then return back to the new earth with Christ Jesus. You will be a priest for a thousand years. Christ Jesus will be your King and he will guide you in your journey here on earth.

Your task while you are on earth is to help reconcile those remaining people back to God. Those individuals who chose again not to change their way of thinking will spend eternity in the Lake of Fire with Satan.

Let's repeat this once more. When the thousand years are completed Satan will be released from his bondage in the earth and he will wage war against those who are left on earth. This carnage will last three and 1/2 years. At the end of this short time Satan will be cast into the Lake of Fire along with all those who did not chose to go with Jesus.

You will spend eternity with God and Christ Jesus in the New Jerusalem on a new Earth.

Contrary to popular opinion the Earth(planet) will not be physically destroyed but cleansed of everything which resembled the old world.

Chapter Twenty Two

The other God.

When I say there is another god in the Universe who desires your worship just as much as THE Creator of the Universe, God, the Father of Christ Jesus, do you have any trouble believing this statement, if so then. . .

There is one and his name is Satan and he is alive and doing very well . . . at least for the time being

Please consider these facts:

Satan does not want you dead, you are useless to him if dead.
Satan does not want you sick, you are helpless if sick.
Satan wants you healthy and whole to worship him.
Satan has his own followers, they are called Satanists.
Satan even has his own bible which he wrote.
Satan performs human sacrifices per his own law.
Satan wants you to enjoy all the sinful pleasures he is offering.
Satan does not cause sickness, he influences its roots.
Satan does not cause death. Christ Jesus took that power away from him when he*(Jesus)* was on the cross.
Satan will lie.
Satan has not been seen since his encounter with Jesus in Matthew 4:1ff.
Satan cannot be everywhere, but his billions of unholy angel spirits can.

Satan's servants will do all his work. Satan is still very angry at God and will make every effort to discredit the true God.

And in conclusion once you have fulfilled Satan's desires he will discard you as a broken shell of a person.

Satan's unholy angel spirits or servants number in the billions and these spirit creatures exist in all the kingdoms of the world, Satan's world. They are continually influencing the devices of man. In **Revelations 12:9 "And the great dragon was cast out, that old serpent, called the Devil or Satan, which deceiveth the whole world; he was cast out into the earth, and his angels were cast out with him."**

Revelations 13:1ff describes Satan's goal here in this world which is to reconcile men and women and children back to him, not the one true God. Satan desires worship just the same as our God does. Satan unholy angel spirits have showed up in many spiritual forms throughout the centuries, especially in Israel. Just about every time Israel got a new king they would begin worshiping whatever Satanic image was available which usually was the Ashtoreth pole. **I Kings 11:5 "For Solomon went after Ashtoreth the goddess of the Zidonians, and after Milcom the abomination of the Ammonites."** For a greater explanation of what went on during those times read **I and II Kings.**

When was Jesus tempted by Satan?

In **Matthew 4:1 " Then was Jesus led up of the spirit into the wilderness to be tempted of the devil." 2 " And when he had fasted forty days and forty nights, he was afterward an hungered." 3 "And when the tempter** *(diabolos-Greek)* **came to him, he said, If thou be the Son of God command these stones be made bread." 4 "But he answered and said, It is written, man shall not live by bread alone, but by every word that proceedeth out of the mouth of God." 5 "Then the devil taketh him up into the holy city and setteth him on a pinnacle of the temple." 6 "And saith unto him, If thou be the Son of God, cast thyself down; For it is written, he shall give his** angel charge concerning thee; and in their hands they shall bear thee up, lest at any time thou dash thy foot against a stone." 7 "Jesus said unto him, It is written again, Thou shalt not tempt the Lord thy God." 8 "Again the devil taketh him up into an exceeding high mountain and sheweth him all the kingdoms of the world, and the glory of them." 9 "And saith unto him, All these things will I give thee, if thou fall down and worship me." 10 "Then saith Jesus unto him, Get thee hence, Satan; for it is written, Thou shalt worship the Lord thy God and him only shalt thou serve."

Back in time. . .

Let us go back in time many billions of years to the creation of the Universe. **Genesis 1:1 "In the beginning God created the heaven and the earth." 2 "And the earth was without form and void; and darkness was upon the face of the deep, And the Spirit of God moved upon the face of the waters."**

What happened between Genesis 1:1 and Genesis 1:2

It is very important to remember when reading God's word there are periods of time between verses of scripture. In the above case the earth was not created whole and complete. It took billions of years to cool and solidify. During this period of time all the prehistoric creatures were born and grew up and wandered the earth, adapted and then died.

What caused their disappearance?

What took place was called *"Pangaea."* About 300 million years ago there were not seven continents but one massive continent. This continent was surrounded by one sea called *Panthalassa*. The formation of Pangaea gave way for the modern theory of plate tectonics. Over time these plates began to shift. The shift resulted in giant land masses breaking apart and forming the new face of the earth. It seems only logical that a great amount of the prehistoric animals living on these continents would through the migration of the plates eventually be affected with extinction. Should you want more information concerning *plate tectonics* go to *livescience.com/38218facts-about-pangaea.html.* Today scientists are finding species of animals which were originally thought to have inhabited Europe and Asia hundreds of millions of year ago now appearing in South America or even North America.

From a biblical stand point, all of the movement of these plates took place between Genesis 1:1 and 1:2. God did not create Adam until around 4,000 B.C.

By this time Satan was waiting for Adam and how did Satan know there would be an Adam. You know Satan's other name was Lucifer and he was second in command in Heaven right next to God. Lucifer was privy to everything God had planned for the creation of the universe including the creation of man, in this case Adam and Eve.

Angels / Archangels

Prior to the creation of the universe God created many untold billions of angel spirits. What was the reason for this event we do not know. *It might be that God had assigned a certain angel spirit to watch over each person on the earth from Adam's time until now, that's why it was necessary to create billions of these holy angel spirits. There is however no biblical scripture to support this theory.* There is biblical scripture to confirm the existence of three arch angels. Michael and Gabriel were given dominion over 2/3rds of these holy angel spirits and Lucifer was given dominion over the final 1/3rd of these holy angel spirits.

Michael, the warrior archangel was responsible for leading all the battles God waged against men, especially those battles involving Israel. Now Gabriel, the messenger archangel was responsible for delivering all those important messages God wanted man to know, and Lucifer, the archangel of light, who was the most beautiful and smartest of all the angel spirits was God's right hand angel.

Contrary to popular opinion angels do not have wings. They are spirit forms. And there have been times in the Bible when they would take on a human form so as to not frighten the humans they were dealing with. For example when Mary was told by the archangel Gabriel she was going to have a baby boy whose name would be Jesus she was told not to be afraid or when the angel announced to the shepherds about the birth of Jesus.

Over time and with the aid of the minds of old painters of the day some angels became cute little cherubim floating around the heavens.

A little more on Lucifer or Satan. . .

Lucifer, the second in command of all the heavens and responsible to God only.

Lucifer became envious of God's supreme position and decided he wanted to be first in the heavens.

God, who had created Lucifer said in His own loving way to Lucifer, *"this will not work"* and thus began an awesome war in Heaven. How long it went on we do not know but we do know the outcome. **Revelations 12:7 "And there was a war in heaven; Michael and his angels fought against the dragon***(Satan)* **and the dragon***(Satan)* **fought and his angels." 8 "And prevailed not, neither was their place found any more in heaven." 9 " And the great dragon was cast out, that old serpent called the Devil and Satan which deceived the whole world; he was cast out into the earth and his angels were cast out with him."**

After the war Lucifer's name changed to Satan. Satan in Greek means the hater or accuser. The key words to remember in the above verses are *"serpent"* and *"into the earth."* The only time Lucifer's name shows up in the Bible is in **Isaiah 14:12a " How art thou fallen from heaven, O Lucifer, son of the morning!"**

Where is Satan now?

Quite simply *"in the earth."* He is doomed to wander through the earth, not on the surface of the earth. Some theologians believe Satan is in heaven right now alongside God just waiting out the eons of time to come back, but if that were the case then why this translation of **Revelations12:9 "And the great dragon was cast out, that old serpent called the Devil and Satan which decieveth the whole world; he was cast out into the earth and his angels were cast out with him."**

In due time there will be a *"gathering together"* of the bride of Christ, which is you along with all the other millions who believed in Jesus and his Father God. Then Satan will be locked in the bottomless pit for one thousand years.

After the *"gathering"* all those who were faithful to God and Jesus Christ will be rewarded with priest hoods. **Revelation 5:10 "And hast made us unto our God kings and priests and we shall reign on the earth."**

At the end of the thousand years Satan will be loosed so he can begin his final battle with those who remain on the earth. **Revelations 20:7 "And when the thousand years are expired Satan shall be loosed out of his prison." 8 " And shall go out to deceive the nations which are in the four quarters of the earth, Gog and Magog, to gather them together to battle; the number of whom is as the sand of the sea."**

In **Ezekiel 38:1 "And the word of the Lord***(God)*** came unto me saying," 2 "Son of man, set thy face against Gog, the land of Magog, the chief prince of Meshech and Tubal and prophesy against him." 14 " Therefore, son of man, prophesy and say unto Gog, Thus saith the Lord God; in that day when my people of Israel dwelleth, shalt thou not know it." 15 " And thou shalt come from thy place out of the north parts, thou and many people with thee, all of them riding upon horses, a great company, and a mighty army." 16 " And thou shalt come up against my people of Israel, as a cloud to cover the land; it shall be in the latter days, and I will bring thee against my**

land that the heathen may know me, when I shall be sanctified in thee, O Gog, before my eyes."

Magog is the grandson of Noah and where his grandsons went they usually started a city, *"the land of Magog."* Meshech and Tubal were also grandsons of Noah. They established cities where Gog was the chief prince.

Why did Satan choose a snake form?

There is no scripture which states exactly why Satan chose a reptile form. He could have chosen whatever animal he desired but in this verse we may have found the answer. **Genesis 3:1a "Now the serpent was more subtil** *(old English spelling)***than any beast of the field which the Lord God had made."**The emotion of fear had not yet been introduced so Eve was comfortable talking with Satan with whatever form he took.

Satan has been described as a dragon in **Revelations 12:9a "and the great dragon was cast out, that old serpent called the Devil and Satan."** A dragon has always been a violent creature breathing fire and flying around generating havoc on the towns folk of Medieval times. This image goes along with painters of the times when they began depicting Satan as a dragon. A dragon is considered part of the reptile genus.

When you are reading the KJV of the Bible you will find no reference to angels flying down to earth. As I said earlier the only wings angels had were depicted by the old masters in their religious paintings. Angels had spiritual forms which were the same as what Christ Jesus had taken on when he was being seen around the countryside after his resurrection.

Fast forward to today.

Lucifer's name has now become the Devil or a more politically correct name of the Adversary, but in reality his name is Satan. Satan has not changed his behavior since he was cast out of heaven. He still aspires to be worshiped. In fact there are many individuals in our world who worship him today in secret places. They are called **"Satanists."** They have even published their own version of the bible which of course was supposedly written by Satan himself.

The only record in the Bible of Satan taking on human form which God allowed was to confront Jesus in the desert. In **Matthew 4:1 "Then was Jesus led up** *(was permitted)* **of the spirit***(God)* **into the wilderness to be tempted of the devil." 2 "And when he had fasted forty days and forty nights, he was afterward an hungered." 3 " And when the tempter came to him, he said, If thou be the Son of God, command that these stones be made bread." 4 " But he answered and said, It is written, Man shall not live by bread alone, but by every word that proceedeth out of the mouth of God."**

In **Deuteronomy 8:3b "that he might make thee know that man doth not live by bread only, but by every word that proceedeth out of the mouth of the Lord doth man live."**

God knew all this would happen.

God in His foreknowledge knew the temptation would take place and He knew His Son would not yield to Satan. Jesus had to go through with this examination in order to fulfill the prophecy of **Isaiah 53:5 "But he was wounded for our transgressions, he was bruised for our iniquities; the chastisement of our peace was upon him and with his stripes we are healed."** The son of God would suffer a terrible death. A death so awful the true description is just now coming to light.

Jesus was flesh and blood, just like you. When he was cut he bled just like you do. There was nothing supernatural about Jesus. Jesus had to be flesh in order to bear all the sins of all the people who would eventually come to praise and believe in him and His Father God. In his fleshly body he took the power of death away from Satan. Which means Satan does not have the authority or power to cause you to die. In Jesus' fleshly body the stripes he received as he was punished by the Roman guards gave you the power to heal your fleshly body when you are injured simply by claiming His Father's healing through your step brother's name, Christ Jesus. And this is how you would claim healing: You injure yourself or you have a headache or you feel sick. Simply say **"I claim the healing power of God in the name of Jesus Christ."** Sound too easy. Think you need to suffer some more. Maybe do some penance. God would like you to be whole and when you trip up and make a careless mistake God is there to lift you out of your dilemma should you ask Him too. God has the power, all you have to do is exercise it with a petition or prayer.

And when Jesus bled for all of the sins you had ever committed they were all washed away by the Father. Read carefully. Only the sins you committed prior to giving your life over to God and Jesus Christ were washed away. Any sin you commit after your being *"born again"* will be forgiven by your Holy Father when you come to Him with a humble heart and thank Him for His awesome forgiveness. Your Heavenly Father has promised to never remember your sins again. **Psalms 103:12 "As far as the east is from the west so far hath he removed our transgressions***(sins)* **from us."**

And furthermore, Christ Jesus will never be crucified again so he does not have to continue to die over and over again for your sins.

Does Satan cause sickness and death?

Satan personally cannot affect you because he is locked up in the earth wandering to and fro, but he does have billions of unholy angel spirits, the same ones he took with him when God cast him out of heaven. These unholy angel spirits do the bidding of Satan throughout his world which sits on top of the earth. **Ephesians 6:12 "For we wrestle not against flesh and blood, but against powers, against the rulers of the darkness of this world, against spiritual wickedness in high places."**

Because you live in Satan's world there is a natural tendency to want to place the blame on someone or something when a loved one becomes ill or is hurt in an accident. Satan personally did not cause the illness or the accident but his angel spirits through their influence were able to affect how the accident happened. The key word is *"influence."* Do we know how they do it. No! But you will know when you see the result of the influence.

When God created the universe and it was complete and on the seventh day He simply stepped back and rested. I do not know how a spirit being can step anywhere but He took His spiritual hands off the process and released the natural forces of what He had created to begin their own inner action on each other.

When God told Adam and Eve to go forth an multiply they did. And the process kept on going until Noah. At which point everything concerning humans was brought to a screeching halt. All human and animal life as they knew it then was destroyed with the exception of Noah, his wife and his family of three sons and their wives and the animals on the ark. **Genesis 7:2 "of every clean beast**(*clean animals did not have split hooves*)**thou shalt take to thee by sevens, the male and the female and of beast that are not clean**(*split hooves*)**by two male and female."** This also included birds by seven. All were brought on board the ark. The animals were not quite mature enough to reproduce themselves when they came aboard the Ark. One interesting note was Noah did not have to go and collect all these animals. **Genesis 6:20b "shall come unto thee,"** They all came to the ark according to how God dictated. Once the flood was over then the population of the earth began again thanks to Noah and his family and the animals.

At this writing there are seven and one/half billion people here on earth. This does not count the billions who have already died before. So with everybody going out and procreating eventually all those genes getting mixed up with other genes began to cause interruptions in the whole gene pool. What happened? Weak genes were dominated by strong genes and if those strong genes carried an abnormality then you had the beginnings of a disease. The strong gene was mixed with other strong genes and the process continued until you have the result of what you see today, diseases in many people and sickness is rampant throughout the world.

Did Satan cause this? Did God cause this? Neither did. Sickness and disease are only a small fraction of what the earth and time has brought forth. The beauties of this earth go on forever. Remember Satan and his unholy angel spirits can only influence what is already in existence. Satan does not have the power to create anything. God created man in His *"spiritual image."* God is not flesh and blood, He is spirit. He is like the wind everywhere at one time. God spoke to Adam thru revelation. God being Holy Spirit can only communicate with what He is, Holy Spirit, therefore when you were *"born again"* God's Holy Spirit was in you since birth waiting to be energized. You energized it by your commitment to Jesus Christ and his Father God and by believing. Now you can communicate with God anytime day or night.

Green pea versus white pea.

"What do green peas have to do with the 'gene pool." Here is an example of how the *"gene pool"* got mixed up. Remember the Biology experiment you might have done in high school with the green peas. The whole class began growing green peas. As the peas grew an unusual incident took place. One of the green pea plants started producing white peas, totally absent of any green color. So now you take the white pea seedlings and graft them along with the green pea seedlings and you start getting multicolored peas, not white nor green but variegated. This took place in one Biology class during one school year.

Imagine instead of peas you have men and women who mate and produce an offspring who is healthy. He or she grows up and mates with a person who has been sick much of their life. Their offspring are born with a physical defect. Then the child with the physical defect grows up and mates and gives birth to a healthy offspring and a deformed offspring. Are you getting the picture. Multiply the above a billions times over and over and you will see how you can end up with various physically crippling diseases and abnormalities among the human race.

Are you still looking to blame someone. Is it too difficult for you to take some responsibility for your actions or your families or your past relatives.

How does Satan affect us today?

Through these unholy angel spirits today is how Satan can influence your life and eventually your thought processes. Some people would say you are possessed by Satan should you do something terrible. Actually your mind is the battleground in this world and this is where you can go wrong. Should your mind be occupied with God's Word then the influences of Satan's cannot occupy the same space as God's Word. Now if you do not have God's word to rely on then all you have is what you have been taught by the world and since it belongs to Satan you have been feeding your mind with whatever he feels you should know.

When someone murders another individual for whatever reason the person doing the murdering is responsible for the physical act. Should the person who committed the murder come to God and humbly ask for forgiveness your God being a just God will forgive the person assuming they have accepted Jesus Christ as their savior. However, the action this person took is not forgivable in your society and there is a consequence for the action and it could be prison time or death

Wicked thoughts. . .

Without God's word going through your conscious thoughts on a moment by moment basis where applicable your behavior will eventually fall into the snare of Satan and his unholy angel spirits. One of the quickest ways to give your mind over to Satan is with drugs of any sort, whether physical or visual. And once you start down this path the return will be very hard. There may come a point in time when you will lose control of your righteous habits, bodily functions, truthful speech, glorious sight and hearing. All of your five senses will fall into the spiritual hands of Satan unless you make a change in your life now and what comes next spiritual death. **What causes death?**

Let me clarify one point. I am talking about death from natural causes, not those caused by war, murder, accident or disease.

God designed the human body to fail within 120 years. In **Genesis 6:3 "And the Lord said, My spirit shall not always strive with man, for that he also is flesh; yet his days shall be an hundred and twenty years."**

Neither man nor woman will live longer than this. Why? God could have been getting tired of the constant bickering among His chosen people. (Read the account of the exodus of the Jewish people from Egypt). Considering the population growth which was taking place then, people would continue to live 400, 500, or even 900 years. So who then causes death? No one. Remember God designed your body to fail or wear out at an undisclosed time in your life here on earth. Some bodies will wear out faster because of sickness or genetic disorder.

In the Old Testament, God would continually keep His hand of protection over His people from King to King as long as Israel worshiped Him as their one and only true God. When Israel would go to war God's hand was upon Israel's troops until they had victory. As soon as Israel would get a little over confident and began worshiping idols of all sorts including their leaders, one of the opposing Kings would declare war on Israel. Israel would go to war expecting to be victorious and they would be wiped out, why? They took their eyes off of God and He in turn took His hand of protection off of Israel.

Did God cause those thousands of warriors to die? No! God set a condition and Israel chose of their own free will not to follow God so. . .God said worship me and only me and I will protect and prosper you. Stop the worship and I will stop the protection and the prosperity. All which will lead to slavery, again.

Now some say Satan causes death but he does not have the power to cause death anymore. Jesus Christ, on the cross, took the power of death away from Satan. **Hebrews 2:14 "Forasmuch then as the children are partakers**(*share fully*)** of flesh and blood, he also himself likewise**

took part*(Mary's son)* **of the same; that through death he** *(Jesus Christ)* **might destroy***(paralyzing the death power of Satan)* **him that had the power of death, that is the Devil***(Satan)."*

So to answer the question, no spiritual being causes the natural death of any human. God does not take old people away, nor does He take small children and babies away.

The problem. . .

The problem existing is men and women cannot accept the responsibility for their lives. They constantly have to find someone or something or some company to blame for whatever circumstance happens to them. God, for centuries, has had to take the *"rap"* for all the little babies who die or the very old parents of young children or the father of two baby girls or the mother of three sons all who die naturally. God had nothing to do with these deaths. For this to happen God would have to be a *"respecter of persons,"* which He is not. **Romans 2:11 "For there is no respect of persons with God."** And Satan is not responsible for people dying naturally, but spiritually dying yes.

When your body, as a believer, wears out and you give up your last breath, your personal spirit goes to Paradise to wait for the Gathering. The whole thing is just this simple, just the facts.

In conclusion

Satan is alive and well and still walking to and fro within the earth encouraging his unholy angel spirits to do whatever they can to make your walk in his world as bumpy as possible. In doing so you might just break fellowship with your heavenly Father. You must do everything you can to keep your Father God's glorious Word in your heart and in your conscious thoughts. Following this path will keep those unholy angel spirits at bay.